THE SPIT-SHINE SYNDROME

Recent Titles in
Contributions in Military Studies
Series Advisor: Colin Gray

The Spit-Shine Syndrome

ORGANIZATIONAL IRRATIONALITY IN THE AMERICAN FIELD ARMY

Christopher Bassford

Foreword by Robert M. Elton

CONTRIBUTIONS IN MILITARY STUDIES,
NUMBER 76

Greenwood Press
NEW YORK · WESTPORT, CONNECTICUT · LONDON

Copyright acknowledgments

The author and publisher would like to gratefully acknowledge the permission of A. L. Hite for the use of his words, which are contained in a letter dated December 10, 1985.

Library of Congress Cataloging-in-Publication Data

Bassford, Christopher.
    The spit-shine syndrome : organizational irrationality in the American
Field Army / Christopher Bassford.
        p.   cm. — (Contributions in military studies, ISSN 0883-6884
; no. 76)
    Bibliography: p.
    Includes index.
    ISBN 0-313-26215-2 (lib. bdg. : alk. paper)
    1. United States. Army—Management. 2. United States. Army—
Officers. I. Title. II. Series.
UA25.B27   1988   87-37551
355.3'0973—dc19

British Library Cataloguing in Publication Data is available.

Library of Congress Catalog Card Number: 87-37551
ISBN: 0-313-26215-2
ISSN: 0883-6884

First published in 1988

Greenwood Press, Inc.
88 Post Road West, Westport, Connecticut 06881

Printed in the United States of America

The paper used in this book complies with the
Permanent Paper Standard issued by the National
Information Standards Organization (Z39.48-1984).

10 9 8 7 6 5 4 3 2 1

CONTENTS

TERMS AND ABBREVIATIONS

AGI	Annual General Inspection
Air-Land Battle	The U.S. Army's current war fighting doctrine
ARTEP	Army Training Evaluation Program; also the evaluation itself
Bundeswehr	The modern West German armed forces
COHORT	Cohesion and Operational Readiness Training: a program for training and deploying units, keeping personnel together through a three-year tour
CONUS	Continental United States
CPX	Command Post Exercise
CTT	Common Tasks Test: a standardized test of a limited number of common military skills; administered to soldiers annually
DA	Department of the Army
DCP	Divisional Command Package, a proposed solution to the problem of personnel stability in commands and staffs
DOD	Department of Defense
DRS	Divisional Rotation System: a proposed system for stabilizing army units and personnel
DS	Direct Support: the maintenance echelon directly above the field unit
EER	Enlisted Efficiency Report
EXEVAL	External Evaluation: as used here, a proposed system for inspecting military units

FTX	Field Training Exercise
"grunts"	infantrymen
LANCE	A short-range tactical surface-to-surface missile (SSM), capable of carrying either a conventional or nuclear warhead
MILES	Multiple Integrated Laser Engagement System
MILPERCEN	The army's Military Personnel Center
MOS	Military Occupational Specialty
MTO&E	Modified Table of Organization and Equipment, the document that authorizes a unit to have its personnel and equipment
NRAS	Nuclear Release Authentication System: the code system used to send and verify messages relating to nuclear weapons
NV	Night Vision: infra-red and star-light scopes for night observation
OBC	Officer Basic Course
OCS	Officer Candidate School
OER	Officer Efficiency Report (see example pp. 80–81)
OPFOR	Opposing Forces, usually meaning a simulated enemy
OR rate	Operational Readiness Rate, supposedly reflecting the maintenance status of a unit's equipment
REFORGER	**RE**turn **O**f **FOR**ces to **GER**many: an annual exercise to test U.S. capability to reinforce NATO
ROK	Republic of (South) Korea
ROTC	Reserve Officer Training Corps
ROKA	South Korean Army
S–1	Staff officer concerned with personnel issues
S–2	Staff officer concerned with intelligence issues
S–3	Staff officer concerned with training and operations
S–4	Staff officer concerned with logistical issues
S–5	Staff officer concerned with civil-military issues
SACEUR	Supreme Allied Commander, Europe (always an American)
SOP	Standard Operating Procedure
Spetsnaz	Soviet special forces

SQT	Skill Qualification Test: administered to soldiers to measure their skills in their military specialties
"Team Spirit"	A major annual exercise to test U.S. capability to reinforce the Republic of Korea
TFI	Tactical Forces Inspectorate: a proposed organization for determining the military readiness of army units
UCMJ	Universal Code of Military Justice
USAREUR	U.S. Army, Europe
VOLAR	Volunteer Army, a term used mostly in reference to the 1970s
XO	Executive Officer

FOREWORD

For over thirty-three years, I watched the quality of young Americans as they entered our army to serve their country in enlisted or officer status. That quality has varied significantly over time, but clearly, as individuals, they are the most outstanding today that I have ever seen. They are meeting the challenge of a new doctrine and high tech equipment. The potential is there to mold a truly great army. Yet, I am concerned that in the long run we will not be able to retain "the best and the brightest," but that in a sophisticated army with great lethality we will drive away those very individuals who would make us great. The question is one of priorities.

What is our first priority? Maintaining deterrence is a complex mission even when viewed through the landpower prism alone. For our army there are many factors competing for today's shrinking resources: training, modernization, accessions, logistics, research and development to name a few. All are important in today's defense equation. Yet, they do not respond to a fundamental principle which we have lived with but suppressed since the beginning of the Korean War. That is: wars in our future will be "come as you are" for Americans. Mobilization may take place for those conflicts that need it, but any long prior build-up is out of the question. This fact has never really been disputed, even in our most unlikely scenario—Central Europe. The logic flow then is this: with "come as you are" the imperative, what cries out as our first priority as an army? I believe it is the development of stabilized, cohesive units. Units where the leaders are competent in the profession of combined arms warfare; units whose soldiers, NCOs, and officers know and are committed to each other and the success of the unit; units whose leaders teach themselves and soldiers tactics and doctrine rather than relying on TRADOC to do it all; units where stability means togetherness for an absolute minimum of three years without interruption; units whose replacements come as cohesive packages rather than parcelled out like poker chips one at a time to meet monthly readiness paper requirements.

Units that are truly able to benefit from the collective training experience of the NTC (National Training Center) or JRTC (Joint Readiness Training Center) because they remain together *after* the training and have the motivation to square away the errors. In today's army, very few, if any, tankers return to their second tank gunnery in the same year in the same crew; most are broken up within six to nine months.

This book is tough and critical. It hits relentlessly at bureaucratic systems, yet does not degrade the officers and soldiers who could, under modernized, thoroughly streamlined systems, operate to their full potential. Still, many will be wounded by its bluntness. Some will throw it across the room in disgust. My entreaty is to pick it up and read on. I personally do not agree 100 percent with all of the author's recommended solutions, but I do agree that a change of focus to unit stability and readiness is needed, and, contrary to other critics, the author has provided thoughtful solutions. A clear priority must be established. We can not continue to do *all things* for *all masters*. Our units must be *ready now*! A C–2 rating (80 percent) with 30 percent turnover of new people is not good enough—even with the superb young soldiers we are recruiting these days. The lessons of history—unfortunately our own—are too numerous to forget. The British, French, German, Israeli, and Soviet Armies *all* emphasize stability and cohesion in their *units*. Why do we ignore it—or why do we agree, but shrug it off saying we have other priorities more important in a peacetime army? The author praises the army's COHORT (Cohesive, Operational, Readiness, Training) program, but decries it as being simply too "timid" in execution. Unfortunately, he is correct, as Dr. David H. Marlowe, Walter Reed Institute of Research, spells out in detail in his Sept. 87, "Unit Manning System Field Evaluation." The program would have been far from "timid" had we been able to make the hard choice the original program envisioned, which was to alter our institutional "individual equity" culture. We never decided on our first priority and then never made our personnel, training and logistics policies, procedures and systems fully support that priority.

Our current Chief of Staff has made "training" his first priority. I agree, but with modification: "training which develops ready units." Units that are stable, free from many of our bureaucratic requirements, can do this quickly. The talent is there! Again, this book screams for someone to listen. It comes from the young officers and NCOs who must launch into combat at the instant the claxon sounds. And, with the notable exception of our magnificent Ranger Regiment, none of our units feel real comfortable about their complete ability to *go now*.

The text calls for changes in our division manning system. Old timers will be reminded of Operation Gyroscope of the 1950s. Having been in one of those units, as was the current Chief of Staff, the Commander of AMC, and the Commander of TRADOC, among others, I can only applaud its concept. Unfortunately, after a few years, we succumbed again to "other important priorities" and that program was scuttled as being too expensive. Further, it was disruptive to the individual replacement system, and personnel managers could not make it work—and man all the other "first priorities." Further changes are recommended to provide hard hitting inspection teams, new promotion, school selection, officer and enlisted evaluation, award and retention systems that put premiums on unit achievement and the contribution made.

Our system will be changed to truly reward service in units—not just treat it as "something on the list to do." An officer's or NCO's professional behavior will be rewarded by command, early promotion, professional schooling. Those not in units will perform meaningful staff work and a decision will be made regarding a "command track" for those who are gifted with soldier leadership skills. When a combat arms officer or NCO scrambles to get back in a unit, then we will know that the culture is correct. There are many opportunities to reduce the size of the "service" portion of the officer corps—many tasks that can be civilianized—better yet "privatized," such as finance, personnel, civil engineer. Why not let our installations or "cities" be run by civilians, responding to the installation commander's civilian deputy? Our experience with management at the NTC may be a reasonable beginning.

The current SACEUR, General J. R. Galvin, has spoken critically of the "grindstone of bureaucratic business" to which we have become accustomed to keeping our noses fixed.

We are led away from the important tasks by the exigencies of day-to-day operations—husbanding sophisticated equipment, doing the housekeeping and administration, balancing this year's budget while justifying the requirements for next year, answering the mail.... We could say, I suppose, that this kind of distraction always must be overcome.... The difficulty begins, however, when these activities cease to be distractions and instead become the focus of all our efforts. (Galvin, J. R., "Uncomfortable Wars, Towards a New Paradigm," *Parameters*, xvi, no. 4, pg. 2.)

These fixes will not be easy, but I suggest that this is the ideal time to set our course. The army (and, in fact, all of DOD) stands at the beginning of a major resource and probably personnel reduction over the next five years. This resource drought can be disastrous if we do not approach it with the "glass half full" attitude. If we do not shape it to meet our clear priority, then the Congress will. The current senior army commanders stand in an enviable position to truly "streamline" our army. It is an ideal time to drive into those years with a clear purpose of what will be our first priority, and make the appropriate reductions in other areas.

Robert M. Elton
Lt. General (USA Retired)
President, Sage Centers for Strategic Research

PREFACE

This book will no doubt be taken as an attack on the leadership of the United States Army. It is not. This book is not about a group of men but about a bureaucratic system, one which has been growing without coherent purpose for generations. This is the system by which we select, train, assign, promote, and utilize the army's battlefield leaders. These are the men who are charged with our nation's fortunes in combat and with the lives of the young citizens who make up our fighting forces. Judging by the military results, it is a system that ceased to work more than a generation ago.

To criticize this system it is not necessary to question the individual qualities of the army's leaders and soldiers, and based on personal observation I cannot accept many of the negative assessments made of these men by other critics of the armed forces. Unfortunately, the army's organizational methods make those qualities largely irrelevant. The great bulk of the army's leaders are intelligent, dedicated men, but they are prisoners of a system that they are nearly powerless to affect. Many have reached their positions not because of the presence or lack of military virtues but by bureaucratic accident.

In general, my experiences on active duty were not unusual, although my duties in logistics and training gave me a rather broader look at the field army than the average junior officer receives. Like approximately 70 percent of new army officers, I received my commission through the Reserve Officer Training Corps (ROTC). I entered basic training in 1979 and served from 1981 to 1986 as a field artillery officer, with tours in both Korea and Germany. My academic background and motivations for joining the army were, however, somewhat atypical for army officers. Like most American soldiers, I saw military service as a duty to the country, but unlike most officers I did not view it as a potential career. I entered the army as a research project, a chance to observe directly the subject of my academic

xvi   PREFACE

studies. I did not expect to be so profoundly disturbed by what I would observe.

I am sensitive to the criticism that as a junior officer my view of the army was too limited to provide a credible basis for the sweeping analysis I make here. Were my subject the making of grand strategy or even operational planning that criticism would have some validity. My subject here, however, is the field army and the organizational techniques that are used to run it. In the United States, I was trained at several major and minor military installations. In the course of my work in Korea, I became familiar with virtually every unit in the Second Infantry Division and many in Eighth Army. I had friends in the Korean army and many Korean soldiers in my unit. In Europe I ran or was otherwise involved in training exercises with units from V and VII Corps Artillery, Third Armored Division, Eighth Infantry Division, and elements of the German army. I have participated in the two largest military exercises held in the free world: "Team Spirit" in Korea and REFORGER in Germany. My window on the army's field units was in many respects superior to that of more senior officers, for my observations were not distorted by the energetic deception efforts made by all units in the presence of higher commanders and staff.

This book is written not only for academicians and military analysts but for the concerned citizen as well. The subject does not lend itself to a detached, academic style of writing, and the approach I have chosen is to blend facts and statistics with a particular historical perspective, and to illustrate them through personal observations. I have documented the latter as well as I can without subjecting any individual to personal embarrassment. The use of a certain amount of military jargon is unavoidable, and a list of the most heavily used acronyms and abbreviations has been included. I have tried to ignore the innumerable but inevitable petty stupidities that can make military life so irritating, and the problems on which I have focused are those that are critical, fatal, but correctable through radical organizational reform. This book offers a blueprint for such reform.

I owe thanks to the many soldiers and civilians of the army who have assisted me in the writing of this work, but it would not be doing them any favor to name them here. I could not have completed the research and writing without the indulgence and encouragement of the history faculty at Purdue University, especially Professors John J. Contreni and Gordon R. Mork; nor could I have done without the kindness and professionalism of my editors at the Greenwood Press, Mildred Vasan, Nick Allison, and Elizabeth Klein. Special thanks go to my advisor, Professor Gunther Rothenberg, who encouraged me when I flagged but also forced me to more clearly define my argument. I must also express my gratitude to Professor Williamson Murray of the Ohio State University, who encouraged me to embark on this project in the first place, it seems now a very long time ago. Most of all, I owe thanks to my wife Sun Yong, who has suffered over this work far more than I have. I am, of course, solely responsible for any errors of fact or judgment contained herein.

THE SPIT-SHINE SYNDROME

1

INTRODUCTION

This book is another in a growing genre of works on military reform. It focuses on the army because that is where my own experience lies, but I believe that the analysis is broadly applicable to the other services as well. To some extent it is a rehash of the existing reform literature, and to a larger extent a critique of previous reform prescriptions. The book contains some new material to help update the debate on military reform. Much of this material is anecdotal, but many of these anecdotes can be documented. Each is included as a worm's-eye view of problems that have been identified elsewhere as fundamental to the demonstrated incapacity of the United States Army to perform real-world missions. They serve to demonstrate that the organizational pathologies that led to disaster in Vietnam are still alive in the army of the 1980s. Anyone with experience in units of the field army will recognize them as characteristic examples of the impact of the army's organizational methodology. The main thrust of the work is prescriptive. The reforms proposed incorporate many that have been suggested before, but I believe that as an integrated program they constitute a new approach.

There appears to be a consensus among informed elements in the nation today, even within the military itself, that something is seriously wrong with our armed forces. Even the *Army Times* routinely runs columns saying things like "Our military performance has been dismal, and little hope of im- provement exists."[1] There is also, as that line implies, a strong sense that nothing can be done about it, the underlying thought being that our military incompetence is rooted in fundamental and irremediable social and political problems. It is tempting to believe that our military incapacity stems from basic social causes, flaws inherent in our political system, or the inevitable complexity of modern organizations. While such weaknesses do in fact exist and have an impact, there is no reason to suppose that they are inevitably fatal to military effectiveness. In any case, none of these factors seems susceptible to conscious reform efforts. Fortunately neither do any of them lie at the heart of the difficulty. Throughout this book it will be argued that the practical problems, that is, those that actually can be addressed, lie in the organizational methods used by our military system. Fundamentally dysfunctional philosophies have been built into the military organizations themselves, and they can and must be rooted out and corrected. Some societal problems, particularly the divorce of the middle and upper classes from military service and the general reluctance to support military action in defense of national interests, may well be more an outgrowth of our military ineptitude than a cause.

Nevertheless, the political and social excuses for military failure are popular among American Army officers, who persist in believing that American military failures have been due to political interference or lack of public support.[2] It is certainly true that the problems of American military organizations are compounded by congressional micromanagement and by the amateurish machinations of the fragmented national security establishment. American forces have repeatedly been committed by the civilian leadership to actions that simply made no strategic sense, where failure in some form was inevitable. On the other hand, there are competent modern armies, some of them belonging to nations with political systems quite similar to that of the United States. One can cite Great Britain and West Germany as examples of such systems. Israel is a somewhat different case, but that does not invalidate comparisons between its demonstrated military competence and American military fumbling. The long catalog of American military failures is entirely unrelieved by anything comparable to the British performance in Malaya or the Falklands, or Israel's Entebbe Raid, a few examples among many of Western military accomplishments in recent times. To the extent that excessive congressional interference in military affairs is not inherent in the Constitution of the United States, it is the incompetence of the military leadership that has opened the door to civilian micromanagement and amateurism. The utter incapacity of existing military units to conduct purely military operations is due almost entirely to self-inflicted wounds.

There are indeed characteristics of American society that have tended to lead us into error, but the "post-Vietnam syndrome" is not one of them. It has long been said that Americans are "warlike" without being "military." That is, we are willing to use force to gain our ends, but we are reluctant to do so in an organized manner. There is no reason to believe that the national character has changed radically in this period during which our military fortunes have been plummeting. The "post-Vietnam syndrome" is not the manifestation of any deep-seated national pacifism, for if it were it would be impossible to explain the recruiting successes of the all-volunteer force in the 1980s,[3] or the deep patriotic chord that Lieutenant Colonel Oliver North evidently struck during his televised testimony before Congress in mid–1987. Military officers continue to enjoy a high status in our society.

The national lack of will to use military force appears to be, instead, a result of American frustration with the dismal record of its military forces. If it is true that nothing succeeds like success, it is equally true that nothing fails like failure.

The historical roots of American military disorganization are not difficult to pinpoint.[4] On the eve of global war in 1940, the regular army had about 130,000 men, completely dominated by a tiny officer corps, and almost wholly stationed in American territory. The existing military structure was fairly well conceived for fighting Indians and Mexican bandits, but not a first-rate military power. During the war it swelled to millions of men, adopting desperate expedients to fill the ranks and to create units out of thin air. This required producing an officer corps of "90-day wonders." In the aftermath of World War II, the army shrank with mind-numbing speed to near-prewar figures, but swelled again for Korea. Today's army was born in the 1950s, and in the process the older, genuinely military tradition was obliterated. In its cycles of growth and shrinkage, the army institutionalized many of the stopgap measures adopted in the course of massive expansion under emergency conditions, which accounts for much of the determined amateurishness of the army today.[5] Meanwhile, the American armed forces have been reconstructed on inappropriate commercial and bureaucratic models under civilian leaders like Robert Mac-Namara, whose roots were in big business. The peacetime standing army now includes about 780,000 soldiers and a third of a million civilians. Overall, the Department of Defense (DOD) employs about 3.3 million uniformed and civilian personnel, scattered around the world. Most people do not realize what a novel, ad hoc, unmilitary organization this is; no nation (including ours) has ever fought a war, let alone won one, with such a bizarre structure.

One practical reason for this development was that America, as a mercantile society, had no other native model to turn to when it was forced to produce a globe-girdling military organization. Second, America was in large part settled by people who came here to flee nations ruled by essentially military aristocracies. We were willing to tolerate a small, specialized officer class of our own only so long as it could be kept isolated. It was trotted out only to meet sudden military emergencies like the Civil War. With Korea, it became evident that a large military establishment was going to remain permanently in existence. Americans began taking a whole new view of the concept of "civilian control of the military." Tremendous fundamental changes were made in every aspect of the military system, from military law to the training of officers. Much of this reform was made in the interests of "fairness," and of preventing abuses of junior soldiers and draftees by an arrogant and arbitrary officer caste. Such abuses had been experienced by many who served in the hastily raised armies of World War II and Korea, with their equally hastily raised officer corps.

In the course of reinventing our forces, we destroyed them. Because we were in many respects all-powerful in the years after World War II, we were able to get away with this, to institutionalize our forces on utterly inappropriate business and bureaucratic models.[6] We even institutionalized our wars, rotating individuals in and out to spread the burden more fairly, while the enemy stayed in place, growing ever more professional.[7] Gradually, however, we have come to pay the price. Traditionally, the United States had begun its wars unprepared, experienced initial defeats, but had been able to mobilize its superior resources and gain the upper hand. Third-, fourth-, and fifth-rate powers like revolutionary China, North Korea, and North Vietnam now are able to defeat our military efforts even in long, drawn-out wars. Evidently, this has not been sufficiently threatening to change our approach to military organization.

In the course of civilianizing the armed forces, we have replaced the old cadre of professional military leaders with a non-threatening class of managers and administrators who are ill-suited and essentially powerless to lead and inspire the men they command, or even to make accurate reports. The current army officer is selected not for any demonstrated leadership ability, but simply because he has managed to get a bachelor's degree in some field (music, for example). He is trained not to lead, not to command, but to find a consensus. After being trained and commissioned, he is put into a position of authority. Suddenly, and usually for the first time, he is exposed to soldiers. The first thing he learns is that he is entirely at the mercy of his alleged subordinates, all of whom have more experience than he does. The current unit commander does not train his troops; he administers a paper system of required forms and manuals. He has virtually no power to train, select, or promote his subordinate officers and senior non-commissioned officers, and what little power he does have is negative. He does not devise, modify, or even comment on tactics; he adheres to manuals drawn up by anonymous scribblers in unknown and unreachable offices. The practical lessons he learns in the field are irrelevant, and they leave the unit when he does. He does not issue tactical commands; he instead "manages" a staff made up of inexpert officers whom he did not train and for whose selection he was, in most cases, not responsible. He knows that there is no great point in thoroughly training any of his personnel, for with as much as 100 to 300 percent personnel turnover per year, they will not be around long enough to justify the effort. At most he will fire a few people with whom he is uncomfortable, hoping that their replacements will be more to his liking. He knows that he himself will not be in his job long enough to make a difference, or even to truly learn it. He is ruthlessly taught that he owes loyalty and obedience not to his immediate commander or to the nation but to a faceless bureaucracy that can destroy his career through a paperwork error or an obscure change in personnel policies. He is promoted not because of his "professional" achievements, but because he has avoided drawing unfavorable notice. He is in constant competition with his peers, has no reason for any but the most superficial cooperation with them, and against his will he must rejoice when one of them fails. Whatever his personal patriotism and military interests, his practical goal becomes personal career survival.

To criticize individual military officers for the poor performance of American forces over the last forty years is a waste of time. None of us could have done any better under the debilitating circumstances America has foisted on its soldiers.

The fundamental problems of today's army are related to two connected anachronisms: that the army's leadership has never adjusted to the change-over from expandable-army thinking, and that the overall military system has never adjusted to the existence of large standing forces. The field army is treated as a mere projection of the bureaucracy in Washington, a circumstance that grows naturally out of the creation of temporary armies earlier in this century but that is now inappropriate. The post–Korean War field army has never been allowed the institutional independence that is dictated by its new status as a fighting force-in-being. Behind all of the army's problems lurks the question of the proper relationship of the army's field forces to the military bureaucracy. That bureaucracy has the three distinct functions of providing services, gathering information, and exercising political control, but these missions have become hopelessly intermixed. Information gatherers have usurped command powers and turned soldiers into their servants. Service organizations have done the same. All of the reforms proposed herein are designed with the purpose of sorting out these various functions, creating a customer-service relationship between the field forces and the support bureaucracy, restricting information gatherers to gathering information, and requiring that political control functions be exercised through a military chain of command rather than through a fatally disruptive set of parallel chains and short circuits.

WHY REFORM NOW?

Presumably, the United States has some reason for maintaining an army of 780,000 men. Obviously, this force is intended to have some sort of utility. Equally obviously, it does not. Military reform is therefore justified by those features of the modern world that justify having the army in the first place. Such questions are beyond the scope of this book, but we must not lose sight of the fundamental fact that war, even "conventional" war, threatens torturous injury and death not only for individual soldiers but quite possibly for entire societies or civilizations. In the age of nuclear psychosis it is common to lose sight of that fact, to forget the monstrous results—revolution, enslavement, and genocide—suffered by the losers of the conventional conflicts of the twentieth century.[8] The social unrest experienced in the United States as a result of the lost Vietnam War was a very mild example. Consider the possible domestic impact of a similar defeat in a war of greater relevance to fundamental American interests. Oil, for instance.

However, there are some newly pressing reasons to proceed with sweeping reform of the army and to do it now. The regular recurrence of mass military funerals for personnel killed in futile parades of U.S. military muscle has awakened a national concern. Second, recent scandals, particularly the Iran-Contra affair, have once again disclosed serious ethical problems in the officer corps. It is becoming apparent to the densest patriot as well as to the most pacific dove that the current military system is producing some dangerously uncontrollable characters. These are capable men who like to get things done, and they are finding their ways to the top of the military hierarchy. It is clear to them that it is impossible actually to accomplish anything, however noble or expedient, through the absurd apparatus we have concocted to protect our national security. They therefore have developed the habit of short-circuiting the system, and that approach has proved to be both easy and effective. Politicians who have sought to restrain the power of the military by wrapping it in red tape should be aware that this strategy has reached the point of diminishing returns. Our incompetent military machine has become the breeding ground for very dangerous tendencies.

Recent moves to cut intermediate nuclear forces will also serve to create an opening for reform. Supporters of a strong defense will want to balance actual reductions in our nuclear deterrent with strengthened conventional forces. Those interested in creating a less threatening U.S. military posture also want to strengthen conventional forces, for two related reasons: first, to make less likely a resort to nuclear weapons in the event of an East-West confrontation, even to permit an actual renunciation of NATO's "first-use" policy; second, to create a basis for consensus on further nuclear arms control.[9]

The problem with these convergent desires is that no more money is likely to become available for conventional forces, and certainly no more manpower. Cutting nuclear warheads is not going to free up much of either for conventional uses. Financial limitations and the hardware commitments of the last decade preclude substantial changes in force structure or equipment. We must improve the quality of the forces we have without infusions of money, manpower, and material beyond those already planned. The army needs to decide now on new directions for the coming period of financial constraints. Unless we are to be satisfied with another inconsequential "do more with less" poster campaign, this means, ipso facto, radical organizational reform. A radically different approach is required, for proceeding down the bureaucratic paths that we have followed for the past few generations is only going to lead us deeper into the morass in which we already find ourselves.[10]

THE FAILURE TO REFORM

If we were to read about a thirty-five-year string of failures by Mussolini's army, we would be amused and put it down to stupidity, corruption, or simply the "peace-loving nature of the Italians." However, the leaders of the American armed forces are not stupid; many are brilliant, as individuals. They are not corrupt in any legal sense. Few have ever accused them of being peace-loving (although the military hierarchy seems to have become a suspiciously strong advocate of moderation in the use of force). Nevertheless, the American military has compiled a remarkable record of failure. Virtually every American military action since the 1950s has demonstrated the inability of the nation's armed forces to handle real-world problems.[11] It would seem reasonable to expect serious steps toward reform to have been taken.

For some reason, however, real reform has not occurred. Some serious alterations to the national military system have been made, such as ending the draft and implementing the all-volunteer concept, but none of these have been aimed at improving the services' performance. We have paid for some very necessary improvements in hardware, which has enhanced our fire-power without enhancing our ability to use it effectively. The recent effort to reform the joint command structure was intended as serious reform, but from the standpoint of the field army it was merely another reshuffling of office space. It appears that its intended benefits are already being eroded.[12] Beyond an occasional memo and a handful of tepid, toe-in-the-water programs like COHORT,[13] the factors that produced military collapse in Vietnam have not been addressed. In the wake of Korea, *Pueblo*, Vietnam, Sontay, *Mayaquez*, Iran, Beirut, Grenada, and *Stark*, there has been no significant attempt to reform the American military system. None whatsoever. The officers who presided over these debacles have, with few exceptions, continued to receive their promotions on schedule and advanced to impose their failed leadership on their entire organizations. The armed forces seem incapable of meaningful self-reform, and it is difficult to avoid the suspicion that nothing short of sweeping military disaster will motivate the government and people of the United States to force meaningful reform upon them. By "sweeping disaster" is meant something on the order of Dunkirk, 1940, since it is apparent that Vietnam, Iran, and Beirut have not sufficed to arouse a strong political constituency for reform.

Serious reform must originate in one of three places: the armed forces themselves, Congress, or the Executive. The services are run by the product of two generations of military failure, and it is unreasonable to expect today's military leaders to condemn as a failure the system that has brought themselves to the top. Nonetheless, a great many officers are aware that the army's organizational methods do not work. A 1984 army survey showed that 49 percent of army officers took the extreme position that "the bold, creative officer *could not survive*" in the army.[14] Characteristically, the Army Chief of Staff reported this to the public by saying that the majority of officers believed that "the bold, original, creative officer can grow and develop (i.e., survive)."[15] Some of the most active reform-seekers are former active-duty officers, and they receive a lot of practical support from those still in uniform.[16] Military analyst Edward Luttwak, for all his blunt criticism of the armed forces, is by no means persona non grata around the Pentagon. The great majority of officers would like to see the system fixed.

However, fundamental self-reform is probably impossible in any large military organization, owing to the very nature of such structures. For an officer even to acknowledge that something is seriously wrong within the military organization itself is awkward in the extreme, since any example chosen for criticism is going to reflect directly on the current leadership. In any case, organizational self-criticism runs counter to the mentality of the American officer corps, which for various reasons (see chapter 3) is extremely intolerant of any form of negativism. Some prominent officers are willing to speak up after retirement. For example, both former Chairman of the Joint Chiefs of Staff General David C. Jones and former Chief of Naval Operations Admiral Elmo R. Zumwalt have acknowledged grave deficiencies in the armed forces and admitted that reform from within is extremely unlikely.[17] Power within the services is simply too diffused to permit the effective wielding of any big stick in the service of reform.

What about Congress and the Executive? Many of the military operations undertaken by American forces have been foredoomed because they simply made no strategic sense. Presidents quite properly have resisted the temptation to make scapegoats of the military leadership, but in doing so they have ignored the purely operational screw-ups that have turned mistaken policy into military embarrassments and disasters. The Executive has therefore imposed no sweeping command shakeups that might have brought determined, reform-minded leadership to the fore. Congress, on the other hand, has shown no reluctance to interfere with the most picayune details of military planning and budget requests. Why has it not pressed for overall reform?

One problem is that Congress thinks that the army lives in Washington, D.C. When congressmen think of reform they naturally think in terms of the military bureaucracy in its hives and warrens just across the Potomac River. They think in terms of grand national strategy and the high command structure. They never seem to grasp the simple fact that the best of all possible strategies, handed on a platter to a team of military geniuses at the Pentagon and passed on by the most efficient administrative apparatus in the world, is going to go nowhere when its execution devolves on the field army. Congressmen appear to believe the endless reams of propaganda on training and equipment readiness which DOD churns out. Despite their willingness to question relentlessly the petty details of every line item in the military budget, they remain oddly timid and naive in matters of fundamental military policy. Despite all evidence to the contrary, they appear to retain a childlike faith in the professional judgment of the nation's military leaders. Political leaders see the pictures of M-1 tanks and well-dressed American soldiers and think they are seeing an army.

The reality is quite different. The field army is made up of capable human beings, with a plentiful supply of reasonably good equipment, who do not know their jobs, their missions, their leaders, or each other. It is led by perfectly decent men that soldiers *cannot* trust, partly because of their habitual dishonesty (imposed on them by the reporting and promotion systems), partly because of their obvious inexperience, and partly because of their oft-demonstrated powerlessness to affect their own situation. Units that appear moderately cohesive in peacetime go to pieces in combat because the web of administrative sanctions that previously has kept them in line becomes totally irrelevant in the face of violent death. This is the famous "pucker factor," which is left out of peacetime calculations.[18] There are no other bonds. Is there any rational reason why a recently graduated twenty-year-old math major should be placed in command of seasoned veterans? Is there some mysterious benefit, peculiar to military organizations, gained from annual unit personnel turnover rates in excess of 100 percent, or even 300 percent? Is there some military necessity for a ratio of one leader for each junior enlisted soldier? These are the features of the American military system that have produced chaos in the field army. This is the environment from which emerges the military bureaucrat with whom Congress deals. Is there anybody on Capitol Hill who could run his office under such circumstances? No. Why then does Congress appropriate billions of dollars each year to inflict them on the nation's fighting forces? No one knows.

A deeper block to the schemes of would-be reformers, however, may be the long-standing fear of a powerful, competent military command body which American political leaders have shown since colonial times. Historically, societies or rulers distrustful of their soldiers have shuffled leaders around in order to prevent them from developing a regional power-base of their own. We may simply have gone one step further, shuffling not only the leaders but their drivers and file clerks as well. Notwithstanding the fact that our military leaders have never seriously threatened the republic, political leaders remain reluctant to place a powerful military individual or staff at the center of the military machine. This factor explains why there is today no overall commander of American field forces outside of the president, and he obviously cannot exercise genuine control. Each of the uniformed services is, in effect, leaderless.

For much the same reason there is no true General Staff on the Prussian/ German model. Most serious schemes for military reform involve creation of one, albeit sometimes one disguised as something else. These schemes founder on the fixed disinterest of the civilian leadership in creating such a body. Beyond any threat a truly effective General Staff might pose to American liberty and world peace, such a body might offer serious bureaucratic competition to Congress, its committees, and the horde of civilian agencies that have their fingers in the national security pie. Such proposals usually fail to take into account the fundamental differences between American society and that of nineteenth-century Germany, and the traditional American fear of such a body. Also, given the current up-or-out promotion system, in which all officers are in effect competing for a relatively few top jobs, creation of an elite body such as a General Staff would be perceived as a threat to the rest of the officer corps. Resistance would be furious, and probably successful. This is why the Special Forces have been so isolated within the army and why their influence is so restricted. The General Staff route to reform is therefore a dead end. Regardless of the proven military benefits of that system, we must look elsewhere for effective methods of reform.[19]

Congress, of course, has its own problems, and the decision-making process on the Hill, particularly as it relates to military issues, appears to be badly confused and misdirected. Senator Barry Goldwater attributed this to a simple lack of interest.[20] This lack of interest derives from the fact that there is no active constituency for military reform outside of a few academicians and disgruntled ex-soldiers. The most obvious potential constituency for reform of the army is the men who stand to suffer the most from its shortcomings: the army's mid- and lower-level leadership. However, most reform schemes presented to date have posed a more alarmingly immediate threat to these people than any hypothetical future conflict. This is because many of them aim at even tighter regulation of an organization already strangling in red tape, at punishing the officer corps for ethical transgressions mandated by the existing reporting, evaluation, and promotion systems, or at replacing the current leadership with some mythical better class of society. The proposals made here aim at both long- and short-term reform measures that should not be perceived as threatening to the bulk of the current leadership and that, in many cases, may be attractive. Current military personnel will stand to benefit from radically improved job security and stability, and will face no cuts in pay or retirement prospects.

Because of the nature of the military hierarchy, this constituency can exert influence only by discrete lobbying within the chain of command and through political pressure on elected officials. Effective military reform probably cannot take place over the determined resistance of the senior leadership, but most of those men are well-intentioned, dedicated public servants. Given the diffusion of power within the uniformed services, and the energy with which subordinates work to shield their eyes from critical shortcomings in the units they command, they are unable to initiate such reform themselves. The actual impetus must come from outside the Pentagon, i.e., from Congress.

PROBLEMS WITH REFORM PRESCRIPTIONS

A considerable volume of literature has been produced on the subject of military reform, and relatively little of the factual content of this book is new. Some writers are hostile to the military on principle, but most are patriotic citizens anxious to see a restoration of American ability—if not necessarily willingness—to use force effectively in the international arena.[21] Some of their work focuses on publicizing the nature and scope of American military ineptitude, some on discerning its origins. Most of their analyses are sound.

What is dissatisfying in much of the writing on military reform has come in the area of corrective prescriptions. Some of these are hopelessly vague, calling for a "restoration of the national spirit." This seems to be rather beyond the capacity of government to provide and, as has been argued, the national spirit is not the problem in the first place. Other than the usual budget-oriented calls for "trimming the fat" from the armed forces, which when enacted usually have the opposite effect, most demands for military reform are aimed at rationalizing the procurement of arms and equipment, at streamlining command and control at the highest levels, or at unifying the services. These are certainly worthwhile goals, and many of the proposals are excellent as far as they go. Unfortunately, streamlining the arms procurement process will only insure that more and cheaper equipment will be lost in combat by forces that, because of their organization and training, are incapable of waging war under any but circumstances of massive manpower and material superiority. Improving higher command may do wonders at the strategic level, and this is by all means worthwhile, but it does nothing for tactical commanders who will remain unable to influence the organization, manning, equipment, training, and utilization of forces allegedly under their control. Many proposed reforms concern details of weaponry, tactics, and doctrine, but it is illusory to try to impose these on a military leadership too obtuse or—and this is more likely—too distracted by bureaucratic infighting to appreciate for itself their (sometimes dubious) benefits. Hardware proposals also entail impossible expense, at least in their initial phases, and are irrelevant in the wake of the Reagan build-up and its expensive commitment to specific weapon systems. All reformers call for improvements in the army's deranged personnel rotation system, but the reforms that have resulted have been piecemeal, superficial at best, and cannot carry over into wartime.

Nor is the problem purely one of inter-service rivalry, and inter-service rivalry has been greatly oversold as a source of American military confusion. Indeed, a strong case can be made that inter-service *cooperation*, often called "log-rolling," is a cause for even more concern. The United States has a long history of being able to produce incompetence within even single-service organizations. For instance, in 1948 General Curtis LeMay assumed command of the Strategic Air Command (SAC). He decided to demonstrate the illusory nature of the nation's strategic bombing power, which at the time was being touted by civilian leaders as an invincible shield against the Russians. He launched bombing raids from every SAC airbase against Dayton, Ohio, an undefended target. Not one bomber completed its mission.[22] If we wish to look further back, we will find that approximately 30 percent of Custer's troops at the Little Bighorn had never fired their army-issue rifles.[23] The great divide between the services is merely a more obvious version of the gulf surrounding each of the various bureaucratic entities created throughout DOD. The same sort of divisions exist between the branches within the army itself, infantry, armor, field artillery, and communications, et cetera, and even within units. These fissures are created by organizational techniques that may be appropriate to a social welfare agency or a pharmaceuticals firm, but not to a fighting force.

Service unification is only the crudest of a whole class of proposed reforms in the structure of the Defense Department and the command flow-chart. Many of these proposals are well thought-out and should be adopted. However, to impose such changes on the military from the outside is to side-step more fundamental problems: even if the congressional decision-making process could be relied upon to produce sensible solutions, the civilian authorities could not possibly identify and solve the pervasive problems of the armed forces in the face of the apathy or active resistance of the vast military bureaucracy. The key question is; Why is it that the nation's soldiers, whose professional interests—indeed, whose very lives—ultimately depend on making military organizations as effective as possible, have not made these often-obvious improvements themselves? The structural approach does not address this vital issue.

One specific solution to the army's problems that is frequently called for is a return to the draft.[24] This allegedly would bring in a better breed of enlisted soldier, or at least allow us to pay him less. Several writers make the point that a draft would cause more college students to join the ROTC, thus increasing the pool of potential officers. From that pool the best could be selected for active duty. Taken in that sense this would be a self-defeating reform: do we really want an officer corps made up of people who joined ROTC in order to evade the draft? Furthermore, based on personal observation I am unable to accept the implication that today's volunteers (officers or men) are a bunch of inferior riffraff.[25] There is nothing wrong with the American soldier.[26] Instead, I accept with certain caveats the old saying, "There are no bad soldiers, only bad leaders," and that our leadership is poor only because it is not permitted to reach its potential. Restoring the draft unquestionably would have many benefits if it were imposed in an equitable manner, but this has not often been the case in American history. It would not address the fundamental issue of leadership. Draftees trained and led into battle by inexperienced young chemistry majors seeking promotion, or by officious bureaucrats and administrators, will not perform any better than today's volunteers. In any case, restoring the draft is not only an essentially political issue but also clearly a dead one.

Most other specific suggestions made by reformers revolve around one of two key concepts: an improved ethics code for officers or creation of a General Staff on the Prussian/German model. Suggestions of the General Staff variety, while rooted in a basically sound concept, remain unimplemented for reasons already discussed. Proposals for an ethics code or an "ethics police force" are based on the idea that by improving the ethics of the leadership we can obtain men who will produce effective forces.[27] While there is unquestionably a vital link between ethical leadership and military effectiveness, trying to go from ethics to effectiveness is an exercise in futility. Legislating morality is notoriously difficult, and to enforce it would require massive further growth in the bureaucratic and legalistic jungle that is already strangling the field forces. It seems more reasonable to demand and enforce effectiveness, knowing that it cannot be achieved by unethical leaders.

The long-term solution to the problem of American military organization must lie in creating an internal "bottom line"—i.e., military effectiveness— that can act as an analogue to the free-market "invisible hand," one that will motivate defense personnel at every level to pursue policies that are compatible with the rational interests of the system as a whole.

THE SPECIFICS OF REFORM

The upbringing of the men who become U.S. Army officers, the constitutional obstacles to the making of rational military and national security policy, and fundamental American social structure and values, all are relevant to the demonstrated incapacity of our military institutions. We must acknowledge that none of them are readily susceptible to purposeful change or reform, and it is doubtful that their "reform" would be compatible with the preservation of those features of American civilization that make it worth defending in the first place.

Within the military institutions themselves, however, administrative and organizational structures, techniques, and goals *are* susceptible to change. They are, in fact, capable of very deep, rapid, and meaningful change, if that change is forced upon them by the national leadership. One proof of this is the manner in which the army has adapted to the all-volunteer concept. Regardless of what one may think of the results, this has been very thorough and in practical terms unresisting. Another example lies in the relative rapidity and thoroughness with which the services have responded to mandatory racial and sexual integration, social policies that the military leadership might have been expected to resist doggedly.[28] Although much civilian interference with military organizations is baneful, it has often been necessary in the past. Neither the infamously successful German *Blitzkrieg* nor the air defense system that preserved Great Britain in 1940 would have been developed without powerful governmental interference with the organizational priorities of the military services involved.[29]

Administrative and organizational factors are therefore the keys to meaningful reform of the American military system. They are the only factors that are both critical in the production of our pitifully incompetent military forces *and* susceptible to rapid, forced, and meaningful change.

Military Reform, in the long term, means reforming the army's leadership from the bottom up, starting with the selection and training of officers, the means by which they are developed, assigned, and promoted, and the ways in which they are utilized. In the shorter term, we must rely on radical organizational changes that will permit the many capable leaders who are already on hand to have an impact on the units they command. Only by producing politically trustworthy but professionally capable military officers, giving them command of units that are stable enough in terms of personnel and equipment to be successfully trained and led, *and making them responsible for the performance of those units*, may we field a force that can effectively wage war at whatever level is deemed necessary by political leaders. The recommendations made in this book are limited to that goal, and questions of procurement, doctrine, force structure, and national strategy, fascinating as they are, are treated tangentially if at all. These matters certainly require attention, but in the absence of effective field forces they are peripheral issues.

The main thrust of the proposed practical reform measures is to correct the army's grossly dysfunctional evaluation systems, particularly as they apply to individual promotion. These measures are based on the idea that the problems of the army's leadership are rooted in organizational absurdities, not in personal incompetence or immorality. Only by divorcing the military reporting system from the promotion process can we insure the integrity and relevance of either. Current evaluation systems mandate a fatal level of dishonesty, distort the chain of command, create a tremendous waste of time and resources, forbid tactical or organizational flexibility or creativity, compartmentalize units into jealously competing fragments, and drive wedges between commanders and their troops. The promotion of officers is effectively unrelated to the performance of the units under their command. Proposed corrections in the evaluation system will force units to compete with one another, yet at the same time will give all soldiers a vested interest in the overall performance of the combined arms team. A rigid connection between unit performance and individual retention and promotion will make possible a "privatization" of the assignments and promotion systems, insuring that individuals are selected by people with a genuine stake in their duty performance.

However, such an evaluation system cannot work in today's units because leaders are effectively neutralized by the confusion induced through massive personnel and equipment turbulence (turnover). Units, particularly above battalion level, do not reflect the abilities and shortcomings of their leaders. Units must be stabilized at a very high level, preferably as divisions, because current efforts at stabilization (COHORT, Regimental System) do nothing to correct the confusion in the army's multi-layered hierarchy of staffs. The present evenly distributed turbulence must be replaced by a steady ripple of change, cycling through the entire army on a four-year basis. The system proposed will convert the existing unit structure into a system of stabilized divisions, taking approximately forty months to absorb the existing field army. It will be self-sustaining thereafter.

Although personnel and equipment turbulence are crippling to the army, their effects are compounded by a command superstructure that is designed for refighting World War II but would undergo sweeping automatic changes in the event of World War III. In peacetime, this superstructure exerts a crushing weight on subordinate units through gross over-supervision. Problems in the rank structure extend down to small-unit level, where the leadership ranks constitute half of all personnel and private soldiers are a scarce commodity. Proposed reforms will correct this imbalance between leaders and led, and create a peacetime command structure that will divorce field units from higher commands and staffs. This will force and permit field units and higher headquarters to focus on their individual missions, while allowing easy recombination for exercise or war-fighting purposes. This structure will also create a field army that has the institutional independence required by the permanent existence of large combat formations.

These are short-fuze reforms, and the process for implementing them is described. Achieving stability at unit level will require toleration of considerable short-term upheaval in the army bureaucracy. This is an acceptable trade-off. Moving to effective evaluation methods will require the creation of an entirely new inspecting body within the army, but many of its elements already exist. Once the decision to adopt reform has been taken, approximately twenty months will be available in which to bring this organization into form.

For the longer term, the most important proposals concern the selection of new junior officers. Although there are many capable junior (and senior) officers in the army today, the weakest link in the command structure commonly comes at company and platoon level, where officer leadership is the most poorly prepared and inexperienced. Methods are proposed whereby the best of experienced non-commissioned officers (NCOs) and junior soldiers can be absorbed into the officer corps, thus increasing its legitimacy in the eyes of soldiers and removing disruptive competition to officer leadership from subordinate ranks. Proposed changes in the source of ROTC cadets, their academic instruction, and the methods used to train them will consistently produce junior officers who will be older and more mature, who will already have military experience, and who will have the academic background needed to understand and apply U.S. military doctrine and political policy.

Each of the following five chapters examines some critical problem area. Each makes specific proposals for phased reforms. These proposals aim only at reorganizing personnel already on hand, albeit redefining their relationship to one another, in the units and with the equipment that already exist. The army may willingly institute some of these reforms on its own initiative. Others will have to be forced upon it against fierce initial resistance. The final chapter discusses the means and results of implementation.

NOTES

1. See Fred Reed's column, "Back Talk," *Army Times*, May 25, 1987, subtitled "Military no worse than the rest of society." Reed's argument is that the military should not be pilloried for its incompetence, since the rest of America is just as screwed up. For other fairly typical examples see Jeffrey Record, "Is Our Military Incompetent?" *Newsweek*, December 22, 1980; James Fallows, "... And If this is just another job, then by God, I'm a sorry suck-egg mule," *Washington Monthly*, April 1981; Jeffrey Record, "Why America's Military Has Joined the Ranks of the Losers," *Washington Post Weekly Edition*, February 13, 1984; Walter C. Clemens, Jr., "Goliath and the Exocet: Have Americans Gone Soft?" *Christian Science Monitor*, August 18, 1987. For perceptions within the military, see Command Information Division, Office of the Chief of Public Affairs, *Results of Professional Development of Officers Study Surveys* (Washington, D.C.: Headquarters, Department of the Army, 1985), and Benjamin F. Schemmer, "Internal Army Surveys Suggest Serious Concerns About Army's Senior Leaders," *Armed Forces Journal International*, May 1985; David H. Marlowe, ed., *New Manning System Field Evaluation: Technical Report No. 5* (Washington, D.C.: Department of Military Psychiatry, Walter Reed Army Institute of Research, September 1987). The view from Capitol Hill appears in Ninety-ninth Congress, *Defense Organization: The Need for Change, Staff Report* (Washington, D.C.: GPO, 1985). A good overview of the reform debate can be found in Asa A. Clark, Peter W. Chiarelli, Jeffrey S. McKitrick, and James W. Reed, eds., *The Defense Reform Debate: Issues and Analysis* (Baltimore: Johns Hopkins University Press, 1984). Numerous major works on military reform are cited elsewhere in the text.

2. See, for instance, Colonel Harry G. Summers, *On Strategy: A Critical Analysis of the Vietnam War* (Novato, Calif.: Presidio Press, 1982). Bob Buzzanco, "The American Military's Rationale against the Vietnam War," *Political Science Quarterly*, issue no. 4, 1986, contains a brief discussion of the "We could have won it" arguments of military revisionists.

3. See James Burk, "Patriotism and the All-Volunteer Force," *Journal of Political and Military Sociology*, Fall 1984.

4. See especially the historical works of Russell F. Weigley.

5. A key work for understanding the impact of sudden wartime expansion on the army's subsequent organizational methods is Robert R. Palmer, Bell I. Wiley, and William R. Keast, *The Procurement and Training of Ground Combat Troops* (Washington, D.C.: Office of the Chief of Military History, 1948).

6. One could draw some sharp parallels here between the American military and American industry.

7. See S. L. A. Marshall, *Pork Chop Hill* (New York: The Macmillan Company, 1956).

8. For a graphic example of an increasingly typical price for losing in the twentieth century, see Alain Resnais's classic film, "Night and Fog" (Nuit et Brouillard). Bring along a medium-size plastic bag.

9. See McGeorge Bundy, Morton H. Halperin, William W. Kaufmann, George F. Kennan, Robert S. MacNamara, Madalene O'Donnell, Leon V. Sigal, Gerard C. Smith, Richard H. Ullmann, and Paul C. Warnke, "Back from the Brink," *Atlantic*, August 1986.

10. See Leslie H. Gelb and Richard K. Betts, *The Irony of Vietnam: The System Worked* (Washington, D.C.: The Brookings Institute, 1979). The authors demonstrate the relentlessness with which these bureaucratic systems will pursue senseless policies and goals even when key personnel in the system recognize that they are unachievable or self-destructive.

11. The Inchon invasion of late 1950 was the last major successful American military operation of consequence. Edward Luttwak makes this point in a number of articles, and it has become the standard PAWEWTH (Point After Which Everything Went to Hell) among military affairs writers. See, for example, Clemens, "Goliath and the Exocet." ("PAWEWTH" is a useful acronym derived from Professor John Lewis Gaddis of Ohio University.)

12. Public Law 99–433, the Goldwater-Nichols Department of Defense Reorganization Act of 1986. See Michael Ganley, "DOD Reorganization Awaits Reagan's Pen after Compromise Bill Clears Senate," *Armed Forces Journal International*, October 1986; William V. Kennedy, "The Military Services Counterattack Pentagon Reform," *Christian Science Monitor*, July 29, 1987.

13. COHORT stands for Cohesion and Operational Readiness Training, a system in which company-sized elements are trained and remain together for a three-year tour, which may include rotation overseas. See discussion, chapter 2. Colonel Dandridge Malone was very enthusiastic in "Dear Army: You've Got Yourself a Winner," *ARMY*, September 1985.

14. See Schemmer, "Internal Army Surveys."

15. Command Information Division, Office of the Chief of Public Affairs, *Results of the Professional Development of Officers Study Surveys* (Washington, D.C.: Headquarters, Department of the Army, 1985), 8.

16. See Richard Gabriel, *Military Incompetence: Why the American Military Doesn't Win* (New York: Hill and Wang, 1985), viii-x.

17. Quoted in Edward N. Luttwak, *The Pentagon and the Art of War: The Question of Military Reform* (New York: Simon and Schuster, 1985), 61. See also

David C. Jones, "What's Wrong with the Defense Establishment?" in Asa A. Clark, et al., eds., *Reform Debate*.

18. The term "pucker factor" refers to the problems individuals experience with sphincter control when suddenly exposed to enemy fire. In a larger sense it applies to the radical alteration in value systems experienced by men in combat.

19. American military reform schemes based on the model of the German General Staff date at least to the 1870s and the works of General Emory Upton. See Emory Upton, *The Armies of Asia and Europe* (New York: D. Appleton & Company, 1878; reprint, Westport, Conn.: Greenwood Press, 1968), and *The Military Policy of the United States* (Washington, D.C.: 1912). The prescriptions made in Luttwak's *Art of War* are essentially a call for a true general staff. Resistance to the concept is partially explained in Robert L. Goldich, "Evolution of Congressional Attitudes toward a General Staff in the Twentieth Century," in Senate Armed Services Committee, *Defense Organization*, 244–74.

20. Senator Barry Goldwater, "Overdose of Oversight and Lawless Legislating," *Armed Forces Journal International*, February 1987. See also Ninety-ninth Congress, *Defense Organization*, 569–613; James W. Reed, "Congress and the Politics of Defense Reform" in Asa Clark, et al., *Reform Debate*.

21. James Fallows, Richard Gabriel, Arthur Hadley, Edward Luttwak, Jeffrey Record, and Paul Savage, among many others, have pointed out most of the problems discussed here. Politician Gary Hart has published a book on the subject. Their descriptions of the failures of the American armed forces and of their causes are generally well written and documented. However, some reform writers are not so responsible, as Fred Reed points out in "Let's Reform the Military Reformers," *Washington Post*, "Outlook," H1.

22. Harry R. Borowski, *A Hollow Threat: Strategic Air Power and Containment before Korea* (Westport, Conn.: Greenwood Press, 1982), 167–68, 181; Fred Kaplan, *Wizards of Armageddon* (New York: Simon and Schuster, 1983), 43.

23. Evan S. Connel, *Son of the Morning Star: Custer and the Little Bighorn* (New York: Harper and Row, 1984), 307.

24. For example, Richard Gabriel makes a strong appeal for a draft in the conclusion of *Military Incompetence*. James Fallows makes a similar argument in *National Defense* (New York: Random House, 1981). It is probably the most common reform prescription.

25. Although such criticism of army personnel has become muted in the later 1980s, it still occurs. See Arthur T. Hadley, *The Straw Giant* (New York: Random House, 1986).

26. For a recent and very upbeat description of American soldiers in basic training, see George C. Wilson, "Our Gung-Ho Volunteer Army Gets in Step," *Washington Post National Weekly Edition*, September 14, 1987.

27. The preeminent theorists along these lines are Richard Gabriel and Paul Savage. See *Crisis in Command: Mismanagement in the Army* (New York: Hill and Wang, 1978).

28. For a recent discussion, see Richard Halloran, "Women, Blacks, Spouses Transform Military," *New York Times*, August 25, 1986, sec. 2.

29. Historically, many advances in organization and doctrine have had to be imposed on military organizations by external government pressure. The Wehrmacht's *Blitzkrieg* and the Royal Air Force's Air Defense System are World War II

examples. See Barry R. Posen, *The Sources of Military Doctrine: France, Britain, and Germany between the World Wars* (Ithaca: Cornell University Press, 1984). Marine Corps amphibious doctrine and the infrastructure to support it were developed under severe political pressure to justify the continued existence of the Marine Corps. See Allan R. Millett, *Semper Fidelis: The History of the United States Marine Corps* (New York: Macmillan, 1980).

2

UNITS

In April of 1985, after nearly two years of needling the battalion leadership about the unit's total lack of practical combat skills, I was directed to launch small ground attacks on the unit's missile batteries. The batteries were informed of the forthcoming assaults, and even notified of the hour at which they would be made. Nonetheless, the first night assault encountered no security forces, wiped out the battery leadership, and captured the Fire Direction Center with all of its classified equipment and documents. These included all of the critically sensitive communications and Nuclear Release Authentication System (NRAS) codebooks. No attempt was made to "destroy" any of this equipment or sensitive material. No use was made of the unit's substantial quantities of night vision equipment for security purposes. Only one soldier, a cook, attempted to resist the attack. This soldier later told me that he had not been told of the planned exercise and at first believed the assault to be a real one.

This was the first attempt made in the memory of the battalion to use a genuine opposing force (OPFOR) to test its defensive tactics and procedures. Had the exercise been real, the little team of aggressors (created ad hoc that morning and consisting of two air defense sergeants and myself) would have killed about thirty soldiers in a leisurely assault lasting perhaps three minutes. This was the type of attack identified by all intelligence echelons as the most likely and most dangerous threat to units of this kind, and it neutralized one-third of a U.S. Army nuclear-capable missile battalion.

In a rational world, the battery commander would have been counseled sharply, if not relieved. However, in that same rational world someone would have been held responsible for putting 350 marines in a dormitory in a war zone in Beirut. In the very different world of the army, the evaluators' report made no mention of the unfortunate incident related above and the battery received a "Pass" score for Battery Defense.[1] No attempt was ever made to correct the flaws in equipment, tactics, or Standard Operating Procedures (SOPs) that had rendered the unit so vulnerable to disaster.[2] Instead, after several later exercises with virtually identical results,[3] the OPFOR program was terminated without comment.

It would be a grave mistake to ascribe this apparent lack of interest in combat readiness to personal failings on the part of the officers involved. The problem is systemic.

PERSONNEL TURBULENCE

Field Manual 6–40, the artillery gunnery manual, contains a definition of casualty criteria.[4] To "neutralize" an enemy unit, gunners aim to inflict 10 percent casualties. To "destroy" it, 30 percent. And yet the U.S. Army's personnel rotation system routinely inflicts such damage on its own units as a matter of policy. The rate of personnel turnover or "turbulence" at unit level varies with the unit, and the overall rate varies considerably over time. A 1975 study of the Second Armored Division revealed personnel turnover rates in component units and staffs ranging from 177 percent to 388 percent.[5] In 1980, 81 percent of the army's officers and enlisted personnel changed assignments. In 1985, 46 percent of officers changed jobs.[6]

In the Second Infantry Division, Korea, personnel serve only a twelve-month tour. This does not translate into a 100 percent turnover rate, however. First of all, many soldiers fail to complete the tour due to injuries, family problems at home, disciplinary actions, et cetera. On the other hand, many soldiers find the environment so congenial that they voluntarily extend their tours. The overall rate for the division in 1986–1987 was 89 percent.[7] At company level the rate is far higher, because soldiers are not transferred and replaced on a one-for-one basis. The transfer or promotion of one individual may generate moves for several others. Gaps develop in particular companies or sections, necessitating constant reshuffles at every level. The average lieutenant in my battalion went through three jobs in a year. The practical level of turnover at company level is two to three times the rate for the division as a whole. The rate was lower in Germany, but still approached 100 percent per year.

Such personnel turbulence, which effectively neutralizes units in peacetime, has been institutionalized in combat. Soldiers in the Korean and Vietnamese wars served one-year tours, prompting the famous statement "We were not in Vietnam once for ten years, we were there for one year ten times." Commanders' time in command was even shorter, averaging less than six months.

Why does the army purposely inflict upon itself such a crippling system? Virtually every other army in the world recognizes that the soldier is a human being and that his ability to function in any organization, especially one that may subject him to the terror of combat, depends on human factors like familiarity, trust, and respect. The American military system insists instead on treating the soldier as a spare part, a "crewman, missile, 15D20." It is a sad irony that a nation with such a profound respect for the individual should treat the men who defend it with such contempt. The current personnel system derives from the emergency measures instituted a couple of generations ago in order to mass-produce a world-class army out of one designed for fighting Indians and Mexican bandits. The tendency to rely on individual rather than unit rotation was confirmed during the Korean and Vietnamese wars. This system was never designed to improve combat effectiveness, but rather to spread the burden of combat "fairly," and the driving force was a perceived need to lessen political pressures to bring the boys home immediately. The system of individual replacements may have been an unavoidable emergency measure when we were forced to build an army from scratch. Individual rotation had some political justification, even though it made no military sense, in wars fought by draftees with no national intention of winning. It is inappropriate for the large, standing, volunteer army of today. The personnel system has never adjusted to this reality.

To a managerial mind, accustomed to moving commodities to market and maintaining inventories, it may seem sensible to treat people like pork bellies. This system does not work with soldiers and never has. It lives on because of its illusory career benefits for officers and its apparent administrative convenience. Most Americans, even those who have served in the armed forces in wartime, have little appreciation for just how badly American units have performed in combat. The victories won through massive manpower and material superiority, in coalition with more experienced allies, have obscured the shocking disparity between the performance of armies professionally organized, trained, and led, and our own.

Recognizing that the division was the unit that actually fought large-scale conventional battles, the army attempted during World War II to raise and train cohesive units of that size, often built around National Guard cadres. Originally envisaging a field army of some 200 combat divisions, we actually fielded 90 of widely varying quality. By the end of the war, the army had run out of divisions. Because of higher than expected casualties (a very large percentage of which were psychological cases), units already committed to combat demanded individual replacements far faster than they were being produced. Accordingly, the army stripped the trained soldiers out of units with later deployment dates and shipped them off to Africa, Italy, and France as individuals. Replacements were taken from highly trained units to be sent to units already overseas. Those formerly highly trained units then drew replacements from units in training, who then drew replacements from divisions newly forming. Between activation and deployment overseas, the 106th Division lost over 12,000 men to replacement duty. The Sixty-ninth Division lost over 22,000, more than the total number of men in the division. The official history of the procurement and training of ground troops during World War II shows that reliance on individual replacements severely disrupted the production of trained divisions and seriously degraded their combat performance.[8] As a direct result, the majority of United States Army divisions could not hold their own against their German opponents without "overwhelming artillery ... and close air support." In the average engagement, only one-third of American infantrymen in combat would even fire their weapons at the enemy.[9]

One of my professors at Ohio University was a soldier in such a unit. Dr. Gifford Doxsee was then a private in the 106th Infantry Division, fully trained during 1944 and preparing to deploy overseas. Private Doxsee felt confident in his unit and in the men with whom he had trained. Unfortunately, just before embarkation for Europe all of the unit's riflemen and machinegunners were stripped from the unit and shipped to France as individual replacements. The division was then filled up with a hodgepodge of new recruits, excess Army Air Force cadets, and soldiers at home on leave from the Aleutians. The last group of soldiers joined the division two weeks before embarkation and never received any training with the unit. The division went immediately into the line in a "quiet sector." Five days later it was destroyed in the German Ardennes Offensive, generally known to Americans as the Battle of the Bulge. The story of the 106th Division is a controversial one, partly because no one really knows what happened. Most records were lost in the division's collapse. The men did not know each other or their commanders and did not feel any real connection with the unit. Although pieces of the unit put up a serious fight, the army's official history of the battle shows that the division simply dissolved. Private Doxsee spent the remainder of the war as a prisoner.[10]

The army made a sincere effort to train and deploy men in units. In cases where this was successfully carried out, American divisions were quite comparable in quality to those of the enemy. The Eighty-second Airborne and 101st Division are examples, and their names live on in the army today because of their excellent performance in battle. That performance is proof that there is nothing wrong with the American fighting man, given decent leadership and a unit in which he is a man, not a spare part. What happened to the 106th, on the other hand, was not unique, and it foreshadowed events in Korea and Vietnam.

Clearly, the individual replacement system had a devastating effect on units. What was its effect on individuals? Historian Martin van Creveld explored this question and came up with some startling figures. The German army fought on multiple fronts for six years and suffered almost two million killed. During that time, the highest rate of psychological casualties suffered (that van Creveld could substantiate) was 2.7 percent of strength per year, and that was in units in the West during a period of little fighting. In the Afrika Korps the rate was about 2 percent, and in Army Group South, on the Eastern Front, the figure was even lower. These are men who were evacuated because of mental problems, and up to 85 percent eventually returned to their units. The rate of relapse was insignificant. Psychological casualties were not considered a significant problem, even in 1945. By 1943, in contrast, with the United States Army still only minimally engaged in combat,

admissions to psychiatric hospitals were running at an average of 6.76 percent of strength per year, the lowest figure being 3 percent... and the highest 120–150 percent. For combat divisions on the European continent between June and November 1944 the figure was 26 percent, or almost ten times that of the opposing German Army Group D. The overall number of [American] soldiers treated for psychiatric disease in World War II was 929,307, or 8.9 percent of all who passed through the army. Close to 43 million men-days were lost, and 320,000 men had to be discharged as permanently unfit. The number of cases was about equal to that of all battle and nonbattle wounds combined and exceeded the number of those killed by a factor of about three to one. At one time, indeed, more men were being discharged from the army for psychiatric reasons than were being added by induction, prompting General Marshall to set up an investigation.[11]

Van Creveld's findings sparked further research, and it has become clear that the actual number of German psychological casualties is masked by problems of definition and reporting practices.[12] Nonetheless, there still appears to have been a great disparity in this regard between the German and American armies, and the difference clearly was related to organizational and leadership factors.

Consider this comparison of the experiences of a young German conscript and that of a young American draftee.[13] Fritz is from Bavaria. He is inducted into a training unit located not far from his family home. His fellow soldiers are mostly Bavarians like himself. His officers are veterans from the division that he will join when his training is complete, and they will accompany him to the front. During his training he grows close to the other men of his unit, as is natural during a shared period of excitement and learning. Training completed, he and his fellows board a train for the Eastern Front. They arrive in a rest and rehabilitation center behind the lines. Their division is pulled out of the line to come back and integrate them. They meet their new commanders and are distributed in groups to the specific small units that need them. As part of the division they move up to the front to face their first experience of combat.

Fred, on the other hand, is from a small farm in New Mexico. He receives his draft notice and is given a train ticket to Fort Dix, New Jersey. There he engages in a very intense period of training with a wondrously diverse group of fellow draftees, with whom he also begins to form strong bonds. Training complete, he is torn away from his new friends and team-mates and put on a troop train for Norfolk, commanded by a bored second lieutenant that he will never see again. In Norfolk he boards a troop transport that takes him to France. There, he sits alone among many others in similar straits, waiting to be assigned to a unit. One day a truck pulls up, and his specialty code matches the driver's requisition list. He gets in the truck, but the men from his new unit do not even want to know his name. Why should they? Replacements do not last long enough to make good buddies. He joins his new unit in the line. That night he goes out on patrol.

Which man would you rather be? Is it any wonder if Fred shortly joins the list of psychological casualties? Some have argued that the German was simply better suited socially and psychologically to be a soldier than the American. Van Creveld disputes that. But even if it were true, we must ask why then did the Germans go to such lengths, and pursue policies that must have been very inconvenient to administrators, to cater to the social needs of their soldiers? After all, the Wehrmacht did not have a reputation for coddling people. They did it because long experience showed that it was necessary and that it worked. The German army in World War II did not disintegrate until it was physically destroyed.

In Korea, in 1950, the first American units committed to combat often refused to fight, demanding to be sent back to the arms of their girlfriends in Japan. American soldiers threw away their boots so that they could run faster.[14] Generals grabbed bazookas and were captured fighting North Korean tanks, because their soldiers would not.[15] Only when General Walton Walker gave his controversial "stand or die" order, and after they discovered that their friends who had surrendered had been strangled in barbed wire, burned to death in gasoline-soaked foxholes, or castrated and hung, did they begin to fight. The American Army which fought its way out of the Pusan perimeter in September 1950 had learned its trade.[16] However, once the war bogged down and individual soldiers began to rotate in and out of the war, military amateurism resurfaced. S. L. A. Marshall's combat studies in Korea show American patrols, desperately short of military skill, being murdered for the amusement of Chinese troops who remained on the battlefront without relief.[17]

The primary effect of this system was to produce an army of anomic individuals, with no stake in victory and no goal but survival. The end result was a doped-up, officer-killing American army disintegrating in Vietnam. The passive disobedience and irresponsibility shown in Korea turned into active resistance. General William C. Westmoreland, commander in Vietnam and later Army Chief of Staff, defended the one-year tour and the individual rotation policy on the grounds that they gave the individual a goal: survival. One has to suspect that individuals had this goal to start with and would have retained it even if their leaders had not made it the primary mission. The lack of a military goal ("victory," or even "maintaining the status quo"), combined with the fact that their commanders spent only six months in their exposure to the same dangers, led soldiers to view themselves as victims. This is a role that American troops are probably the least likely in the world to accept. They replied in kind. There were between 800 and 1,000 actual or suspected "assaults with an explosive device" (fraggings) recorded in Vietnam as of December 1972.[18] This was not a random venting of the homicidal urge, as the great majority of assaults were aimed at officers and NCOs. These figures do not include actual or attempted shootings, intentional misdirection of artillery fire, or "combat refusals," known in other armies as "mutinies." Combat refusals, in which entire units refused to obey when ordered into combat, numbered in the hundreds per year. Drug use and addiction skyrocketed. Official army statistics show that 5.5 percent of U.S. troops were using heroin immediately prior to their return to the United States. As with all military statistics of an uncomfortable nature, these are probably minimized, if not falsified: other drug addiction studies indicate a rate five times that high.[19]

It does not take many such occurrences to destroy the faith of officers in their men. The faith of American soldiers in their leaders clearly was already gone. The resultant "traditions" lie dormant in the current peacetime army, but they have not been forgotten.

Compare this with the performance of the German army of World War II, which suffered millions of casualties in five years of war but never started killing its officers and never lost cohesion. The French army did suffer similar symptoms in 1917, but only after suffering millions of casualties in years of bloody trench warfare, under incompetent and brutally uncaring leadership. Even then they rarely killed their officers, and they did not become drug addicts. The French army later fought for years in Vietnam itself without suffering a drug dependency problem. No example exists of behavior comparable to that of the U.S. Army in Vietnam by any army in any war in history. From a pacifist's point of view it may be a matter of national pride that it took the Americans a relatively minor war, with quite low casualty rates, to reach this level of military disintegration.

Obviously, the individual replacement system does not work in the stress of wartime. It does not work in peacetime either, for somewhat different reasons. In war, units live and work in the field, and the element of fear sends the "learning curve" shooting almost straight up. In peacetime, units are constantly distracted by all sorts of minor irritants. Training in garrison often becomes impossible as units are disrupted by lawn-mowing details, individuals going on leave or visiting the doctor, and change-of-command parades (which can disrupt a unit for weeks because real field units ordinarily do not practice close-order drill). In one fairly representative example, I took my missile battery to a small training area near Mainz to practice tactical use of their weapons and reactions to a road ambush. Training of this kind had never been conducted before in the battalion and was carried out only once more in the three years I was there. Only 48 percent of the battery could be present for training. Several soldiers were on duty in the unit dining facility, collecting change. The cooks were never available for military training. Ten men were in the motor pool for an unannounced battalion maintenance inspection. One of the survey teams was out in the woods putting in survey markers for a battery land-navigation class, another piece of training that was never repeated during my stay in the unit. Two soldiers were sick; six were on leave; five were in school; one was pregnant. Units try to lock in some minimal amount of real training, usually called "prime time." In my *LANCE* unit such training worked out to about seven hours a week, and usually applied only to missile sections. Personnel transfers quickly eroded any collective knowledge gained.

Officers do not learn their jobs any more thoroughly than the troops do. They may become fairly proficient in certain administrative tasks, but they fall short when it comes to tactical training. During the relatively short time they remain in any one position, they are pressed to spend time training their subordinates when they should be training themselves. Neither task is ever finished, of course. Staffs in particular never learn their own wartime functions thoroughly. I was the first of at least six battalion training ammunition officers who ever had to conduct training under the annual ammunition allocation he had requested himself. Staff officers expend the greater part of their energies in harassing subordinate units, pressing them to learn basic skills the staffs themselves lack. As part of a Seventh Army artillery exercise at Babenhausen, I once spent several hours plotting targets for the *LANCE* conventional warhead. I noticed that almost all of the targets were bridges. Finally, I questioned the battalion operations officer as to the source of all this targeting data. He said that he had received no targets from higher headquarters, and so he was picking some himself. Aside from the fact that this practice would cause total chaos in combat, the targets he had picked were inappropriate for *LANCE*. "What exactly do you intend to do to these bridges?" I asked. "Well, hey, we'll just blow those suckers away to cover our retreat." He was under the impression that the missile's conventional warhead was a solid block of TNT, and that it was accurate enough to knock out a bridge from 60 kilometers away. Quite aside from the accuracy issue, the warhead would have had no such effect. It is a cluster of several hundred grenade-like bomblets meant to destroy personnel or material stocks, not hard or structural targets.

I then wandered over to Brigade Artillery HQ to find out why we had received no targets even after the exercise had begun. There I found no officers to question, only several highly agitated NCOs and warrant officers wading literally knee-deep in printouts from the TACFIRE fire direction computer system. Far from being ready to send targets to us, or even to receive targeting information from target acquisition assets, they were swamped by information they had generated for themselves.[20]

Although the brigade staff did send us targets on occasion, this too was a violation of the chain of command, for the role of *LANCE* missile units is to serve as the corps commander's "hip-pocket artillery." All targeting for *LANCE* comes from him. Yet none of the responsible actors at V Corps understood the capabilities and limitations of the missile.[21] Most thought it was an anti-aircraft weapon. I do not recall ever having been ordered to shoot at a MIG, but on most exercises we never received any targets at all.

One former staff officer I spoke to did understand that *LANCE* is in fact a surface-to-surface missile with both conventional and nuclear capabilities. He argued that *LANCE* could not be used in conventional combat because the enemy would recognize its firing signature and assume that it was a nuclear attack. They would then reply in kind. That is a clever political science argument, but it ignores technical and operational factors that make such a scenario extraordinarily unlikely. This is a good example of just how dangerous a little knowledge can be, but it does not appear to be the reason we so rarely received any targets from corps headquarters.

Commanders are the least likely to learn their jobs. Most company-level commands last between twelve and fifteen months. If we assume that it takes a company commander one year to learn his job, and this is almost certainly an underestimate, it means that 66 percent to 94 percent of the army's company commanders have not learned it yet. After about six months on the job the average commander begins to feel comfortable with his garrison and administrative duties, but his actual time as a tactical commander will remain extremely limited. Even when he has mastered his own tactical responsibilities, something which may never occur given the army's training system, he will remain ignorant of the larger picture into which he must fit his unit's actions. If he is ever to gain an understanding of that larger picture, it will be in schools for higher staff and command responsibilities that he normally will attend, if at all, after his short time in command is over. Battalion and brigade commanders may spend more time in their jobs, currently about two years. Since those jobs are more complex, the competency percentage will remain roughly the same. Some very senior commanders may remain in key positions long enough to become quite effective. General Bernard Rogers achieved considerable respect and influence during his eight-year stay as Supreme Allied Commander, Europe (SACEUR), in an unusual admission of the fact that it helps to stay in a job long enough to learn it.

In Vietnam, commanders were limited to six months in most command positions. Although many excuses were given for this, the most legitimate-sounding explanation was that the army needed to build for the long term and to produce as many officers as possible with command and staff experience in combat. This rationale ignored the pressing need to build an army capable of fighting the war in which it was currently engaged; under commanders who outlasted the usual six-month limit, casualty rates fell substantially.[22] It is belied by the fact that many of the most experienced young officers were thrown out of the army in the post-war reduction in force, largely because their combat credentials were deemed less important than their civilian educational levels. But that is irrelevant, because this rationale is bogus. Commands are rotated at this frenetic rate as a means of sharing the wealth, of punching tickets, of getting everybody on the bus. The army will never cease this ingrained, pernicious practice until forced to by some outside agency.

Aside from the training of small teams of soldiers for critical (i.e., inspected) events, little training can be conducted on post. Real training must await a full-scale Field Training Exercise (FTX). Taking a battalion to the field is a very expensive undertaking but, given the distractions of garrison life and the rapid turnover of personnel, it is the only way to maintain any semblance of a go-to-war capability. The FTX permits soldiers to practice low-order but resource-intensive skills like driving in convoy, but the pace is too hectic to allow training on the fine points. The frequency and duration of these exercises vary from unit to unit. In Germany my battalion went to the field perhaps eight times a year, for no longer than four days at a stretch. Since equipment maintenance problems mounted rapidly and the spare parts supply system broke down whenever we were away from the post telephone system, a quick return to post was mandatory. Besides, four days was about the longest period of time people could stay in the field without having to use the latrine, which is uncomfortable enough out in the open even if a unit is not co-ed. Often, no real latrine was available anyway, because there were no privates available to dig one (see chapter 5). The required four-seater porta-potty was kept on one of the five-ton trucks to meet the field-sanitation requirement. Personnel in need, however, usually sought out a convenient bush.

A more fundamental reason that FTXs lasted only four days was because that was the longest that the unit could sustain twenty-four-hour operations. A *LANCE* unit is not authorized the redundancy in personnel necessary for true round-the-clock functioning, but that is the way its mission is defined. Because no one wanted to get caught sleeping on the job, the FTX became a great endurance contest. Unit operations therefore always collapsed at about the seventy-two-hour mark, permitting a decent night's sleep for the vehicle drivers before hitting the autobahn for the trip home. On only one occasion did the battalion stay longer in the field, and that was when it was dragooned into REFORGER in January 1985. Operations started out as usual, but fortunately the unit collapsed before the actual exercise began and there was time to adjust to a more deliberate pace. No lesson was learned: the next FTX hit the seventy-two-hour wall as usual. This behavior was not dependent on the commander, and all *LANCE* units in Europe function the same way. In any case, such major annual exercises as RE-FORGER have very little tactical content, and they provide very little soldier training considering their enormous cost. Operations stop in bad weather. In REFORGER of late 1985, all combat maneuvers were canceled due to rain and the exercise was ended early.[23]

In Korea, on the other hand, we occasionally went to the field for six weeks at a time. Because civilian-imposed restrictions are few, and virtually all of Korea north of Seoul is a vast military camp anyway, the training environment there was fairly realistic. We fired a prodigious amount of live artillery ammo, and our gunnery people reached a truly impressive level of proficiency just prior to the unit's annual training inspection (the ARTEP). This capability evaporated within weeks of this inspection, because field training ceased in preparation for the housekeeping inspection known as the AGI and because personnel turbulence at battery level was so intense. Most military skills are collective, and this applies especially to gunnery. The loss of one or two people from a Fire Direction Center can be crippling. In Korea it happened monthly.

I expended a great deal of effort on weapons training, since it is, after all, the raison d'être of true military units. In the view of my commanders this was a waste of time, and they were right. I conducted a .50 caliber machinegun range in January 1984. Within weeks, all of the trained crews had been broken up by either rotation or transfers within the unit. I conducted another range in September 1985, and the enthusiastic crews spent weeks in preparation. By December, when the battalion rolled out for its ARTEP, all of these crews were gone. I had to assemble and load all six of the unit's guns myself (with blanks) and show their new crews where the triggers were. This was the only time in the three years I spent in the battalion that the .50 caliber machineguns, our heaviest armament other than our missiles, had ever been used on a battalion exercise. Some would argue that this is not important in an artillery unit. Quite aside from the fact that battery defense has been historically a major problem for artillery units,[24] there are less than 40,000 American soldiers assigned to armor or infantry units in Europe,[25] and a substantial portion of them are support personnel. On the deep battlefield anticipated by Air-Land Battle doctrine, support and service units can be expected to bear a heavy burden of the actual combat mission. In any case, the example of the machine guns merely provides a paradigm for what happens to any military skill which requires more than an individual effort.

The effects of personnel turbulence on training extend to all levels of command and staff. The primary combat doctrine of the U.S. Army is called "Air-Land Battle," and it is designed implicitly for U.S. forces fighting as part of NATO in a battle against the Warsaw Pact upon the plains of Europe.[26] Quite aside from the question of whether it will work even there, and whether it is actually a "doctrine" at all, is the fact that it is manifestly inappropriate for combat in Korea. There is no space for maneuver since Seoul, the great prize, is almost within artillery range of the border. The Korean army is large and heavily armed, but unlike European armies it is not structured for mobile operations. The terrain is radically different from that in Europe, and the North Koreans are not the Warsaw Pact. Nonetheless, the army in Korea passes out training guides with titles like "Air-

Land Battle in Korea."[27] Why not? The tour is only one year, two if you are not in the Second Infantry Division. Why bother to learn a whole new set of tactics?

The fact that everyone at every level in the field army is either just learning his job or getting ready to move has resulted in what may be called the army's "Spit-shine Syndrome." This is an exclusive focus on appearances at the expense of reality. This syndrome accounts for much curious behavior, from the wearing of patent-leather combat boots to the creation of new divisions when the army cannot even man the ones it has. The mirror polish of a spit-shined combat boot is taken as an analogue for dedication to the unit and military professionalism, because those doing the evaluating either cannot judge, do not have time to worry about, or have no interest in the actual capabilities of the soldier. Soldiers actually win or lose promotions on the basis of a shoe-shine, and units that report an equipment Operational Readiness (OR) figure of 98 percent are given maintenance awards even though 42 percent of the tracked vehicles break down within twenty-four hours of the start of an exercise.[28] A soldier's duty performance, even coupled with a good score on the physical fitness test, will not save him from involuntary discharge if he looks overweight. This is dealt with in more detail in chapter 6, but it deserves a mention here. We do indeed have what former Army Chief of Staff E. C. Meyer calls a "Hollow Army," hidden behind a layer of shoe polish.[29]

Cumulatively, these factors have resulted in an army that hardly deserves to be considered a military force at all. The security procedures followed in Beirut are often portrayed by military leaders as atypical, but marine precautions in Beirut were not much different from those taken by army units around the world.[30] For example, a soldier on my installation in West Germany was murdered by terrorists in order to get his identification card. They used it to get a car-bomb onto the airbase at Rhein-Main.[31] The soldier's body was found on our rifle range. Immediately, post security precautions were tightened up. Troops with rifles and radios were placed on twenty-four-hour patrol of the camp perimeter, a requirement that removed an entire company-sized unit from training operations each week. These soldiers were forbidden to carry any ammunition. Within a week, they were forbidden to carry firearms at all. Some were then issued billy clubs, but these too were soon forbidden. What precisely were these guards there for? No one knew, but I suspect that the purpose was to reassure the troops of their commanders' concern for their safety. The troops were not impressed. The murdered soldier had been picked up by a terrorist couple in a bar downtown, not kidnapped in an assault over the camp's barbed wire. His body was dumped on a rifle range outside the camp's security fence. For practical purposes the post was protected by armed local civilian rent-a-cops, many of whom were actually Turkish or Yugoslavian college students working part time. *They* had live ammunition. Their major security tool was a spot-search of cars coming onto post. One day I drove through the gate with a trunk full of Bulgarian AKM rifles, a dummy anti-tank missile, and an RPG–7 grenade launcher. Through bad luck I was stopped and searched. The guards looked at this arsenal (which I had an authorization to carry, though no one asked to see it), scratched their heads, and waved me through. I reported this behavior to the post commander, with undetectable results. The guards were not subordinate to him anyway, but to the Community Commander across town.

My installation in Korea was also guarded by armed local nationals, albeit ones who were considerably more intimidating than the part-time college students used in Germany. I was never able to get them to close off several holes in the fence, which were used by the troops to sneak out without their passes and to smuggle in hookers from the "ville" that nearly surrounded the camp.

American soldiers (aside from certain elite units like the Panmunjom guard troops) are almost never trusted with live ammunition except on the range, and then only under very tightly controlled conditions. While the Korean soldier's rifle is kept by his sleeping pad in the barracks, with ammunition piled by the door ready for instant use, the GI's weapon is locked up and often takes an hour or more to issue. This was true in West Germany. It was also true in Korea, and my installation there was only a few kilometers from the North Korean border. During FTXs my units were almost naked from the security point of view. The soldiers had no ammunition for their weapons, usually not even blanks. A few clips of pistol ammunition were kept under lock and key. Only border units carry a fighting load of ammunition to the field, and that is normally sealed in a locked container. My units did not even issue the soldiers their bayonets (though some units do), and usually forbade the carrying of any blade larger than a penknife.

One reason for this state of affairs is the peculiar workings of the army's disciplinary system, which refuses to place on the private soldier any significant responsibility for his own actions while holding his superiors responsible for much that is beyond their control. Another is the low state of weapons training possible in the chaotic training environment the American Army imposes on itself. Also, any requirement for real-world diversions like guard duty interferes with the ever-present need to conduct retraining to maintain the most minimal unit skills. Related to both of these problems is the simple lack of familiarity and trust between officers and enlisted men. There are many memories of assaults on leadership personnel during the Vietnam era and the early years of the Volunteer Army (VOLAR). The legacy of Vietnam is still alive, although most officers today fear their troops' irresponsibility and ignorance more than their possibly malevolent intentions. It is asking a lot to expect an officer to trust his soldiers with live ammo in either peacetime or wartime, and most do not.

One of these days the United States is going to be badly embarrassed when a couple of terrorists hold one of its forward-deployed field units hostage, and it emerges yet again that American soldiers are not trusted with live ammo or knives.

There are some other curious features of army life, also related to personnel turbulence and the resulting demoralization of soldiers. When I arrived at my new unit in Korea, I received the standard Venereal Disease (VD) briefing. I asked what was the current VD rate in the battalion. The "Doc," actually a warrant officer "physician's assistant" (PA), told me 11 percent. That did not seem too bad for a one-year tour in a rather primitive environment. No, he said, that's 11 percent *per day*. The then-current commander was a Baptist fundamentalist who took a negative view of soldiers consorting with the local prostitutes. He could do little about the behavior of junior enlisted men, but rumor had it that he had threatened to record the illness on the official efficiency reports of any officer or NCO who caught VD. Many soldiers therefore put off treatment, trying home remedies until major damage had been done. Whenever a really spectacular case came into Doc's office, he would take a Polaroid photograph of the afflicted member and display it in the infirmary window. His favorite was of a soldier's eye infected, he said, with gonorrhea. He entitled it "Looking for Love in All the Wrong Places." The next commander's attitude was different, saying, "We're going to make this town safe to party in." The VD rate dropped to 4 percent.

The first time I drew duty as Courtesy Patrol (CP), during which I had to patrol the local "ville" armed and in uniform, I found out why the rate is so high. There are about forty bars and clubs along a 200-meter stretch of road just outside the camp gate. The Korean police agent on post told me that there were 2,800 registered prostitutes in the town. This number seems, from observation, to be too high by a factor of about two. The discrepancy probably derives from the fact that Korean officials regard any woman who works for the American Army as a prostitute, whether she is in business or not. Still, it makes for a formidable ratio of hookers to GIs, as there are only about 1,000 GIs on the post. Other U.S. posts have their own villes. Korean civilians stay out of GI bars out of a deadly fear of disease. The ROK Army has its own brothels. Therefore, there are about 1.4 hookers per available customer. The going rate for a "short-time" was ten dollars. An "overnight" went up to twenty, but only around paydays. In between, the price sometimes fell precipitously. During "Team Spirit," an annual exercise that brings American reinforcements to Korea for a couple of weeks, all of these hookers "go home to visit their mothers." That is, they load up on buses and head down to Kimpo, where stateside GIs are accustomed to paying a higher fee. Officers were not permitted in the local clubs because they tended to bid up the price, thus injuring troop morale.

Many military leaders, those who have little control over or respect for their men, regard the bars as an ideal way to let their soldiers blow off steam. Rather than deal with soldiers' social needs in a more uplifting fashion, they tend to them in the most demoralizing manner possible, just as in Vietnam they tried to keep soldiers' morale up by bringing over Playboy playmates for massive USO shows. Raquel Welch compared this to dangling raw meat in front of a caged shark. On most U.S. installations in Korea there operates an official concession, the combination steam bath/massage parlor known colloquially as the "Steam & Cream." Questionable sexual behavior is thus countenanced by the chain of command. As a result, operational security is non-existent. Whenever my battalion went to the field, even if it was on a surprise alert at 2:00 A.M., the unit's "Odjimah"—a local woman who accompanies U.S. units to the field, selling cokes and cookies, and occasionally peddling booze and bovine peasant prostitutes— would be waiting at the gate. Anyone who regards as atypical what appears to have happened to the marines in the Moscow embassy is thus missing one of the prime features of U.S. military management technique.

I have no quarrel with this on moral grounds. For very practical reasons many armies have maintained auxiliary units of prostitutes who wear uniforms, though not, obviously, on the job. The personal morals of many of the B-girls in Korea—as opposed to the ones at Fort Sill—are exemplary. A great many neither drink nor smoke, and their personal goals are to get married and have a family. Many do marry GIs, and I have seen soldiers completely reform themselves under the influence of their new wives. From a moral point of view, the most disturbing problem is the "Madame Butterfly Effect." This results in much heartbreak and many fatalities among the girls, who sometimes take their boyfriends with them. I was required to inspect the unauthorized off-post homes of my soldiers to insure that there had been no tampering, accidentally or on purpose, with the *ondol* heating systems often used to induce a peaceful death through carbon monoxide poisoning.

What is so disturbing about the situation in Korea is its sheer scale and the fact that its management (except possibly for the "Steam & Cream") is left entirely to the locals. Similar situations exist wherever U.S. forces are deployed. The medical costs are high, although in Germany tight local health regulations help a lot. However, the sexual life-style of soldiers has effects quite beyond the VD rate. Some are beneficial: in Korea, I was able to get the battery commanders to use their night vision equipment in the field, because infrared goggles were useful in keeping the field whores and "slicky boy," the famous local thieves, out of the perimeter at night. Most effects are not so benign. GIs come to regard all Korean women as prostitutes, a gross distortion of reality. Such anti-American sentiment as one finds in South Korea, an important ally, is often related to the behavior of U.S. soldiers and the Korean perception that America regards Korea as a dumping ground for diseased and lecherous sexual deviants. The impact on troop morale is mixed: the troops become fairly docile, but they also come to spend all of their spare time and money in the clubs. Their work performance and personal standards decline accordingly. The impact on their social and sexual attitudes upon their return to the United States is unknowable but certainly not healthy. The army is full of people who regard ten-dollar sex and cheap booze as the primary benefit of military service.

EQUIPMENT TURBULENCE

There is another form of turbulence that affects the readiness of army units. That is equipment turbulence. Because personnel come and go but the unit's equipment set stays in place, it must constantly be updated. Problems arise when, as often happens, the equipment the army has contracted for is not delivered when expected or is defective when it arrives. Changing one item on a unit's "MTO&E,"[32] the document that authorizes the specific equipment and personnel a unit is to have, often requires changing many others. What is not required is forbidden. Therefore, it is very difficult to prescribe exactly what a unit should have and when it should have it. Owing particularly to the modernization program that has been going on since just before the Reagan administration took office, MTO&Es are constantly changing. This often necessitates the incorporation of radically new equipment, which affects every other aspect of the unit. When we received the new fire direction computers, the battalion was thrown into tactical and logistical confusion for about one year.

As a battalion supply officer, I was expected to keep up with all of the various changes in authorizations, to order what we were short, and to turn in what was excess. As an "aid" in this process, I had to turn in a monthly MAD report. MAD stands for "Material Assistance Designated." Clearly, they named the report before they decided what the acronym should stand for. The MAD report listed only a portion of the equipment the unit was short, and also had to indicate what had been done toward getting it.[33] I did part of the report for months without understanding it, until my boss left Korea and I inherited full responsibility for it. Once I understood it, I realized that it could be a useful tool rather than the mere paperwork drill we had assumed. I prepared a private version of the MAD that listed all of the authorized equipment we were short, and began acquiring it. Meanwhile, we were given a new MTO&E, to take effect in six months. I therefore had to do another report, called a Special MAD, based on this prospective MTO&E. Later, yet another future MTO&E appeared, and so each month I had to turn in a MAD Report, a Special MAD Report, and a Special MAD#2 Report. In theory, I was supposed to be simultaneously ordering all of the equipment listed on each MTO&E while getting rid of all of the equipment that was not. Since there were literally hundreds of conflicts, I tried to order equipment that was compatible and to avoid turning in anything until its replacement had arrived. Fortunately, no one at our higher headquarters appeared to understand any of the MAD reports, and I was able to get away with this.

Supply at unit level is terribly confused because unit supply officers are normally officers of whatever branch specialty tends to populate the battalion. No combat arms officer wants to be a battalion supply officer, as it is seen as a "non-career-enhancing" position. Most officers who draw such duty do not remain there long. Actually, "Assistant S–4" is not an authorized position at all, and I was rated fictitiously as a Fire Support Team chief. The actual S–4 is also the Service Battery commander, and he has no time for the finer points of logistics.

However, S–4 is an odd sort of position: if you do an exceptionally good job, they keep you there because you are so useful. If you do a bad job, they keep you there to punish you. Regardless of which category I fell under, I stayed there for my entire tour, a very unusual circumstance. I read manuals, talked to supply people, and thrashed around trying to get a handle on the job. After about four months, I came to realize that the key document in DLOGS (the computerized Division LOGistical System) was a printout called the "battalion roll-up," which lists all organizational property by type, stock number, and owning sub-unit. Properly maintained, it also shows MTO&E required and authorized levels, equipment which has been ordered but not yet received, and the budget category under which it falls. If the roll-up can be made both administratively correct and physically accurate, the unit will be fully equipped, balanced, and accountable. It normally receives little attention because it is not an inspected item, being a composite of other documents that are considered more important. Accordingly, it comes to contain innumerable errors and becomes useless as a working document. When I belatedly realized its potential usefulness, I studied it carefully. Ours contained at least 246 serious errors regarding authorizations, equipment on hand, and its distribution in the unit. Some of these were paper errors, and some represented serious equipment shortages or maldistribution. Equipment due-in information was entirely jumbled and unreliable.

Because the warrant officers at division had no faith in the abilities of unit S–4s, and because they relied on the unit roll-up as a quick reference, they rejected literally hundreds of our legitimate equipment requisitions. They did this either because the roll-up showed us as overstocked or because we were ordering certain items that they regarded as being in their province to order, even though they never had time to do so. They did not bother to inform us of rejections but simply threw them in the trash. It took us a couple of months to realize this. Finally, I went down to division HQ and sat with them for several days, demonstrating both our legitimate requirements and the fact that we knew what we were doing. Hundreds of requisitions went into the machine that week, and thereafter our requisitions were passed on without interference. We then were able to abuse the system by ordering things we needed but were not authorized to have, like a ground-mount for our machinegun.

In our quest to make up material shortages quickly and cheaply, we began to examine the roll-ups of all the other battalions in the division, looking for equipment that was overstocked and that we could requisition at no cost to the battalion budget. All of the roll-ups were in the same condition that ours had been, showing large shortages and overages, and many obvious errors. Where the overages shown were in fact present, we were able to obtain large amounts of needed gear.

In Germany I had no control over supply. I had .50 caliber machineguns, but no mounts. As a Fire Direction Officer, I rode in a tracked command post vehicle and therefore had to wear the M25 gas mask, designed for tank crewmen. The M25 is a decent mask in many ways, but it is designed to be hooked up to a forced-air vehicular chemical agent filtration system. It therefore has an air intake that is approximately an eighth of an inch in diameter. We had no vehicular filtration systems. When forced to wear the mask, usually for a six-hour mandatory training period, I found that I could breathe adequately as long as I was asleep.

A unit that discovers a problem with its equipment authorization can, in theory, request a change. However, few people in combat units have the requisite expertise to do so, since unit supply officers are usually combat arms specialists. Warrant officer supply-types know better than to try. I learned how to submit a request, which required an extraordinary amount of paperwork. Such requests went nowhere, because higher staffs either did not understand them or disapproved of them on principle. They simply disappeared into the great maw of the army bureaucracy.

Another MTO&E-related problem for many units, including *LANCE*, is self-defense. The *LANCE* missile has a range of something over 100 kilometers, depending on the warhead used. Units therefore need not be on the forward edge of the battle area. However, to be effective at the deep battlefield interdiction which is their mission they do have to operate fairly close to the front lines. During REFORGER one of our batteries was actually overrun by Blue Force tanks. *LANCE* units have no defense against such heavy elements, and efforts to provide a real anti-tank capability would probably be fruitless. When I was a battalion supply officer in Korea, I found on the unit's property listing an item called a "Tracker, Infrared Guided Missile." I had never seen any missile launchers in the unit, and I knew that we did not have any missile ammunition in our go-to-war stocks (the "basic load" of ammunition). There were supposed to be several of these Trackers on hand. I talked to the supply sergeants. Yes, they had something by that name, in cans that had never been opened. It turned out to be part of a *Dragon* medium anti-tank weapon. Further investigation revealed over a million dollars worth of *Dragon* equipment on hand, but it was never used, inspected, or trained with. *Dragon* is not the kind of weapon you pull off of the shelf and kill tanks with on the spur of the moment. Commanders I talked to expressed surprise that they had this weapon at their disposal, but they were not interested in training with it. There was no time, and besides, we were an artillery unit. Let the grunts kill tanks. One commander even grew hostile, thinking that I had ordered the damned things.

It would be unreasonable to expect *LANCE* units to kill tanks. However, it was clear that they were also unable to guard against any other kind of threat, including the one identified by all intelligence echelons as the most likely danger faced by missile units. This was the threat of attack by small light infantry or *spetsnaz* units.[34] I suggested a change to the MTO&E when my own raids on the *LANCE* batteries revealed that their night vision (NV) equipment, mostly in the form of infrared sniperscopes, was inappropriate for the security mission we were supposed to use them for. Like many other apparently sensible readiness-related initiatives, this one was pointless, because having the right equipment does no good since the soldiers do not know how to use it, and because most units have no batteries for their night vision gear. Both of these handicaps are related to personnel turbulence. Unit supply rooms are staffed according to MTO&Es designed for tactical environments. They therefore lack the personnel to deal with the never-ending need to inventory unit equipment as it constantly changes hands. At company level, there is a 100 percent "change-of-command" inventory about every twelve months. New commanders sign a "hand receipt" listing every item of organizational equipment (and another listing installation equipment like desks, coffee-makers, and vacuum cleaners). They are "pecuniarily liable" for the loss or damage of said equipment, to the extent of one month's pay per incident. Much of the practical art of command consists in sub-hand-receipting this equipment to subordinates so that they may absorb the potential costs and embarrassment. Because sub-hand-receipt holders are constantly changing, unit supply personnel are drowned in paperwork and inventories. They are also expected to do a monthly "10 percent Inventory" just to be sure. They certainly do not desire to *acquire* anything, and even if they do, their commander does not. Battery commanders routinely tore up requisitions sent for their signatures, because they did not wish to assume pecuniary liability for additional equipment in the unlikely event that it should arrive during their period of command. Eventually I was forced to obtain permission to sign requisitions myself. Otherwise nothing would have been ordered.

This is especially true in Korea, because no one really believes that an item ordered will arrive in time to be seen by the soldiers who have requested it. Even if an attempt is made to order it, odds are it will not arrive, because active supply operations (as opposed to inventorying) are very low priority. The army's supply system is reasonably effective *if* a requisition survives the trip from battalion to supply center, but this can be a harrowing journey.

Most unit supply personnel are not very expert in the workings of the supply system, which requires a sophisticated understanding of supply categories, advice codes, authorization documents, et cetera. My Service Battery supply sergeant in Korea was an expert aircraft mechanic, transferred to supply duties because of a hearing loss. His predecessor had been an E–4 cannon crewman. In Germany, I had some expert supply people, but their boss (the battalion Property Book Officer) was a wheeler-dealer who expected something in return for every action he approved or undertook. This made active supply operations a killing chore. He was a not-uncommon type. Such people prosper in the army because they are able to convince the commander that their willing assistance is vital to his career survival. Under the current unit evaluation systems, they are right. I was eventually able to circumvent him on the training equipment and ammo fronts, and I acquired some allies in the unit's supply rooms. Notice I said "allies," because the chain of command is so twisted that the training officer, who is absolutely dependent on logistical support to do anything, has no authority over the supply operation. What supply support I received came through politicking and subterfuge, and it took me two years to obtain reliable collaborators in Germany.

I first noticed the night vision battery problem in Korea. Our unit had a lot of NV goggles, and one commander discovered them in a locker in his arms room. The manual does not contain a stock number for batteries, so he came to me. After a few fruitless attempts to order some through the regular channels, I visited the supply yards at Camp Casey and talked to the yard chief. He said, "Sure, we've got tons of them." And he did, but they could only be issued under the last of seven stock numbers listed in the *Army Master Data Fiche*. If a unit ordered them under any other number it would receive a valid "due-in" but never see any batteries. I picked up several boxes of forty each. I took one to a meeting of all the division's S–4s and asked if anybody needed NV batteries. The question caused a lot of derisive laughter, as everyone knew that they were an unobtainable item. I gave one battery to each of them, and was besieged by calls for the next week. I took a box with me to Germany; my battalion had no batteries, had never used its NV equipment, and never did as a battalion until one exercise almost three years later. For night raids on the *LANCE* batteries, I always borrowed NV goggles from the MPs on my post. They were glad to issue them, since they never used them. The brigade MPs had sniperscopes but had not planned to use them on their ARTEP. No batteries. My next door neighbor in town was an aviation captain and unit supply officer. He saw me come home once, all nasty from a raid, with a pair of goggles still strapped around my neck. He got very excited. I gave him a battery.[35]

Some units do have batteries: ordnance units, because their people understand the supply system and have a natural interest in such gadgets; intelligence units, again because they love gadgets; and some infantry units, because use of the NV equipment is tested as part of their ARTEP. Tanks have NV gear built into their gunnery optics. These considerations do not apply to the bulk of units on the battlefield.

In making raids, I always wore infrared goggles. On a dark night the gun and missile batteries were completely helpless to find me, unless I stood in front of a scope-equipped sentry and told him I was there, then showed him how to turn his scope on. Troops were not familiar with these expensive items because their hand receipt holders did not want to risk issuing them to soldiers, nor to do the paperwork that might have made such issue financially safe. Even if equipped the sentry could not have shot me, because the scope needs to be zeroed to the weapon before it can be aimed accurately. Goggles are much more effective for defensive purposes, hence the suggested change to the MTO&E. No attempt was ever made to submit such a change. Why bother, when the MTO&E was so completely defective to start with? Even if we had had the equipment, we simply did not have sufficient personnel to mount a serious guard force. "A" Battery tried it once, in response to our attacks. The battery commander determined that he could protect the battery for about twelve hours, if he was not required to do anything else.

This is strange. Remember, during a crisis or a war these units would be carrying real nuclear weapons, and even in peacetime they carry important nuclear weapons release codes and other information. A German *LANCE* battalion has a heavily armed Security Battery charged with its defense. So does a French *PLUTON* battalion, which has the same number of missile launchers, but 200 percent more troops. The United States is reportedly negotiating with the Germans to obtain German security batteries to protect the American battalions. It should be interesting to see how well that works, since the Germans require ammunition completely different from that of U.S. units, and it is hard enough to understand what is going on during a firefight even if you speak the same language your security forces do.

There are easier solutions to the battery defense dilemma, mostly through changes in tactics. Unfortunately, a U.S. unit commander has about as much to say about the tactics he uses as about the equipment he receives. The ARTEP manuals and other key training documents contain tactical checklists that implicitly limit acceptable tactical procedures.

There are many other critical problems with the organization of current army units. Basically, there are too many of them, and even those that are forward deployed, in areas where war could occur with little warning, are not manned or equipped at a wartime level. Some divisions in Europe are short entire brigades, which are supposed to appear miraculously in the event of war.[36] That is satisfactory from the standpoint of the *LANCE* units, since the appearance of their live ammunition will be equally miraculous in any emergency mobilization. MTO&Es contain two lists of personnel and equipment, one a "required" list often much higher than the "authorized" list that designates the levels permitted in peacetime. A unit may "require" 607 rifles, but be "authorized" only 558. There seems to be no justification for the existence of many of these units except to provide more command slots for the army's horde of command-hungry officers. There is little or no prospect that additional personnel will arrive in time to participate in the wars these units are liable to find themselves in. West German units are similarly dependent on an emergency flow of reserves to active units, but then those German reserves live in Germany and they know where they are supposed to go in the event of an emergency. The army, far from trying to consolidate its people to field the kind of units it claims to need for the "come as you are war," has instead further scattered its resources by fielding additional divisions of light infantry, none of which can be maintained on a wartime footing, and all of which have missions that do not seem to permit any time for reinforcement.[37]

ATTEMPTS AT CORRECTIVE ACTION

Some units have evolved their own unique methods for achieving a modicum of cohesion, at least among small leadership groups. The Special Forces have their famous "prop-blast" parties. The Second Infantry Division, because of its extremely high turnover rates—and also because no one has a car, so no one needs to fear the dreaded drunk-driving citation—has evolved perhaps the most complex and pervasive set of rituals and customs to strengthen individual identification with the unit. Every officers' club has its brass bell, the focus of many rites. There are rituals for entering and leaving the unit; getting promoted; getting a vehicle stuck in the mud; spilling the salt. The installation to which I was assigned was dominated by my artillery unit, and thus the welcoming ceremony was dictated by the artillerymen. The new arrival, be he engineer, "red-leg" (artillery), or chaplain, was ceremonially redefined as a howitzer. Before the bar, beneath the bell, he stood with mouth open, awaiting a Fire Mission. On the command "Load!" a glass containing a raw egg (the bullet) and some appropriate beverage (the propellant) was held to his lips. At "Fire!" the round was swallowed. Failure to completely drain the glass (which was nearly impossible to do) would result in the observation "Rounds incomplete!" after which another shot would be fired. This would be repeated until it was perceived that the eggs were about to come back up. In case of a miscalculation on this point, a brass "misfire pit" was positioned in front of the celebrant.

At first I was rather skeptical about the value of such rites, but they really do create a bond that permits a small, rapidly shifting leadership team to maintain some sense of corporate identity. The bond is most effective if the glue is about 90 proof. One new arrival's heart stopped when he refused to throw up after seventeen eggs. However, Doc was standing by with a defibrillator. After that, we were more understanding about officers who chose the non-alcoholic option. Such customs have limited applicability and are dying out as the army more and more adopts a suburban life-style and mind-set. It is unlikely that the human howitzer can be fired effectively using Perrier water.

The army leadership recognizes that the individual replacement system is dangerously ineffective and has made some extraordinarily timid attempts to correct it. COHORT stands for Cohesion and Operational Readiness Training. COHORT units are company-sized outfits that train and deploy together, staying intact for a three-year tour that may include rotation overseas. COHORT companies are very impressive. Many hum with a quiet efficiency. The tensions, conflicts, and confusion that plague most units are dramatically reduced, or at least hidden from outsiders. Decision-making power seems to rest at much lower levels and the units respond to changes and new requirements easily. They remind me of German units I have seen. COHORT is a good idea. Unfortunately, it is simply too timid, on too small a scale, to correct the army's deeply rooted problems. Army studies show that the COHORT format dramatically improves "horizontal" bonding, that is, the bonding among the junior enlisted soldiers, but it has been rather less successful in terms of "vertical" bonding.[38] The reasons for this are open to speculation, but I would suggest that it is because of the inherent lack of perceived legitimacy on the part of the junior officer corps (see chapter 6). In practice, the program applies to combat arms units only, leaving the vital logistical and other support units, even those organically a part of combat organizations, in the traditional confusion. High combat casualties will quickly overwhelm the fragile COHORT training base, forcing a return to the individual replacement system. Many COHORT companies are lone islands of stability in units otherwise made up of regular-style sub-elements. Because they do not share in the constant interbreeding that characterizes most units, they stand isolated and apart, often the objects of hostility and suspicion. Worst of all, COHORT does not affect the chaos that prevails at battalion-level staffs and higher, and may even intensify it because COHORT officers are not available for sudden transfers to plug gaps in local staff positions.

The internal resistance to even so sensible and mild a reform as COHORT is so great as to prove the inability of the army to reform itself. The basic idea was proposed as early as World War II,[39] and the current program has its roots in the Vietnam experience, but COHORT is growing at a minuscule rate: in 1984 6.5 percent of combat arms companies were COHORT, in 1986 10 percent. A small number of battalions have been created in the COHORT format, 25 as of 1987. The army expects that 71 percent of its combat arms companies will be COHORT units by 1999, a full generation after the end of the Vietnam War.[40] This is a remarkably hesitant approach by an organization that two generations ago was able to expand itself 5,400 percent in five years and still produce an effective, if not first-class, fighting organization. Resistance derives from management systems that were designed around the individual rotation system and have so pervaded the army bureaucracy that they cannot be rooted out in an acceptably pain-free manner. Nonetheless, COHORT is a step in the right direction, and its successes show the potential embodied in its underlying concepts.

The Marine Corps has also enjoyed considerable success with its Unit Deployment Program, a COHORT-like system for marine battalions. The marines' training cycle is twenty-four months long. In the first six months personnel turbulence is high, as personnel shifts are concentrated in that period. A twelve-month training cycle follows, building from individual to small-unit to battalion exercises. Personnel turbulence is reduced to about 10 percent. For the last six months, the battalion deploys overseas or aboard ship and turbulence is cut to zero.[41]

Another—less successful—attempt to stabilize the army is called the "Regimental System." The idea is to restrict an individual's assignments, particularly those of officers, to a relatively small group of similar units. Thus, a newly commissioned second lieutenant, field artillery, would expect to receive all of his future troop-duty assignments (up to the rank of lieutenant colonel) in one of four or five battalions scattered worldwide but sharing a common personnel pool. One unit in Korea and a few others at some stateside installation might constitute a "regiment," with sentimental but no practical connections. This system works erratically if at all. After a period during which implementation seemed to be stalled the Regimental System seems to be catching on, but only at the price of compromises that nullify the value of the system. Regimental affiliation is voluntary and can be switched at any time, there are no quotas for membership in any given regiment, and regimental preference is only one of several considerations in making personnel assignments.[42] Theoretically, a career serviceman could receive all of his unit assignments within his regiment and still never work in the same battalion twice. Soldiers still rotate as individuals, and the system will become irrelevant very quickly in the event of a military emergency. Up-or-out and the Regimental System are probably incompatible, and the rank and specialty distribution of officers and officer slots does not permit much practical impact for a system with only theoretical benefits.

Therefore, if the United States were to become involved in a sizeable ground war today or in the reasonably near future, there would exist no option except to rely on the individual replacement system which has proven so disastrous over the past fifty years.

A MORE RADICAL APPROACH

These problems are of long standing, but the army shows little real interest in solving them. Although there are many organizational and bureaucratic factors that underlie this lack of interest, they are largely rooted in two realities. One, the army's organizational structure does not reward people who press for the creation of actual military utility, resulting in what has been called the army's "War Will Never Happen" strategy.[43] Two, the basic tenet of that strategy is correct: the war for which the army claims to be preparing, that is, a World War II–style Soviet invasion of Western Europe, ranks among the least likely of all possible occurrences. A great percentage of the American armed forces is held hostage in a land where it most likely will never face combat.

However, this book is written on the assumption that the American people want to obtain something real for their money. While it is fairly certain that American units will not be fighting on the Rhine, it is not at all certain that they will not be fighting somewhere else. In a genuine national emergency, U.S. forces currently earmarked for NATO will be employed wherever we may need them, against real enemies who will quickly recognize the virtual helplessness of the American forces they face.

If that helplessness is to be eliminated, it can be done only through radical organizational reform. For good or bad, the nature of army equipment has been fairly well determined by the Reagan-era modernization program. No short-term changes are in prospect, due to financial constraints. The force structure is to a considerable degree determined by military-political commitments not subject to reform. Changing organizational methods may eventually bring in new sources of leadership and change the relationship of American society, particularly its most privileged elements, to the armed forces that defend it. In the near term, say the next five years, the social character of the armed forces is not going to change. To be practical, reform must therefore be based on the units, personnel, and equipment already in place. It must not be aimed at creating some mythical "ideal" structure, but rather at producing an organization capable of identifying and correcting its own deficiencies.

The first requirement for fixing the army is to halt the personnel and equipment turbulence that now makes the creation of reasonably well trained, cohesive, disciplined units impossible. We want to replace the evenly distributed chaos of the current system with a steady ripple of personnel and equipment change, sweeping through the army on a regular cycle. COHORT is a good start, but it does not affect the turmoil above company level or the problem of equipment turbulence.

If the army's divisions were standardized and interchangeable, the ideal solution would be to create COHORT divisions with a fixed MTO&E based on equipment on hand and available at start-up. A division cadre would be built and trained in the course of a year. It would then take over an existing division's equipment set, fill up with recruits and junior personnel, train for a year in the continental United States (CONUS), spend a year in the CONUS-based strategic reserve, then rotate overseas (sans heavy equipment and dependents) for one year. The existing equipment set in CONUS would then be updated to a coherent new MTO&E and be taken over by a newly forming division. This would achieve personnel and equipment stability, and provide for orderly modernization. It would also place the most highly trained units in the most exposed positions, without the dangers and expense of shipping over the soldiers' families and household goods.

It is interesting that the problem of equipment turbulence, rather than concern for the human factor, has prompted some members of the army's high command to make similar proposals. Major General Robert Sunnell has proposed that a new family of combat vehicles be designed, to be built around several common chassis, power trains, and subsystems, in order to simplify the logistical and training burden imposed by the army's current multiplicity of vehicle types and configurations. This is a worthwhile idea in itself, but Sunnell further suggests that the army should "equip, train, and deploy the new force in divisional sets." This is reminiscent of "Operation Gyroscope," a failed attempt by the army in the 1950s to field entire divisions in stabilized blocks.[44]

This may be a good long-range goal to shoot for, but it is not practical in the near term because the army's divisions are not standardized and cannot replace each other on a one-for-one basis. While the entire Warsaw Pact gets by with just three types of division, in a far larger and multinational army, the United States alone has some seven different types of ground divisions in the Regular Army, and more in the reserves. The marines provide yet another form of division for land warfare. All Regular Army divisions are somewhat different, none are fully manned, and many are incomplete, relying on reserve "round-out" brigades to bring them to war strength. Meanwhile, there are a large number of separate brigades and regiments with virtually no common pattern. The 101st (Air Assault) Division is essentially a light infantry division with a great deal of organic helicopter assets. The Eighty-second Airborne is a very large light infantry unit, roughly twice the size of Soviet airborne divisions. The Ninth Infantry is an experimental motorized infantry unit, but it lacks the equipment to fulfill its tactical concept and probably will not get it within the next five years.[45] The Second Infantry in Korea is a strange mongrel with no counterpart elsewhere in the army. The multiplication of U.S. divisional types has been attributed to the wide range of possible missions U.S. forces face, but the true reason appears to be the endemic fragmentation of effort produced by the army's compartmentalized leadership.

Standardization has been proposed before, usually based on three types (armored, mechanized infantry, light infantry).[46] The concept has foundered on a lack of interest. In the long run, the question of standardization breaks down into two choices. We can achieve large-unit rotation using three divisional types that because of their greater cohesion and superior training can adapt to a wide variety of missions. That adaptability will be increased if certain unique assets, like the aviation components of the 101st, can be separated and formed into smaller, more easily transportable, specialized support units. Or, we can have a multiplicity of divisional types allegedly configured for specific missions that, if history is any guide, are unlikely to emerge in predicted form. These divisions can never reach the standards of cohesion and training of the standardized, rotatable divisions because they must be maintained in permanent being, with all the personnel and equipment turbulence that implies. Thus they will never reach the training standards needed to take advantage of their unique but theoretical capabilities. The advantages offered by their specialized structures are illusory.

Considering the current diversity of American divisions, the creation of a simple divisional shell game would be extremely difficult to achieve in any reasonable time frame. In any case, it would not be useful in dealing with the wide variety of separate units (artillery brigades, armored cavalry regiments, et cetera), many of which are unique in configuration.

On the other hand, many of the benefits of such a system might be obtainable through an expansion of the COHORT concept. COHORT companies are fine, but inserted into a current division they are like diamonds in a setting made of cheese. We should create cohesive divisional command packages (DCPs), in themselves small units that can be configured to match each one of the existing mishmash of divisions. By keeping the DCP small, we can obtain the benefits of stability at the level of division staffs while avoiding the administrative problems caused by the movement of manpower in chunks larger than company size. A DCP would consist of all of a division's commanders, primary staff, and primary staff sections at division, brigade, and battalion levels. It also would include the commanders and staff of the division's support command (DISCOM) units. Similar command packages can be created for non-divisional units. After assembly and training, the DCP would move to a CONUS installation or overseas and replace as a block the existing command structure of the target division. It would remain in place for three years, and then be relieved by a new DCP. All MTO&E changes would be made at the time of changeover. Subordinate companies (including headquarters companies) would be organized in the COHORT fashion, serve two years in a CONUS unit, then rotate overseas to a DCP stationed in Europe or Korea. Each overseas unit would have to draw on at least two stateside units for its COHORT company replacements. It would be wise to formalize the relationship between these units, thus achieving the purposes of the Regimental System without its artificialities.

Creation of the DCPs can begin immediately after the decision to do so has been made. There are eighteen divisions, so six will be created in any given year, with one being activated every two months. This system will give us an incidental benefit that will be of use should a major emergency expansion of the army ever be needed, for there will always be six uncommitted DCPs (and numerous non-divisional command packages) in the process of forming. It will also permit key personnel to attend necessary schooling without pulling them out of active units, a process that now produces major disruption.[47]

Let's take for an example the Third Armored Division, currently located in Wurzburg, West Germany. Set the first change of command date as D-Day. Extend current commanders until that date. At D minus 365, appoint the new division commander. Allow him to choose his principal subordinates and to draw them from their current jobs (excepting, of course, members of an existing DCP or COHORT unit). Immediately transfer them to the assembly installation, say Fort Hood. In turn, allow any subordinate commander or primary staff officer in the growing DCP to choose his subordinates from the available pool and to assign them wherever he sees fit. Fill up remaining slots by drawing on the army school system. For example, take all the needed artillery captains from the same advanced course at Fort Sill. Take more senior types from the current classes in the Command and Staff College at Fort Leavenworth. This may require starving existing units of graduates from those schools and changing projected assignments on short notice.

Within a few months the new DCP will be collected. Sign all of these people to a contract, obligating them to remain in the unit until D plus three years and obligating the army to keep them there. This unit will have three missions: training itself to command and control an armored division; learning the missions of its target unit; and working with the army's logistical experts to design an up-to-date, coherent MTO&E, based on equipment that actually will be on hand and available on D-Day. That divisional MTO&E will remain fixed for the three years of the DCP's command cycle, save for relatively minor changes initiated by the DCP itself on the basis of experience. Measures outlined in later chapters will guarantee that commanders will design their MTO&Es and make incremental changes with the purpose of increasing their units' combat capability, and that wrong decisions will carry a real penalty.

At D minus one month, move the DCP to Wurzburg with families and household goods. Match up the new personnel with the people they will replace for on-site job familiarization. On D-Day, hold one massive change-of-command ceremony and ship the old leadership home.

At D plus two years begin the creation of a new replacement DCP, but give it a new divisional designation, say "Twelfth Armored Division." When it replaces the Third Armored DCP the latter unit will return to the States and stand down, but it will not be disbanded. The division is a coherent, discrete, combined arms organization, and it is the natural focus for the loyalties of American soldiers. Therefore it should remain in existence. The personnel of the Third DCP will go in a number of directions. Many will leave the army at the end of their tours to return to civilian life. Others will request transfers to other duties. Some may have qualified, by virtue of their units' superior performance, for promotions that will require their transfer to new units now forming. Some will go to commands and staffs outside the division structure. Others will elect to stay in the Third DCP, possibly in the same duty positions. These people will make up the core of a new division cadre that will spend a year collecting the remainder of its personnel, attending schools or other training, and preparing to become once again an active division. The Third DCP will not be going back to Wurzburg, and may not even remain an armored division. It may be reconfigured into a different divisional type, which will require relatively minor personnel changes. What is important is that it will remain a coherent unit with a continuing designator (Third Division), a genuine form of continuity and tradition, and a real "institutional memory." It will provide a command instrument light-years beyond what the army has now.

A command instrument is not worth much without units to command, and the army has been proceeding far too slowly with its COHORT program. Rather than attempting to raise all COHORT companies from scratch and then letting them disappear after a three-year tour, what is needed is a program to convert existing companies of all types to COHORT format and to give them continuity. Initially we can ask for existing company cadres to volunteer for long-term stabilization. Most commanders will jump at the chance to extend their command time, but they will be inhibited from doing so if they are unhappy with their current subordinates. If we make "volunteering" contingent on the assent of 75 percent of company personnel E–5 and above, unhappy units will not be participating. Offer each group a one-, two-, or three-year contract, depending on scheduling requirements. Pull the unit out of its current parent unit (this may not always be necessary), transfer out the troops who have not volunteered, and fill it up with soldiers whose remaining obligation matches the unit's contract. Put the unit into a new parent unit, so that each division has an equal spread of one-, two-, and three-year sub-units. Each COHORT company should have its own unit designator, say "4077th Infantry," even though it may rotate from being A Company, 1/9th Infantry to being B Company, 2/32nd.

Units that do not choose to participate can remain under the current system for a time. As personnel change, such units may find themselves wanting to volunteer for stabilization. Otherwise, they can be replaced gradually, over a three- to four-year period, with newly created COHORT companies.

After the completion of the initial commitment, each company will stand down. Personnel who are promoted beyond unit requirements and those leaving the army will depart. If his unit's performance has been successful, the commander will be allowed to retain his position or to apply for promotion or assignment elsewhere. As far as possible, new commanders and cadre members should be promoted from within the unit. During the months following stand-down the company will fill up with replacements, send its personnel to required classes and training, and, in the last sixteen weeks or so, absorb and train its quota of new recruits. The unit will then be reactivated and sent to a parent unit in CONUS, preferably without changing installations. After two years there, it will rotate overseas.

For overseas rotation, men will carry only their personal weapons, uniforms, field gear, and a bag of civilian items. If a soldier wants to take his stereo, he can mail it parcel post at his own expense. Troops will draw their heavy equipment primarily from the POMCUS stocks already overseas.[48] Equipment not available from POMCUS (usually communications gear and helicopters) will have to be inherited directly from the units being replaced. Some units' movement to Korea can take place within the context of "Team Spirit," an annual tactical exercise that currently brings extra troops there for a couple of weeks and then brings them home while the soldiers actually stationed there fly to and fro on TWA, the commercial carrier. Total travel costs should be no higher than today, for while more soldiers will be flying to and from Europe annually, they will not be taking their families, dogs, furniture, and cars with them. The greater predictability of transportation requirements should permit more economical use of transportation assets.

The one-year overseas tour is a necessary concomitant to stabilization, as well as an economy measure. Troops deployed overseas should not have to worry about their families should the theater become a war zone, and hundreds of thousands of U.S. civilians should not be put into the position of being hostage to both ally and enemy. The army alone has over 200,000 dependents living overseas. We cannot, however, reasonably expect to send troops overseas minus their families for more than a year at a time. Former Chief of Staff Meyer blamed this factor for contributing to the defeat of his efforts to stabilize officer tours.[49] DCP personnel will be allowed to bring their dependents, of course. Their evacuation in an emergency will be much simpler than the current Non-Combatant Evacuation problem, which is a source of frequent headaches and disruption for overseas units.

Let's name this system of DCPs, command packages for non-divisional units, and COHORT companies collectively the "Divisional Rotation System" (DRS). Large-scale unit stability will have many benefits in terms of discipline, cohesion, and training. Perhaps most important, it will mean that a real "training cycle" can be conducted.

Army units used to have such a cycle, as draftees were usually funneled into a unit in large groups about twice yearly. The term "cycle" still is used to describe unit training schedules, even though it is entirely meaningless given the more or less constant turnover under the present system. The division training cycle will permit time for the military socialization and training of individual soldiers and small units within the COHORT company, then move to the training of small combat, logistical, and staff units, then to integrated training of the combined arms team.

One of the principal benefits of personnel stability is something that is quite impossible now, effective cross-training of individuals and units. Such cross-training will tremendously enhance the flexibility, utility, and endurance of the organization. There will be no reason why various units cannot trade missions and equipment for training, thus allowing the division when in combat to optimize whatever arm is needed. Most infantry units will be able to learn air assault, mechanized, and light infantry tactics. Most light, mobile units will be able to learn reconnaissance functions. Within units, it will be possible to train cooks and bottle-washers to man howitzers or air defense weapons, thus increasing (actually creating) the capability for sustained around-the-clock operations.[50]

COMBAT REPLACEMENTS

In combat many units will suffer casualties, yet (we may hope) few will be destroyed entirely. This will generate a demand for individual replacements. To some extent, this factor will be mitigated in well-trained, cohesive units, because they will be able to continue to function at well below full MTO&E strength. The phenomenal ability of World War II German units to sustain their combat power despite drastic losses is one main basis for the high regard in which the old German army is held. The ability to do so is critical to any combat organization for, as one American general put it, "I have never seen a company, platoon, or squad take a hill at full strength."[51] Still, at some point units must be rebuilt. One idea has been to provide combat replacements in "packets," that is, in small, cohesive teams: a tank crew, a howitzer section, et cetera. This idea has a lot of merit, but casualties will rarely occur in neat, matching packets. Therefore, replacement packets will almost invariably be broken up upon arrival in a unit. Even if the program were successful in replacing small groups like tank crews, it would not apply to the various support groups which make up the bulk of the field army and even large chunks of front-line battalions.

Rather than dribbling in individual replacements, however, the best method is for depleted units to be combined, or for the troops of shattered companies to be used in groups as replacements to fill out sister units. Companies that disappear in the shuffle should be replaced by cohesive replacement units.

Unfortunately, it is unlikely that sufficient unassigned COHORT companies will be available for replacement service, and the army is likely to draw them from undeployed larger units. That is acceptable to some extent, but done to excess it will destroy the uncommitted Regular Army divisions before they can deploy as units.

In theory, the Army Reserve and National Guard stand ready to provide replacement units and even major portions of Regular Army units making their initial deployments. In practice, however, few reserve units are actually capable of deploying as units. It would be highly impractical to deploy large numbers of reserve units above company- or at best battalion-level. Converting National Guard divisions into deployable field units would take many months at minimum. With the DRS in place, Regular Army DCPs could probably absorb new recruits and equipment and still deploy faster. This is true despite the fact that the Reserve forces contain many very capable and experienced soldiers and leaders. Politically, it would be difficult to use National Guard or reserve personnel as individual replacements, and impossible to abolish their higher-level headquarters staffs. Individual replacements will have to come initially from soldiers already in basic or advanced individual training centers, and then from new draftees, a source that will not begin to provide substantial numbers of soldiers for at least 180 days. Under current circumstances, this will again cause cannibalization of other regular units that have not yet been committed. We have seen where that will lead.

The solution is to focus peacetime reserve training funds, personnel, and equipment on company- and battalion-sized units. Encourage the National Guard to concentrate its personnel in fully manned companies, leaving others in cadre status. Keep the divisional structure in place for the purposes of individual state governmental use. In the event of national emergency, probably the only circumstances under which reserve units can be called up anyway, these ready companies can be activated and used along with newly trained COHORT companies as cohesive replacement units. Regular divisions that have suffered serious losses will consolidate their own personnel into functional sub-units (though not necessarily full MTO&E-strength), and integrate the new companies or battalions into the division structure. If the military situation seems to call for new divisions, excess surviving unit personnel can be sent back to the activated National Guard division to assist in training it. Otherwise they can become cadre for newly raised COHORT replacement units being created in the army's regular training centers.

National Guard and Army Reserve units currently maintained in high readiness status should continue to be supported as at present. Let us, however, drop the fiction that they are "round-out" units that will go to war as part of larger regular formations. Treat them as independently deployable units whose use will be purely situation-dependent.

This program will respect the nature of National Guard and Army Reserve units, which are local community organizations, and deal realistically with the political peculiarities affecting their use. It makes minimal changes in their peacetime organization and mission, but gives them a wartime role that is vital and that they can realistically be expected to fulfill. Such alterations in organization and attitude that are required can be achieved through the carrot and stick of federally provided funding, equipment, and facilities.

Once initiated, the new system will take approximately forty months to absorb the army's current field forces. DRS will replace the current evenly distributed personnel and equipment chaos with a steady cycle of change and modernization. It will bring about a situation in which current personnel will have the chance to learn their own jobs and to train their units. It will place the current force structure onto a credible go-to-war footing, with very minimal adjustments and no near-term changes in personnel or equipment. If supported by changes in the mission of reserve units, it will provide a robust system for wartime unit replacement of casualties by methods that are consistent with the best of America's military traditions and that avoid repeating the worst. It will set in train a process that will force the army to reform the dysfunctional elements of its organizational structure and methods, elements that have created a pathetic military joke of today's army.

It will do all of this at the cost of temporarily creating an upheaval in the army's bureaucratic management systems, systems that currently impose a disastrous and permanent confusion upon the army's field forces.

That is a very fair trade. The army's problems are not susceptible to carefully worked out, thoroughly tested, incremental reforms, but the current institutional mind-set demands that every decision be minutely planned and staffed. All military people are familiar with the acronym "KISS," which stands for "Keep It Simple, Stupid," but this is a golden military rule honored more often in the breach than in the observance. Army officers consistently waste their scarce time and troop resources trying to impose order on an inherently chaotic situation through detailed planning. This always results in programs that collapse when the delicately constructed chain of events fails to materialize. The more detailed the preparations the more disastrously they will be derailed by events or, in war, by deliberate enemy action. The excruciatingly slow conversion to COHORT is an attempt to minimize this familiar effect, but such an approach is inherently inappropriate in an organization whose purpose is to deal with crises.

Imposing order on chaos is a mission for theorists; the role of the military leader is to produce results. To be effective, military reform must be applied in quick, broad strokes, using the colors already on the palette. However, it is unlikely that the army could undertake such reforms on its own initiative, because any such decision would be subject to approval by the army's corporate democracy. If outright rejection did not succeed, the tried and true methods of the "exhaustive preliminary study" would. Many bureaucratic objections would be quite legitimate: the army's computerized supply and personnel systems are not set up to deal with such a radical changeover. They will be thrown into temporary chaos. This reform-induced turmoil will be merely a pale peacetime reflection of the breakdown these systems would suffer if faced by the demands of real war. Let's accept a certain amount of such confusion as inevitable and get on with the job.

Therefore, conversion to the Divisional Rotation System (DRS) must be mandated by the civilian authorities, i.e., Congress, and the requirement for changeover should have a very short fuze. There are many thousands of commanders and bureaucrats at every level who can be relied upon to straighten up the myriad minor messes that forced, rapid change will create, especially when such change carries the promise of calmer seas ahead.[52] Placing such responsibilities on unit leaders is a far better method of training them than is the attempt to minimize change and to choreograph all events from above.[53] If they cannot handle such a mission in peacetime, it is the most hopeless of fantasies to think they will be able to handle it in war.

NOTES

1. Battery ARTEP Report, May 28, 1985.

2. A partial exception was Alpha battery. The Alpha battery commander took very aggressive steps to prevent a similar occurrence to his unit. These steps, while partially successful, did not prevent the destruction of the battery FDC. They did demonstrate, however, that changes to the field tactics employed by the LANCE battery, along with minor changes to the personnel and equipment authorized by the unit's MTO&E, could substantially enhance the security of the battery and radically increase the cost to the enemy. These measures were not sanctioned by the battalion commander, nor were they explored by the staff officers concerned with operations, training, personnel, and logistics, although all of these men were intelligent, diligent, career officers. All of the measures taken to avoid the OPFOR teams were dropped when the battalion's OPFOR program was terminated.

3. Aggressor's After Action Report, April 30, 1985.

4. FM 6–40, Field Artillery Cannon Gunnery (Washington, D.C.: Headquarters, Department of the Army, 1984), H–4.

5. Richard A. Gabriel, Military Incompetence: Why the American Military Doesn't Win (New York: Hill and Wang, 1985), 10.

6. USA MILPERCEN, February 11, 1987.

7. Headquarters, Second Infantry Division, July 28, 1987.

8. Robert R. Palmer, Bell I. Wiley, and William R. Keast, The Procurement and Training of Ground Combat Troops (Washington, D.C.: Office of the Chief of Military History, 1948), 472–74. See also the works of Russell F. Weigley, particularly Eisenhower's Lieutenants (Bloomington: Indiana University Press, 1981).

9. Allan R. Millett and Peter Maslowski, For the Common Defense (New York: The Free Press, 1984), 453. This conclusion is derived from the works of combat historian S. L. A. Marshall, although his calculated average is 15 percent. See S. L. A. Marshall, Men Against Fire (New York: Morrow, 1947), 50–63. Millett and Maslowski's book is cited because it is generally very favorable to the American military, and its negative assessment of U.S. units is particularly hard to explain away.

10. Letter, Gifford Doxsee to Mrs. Edward H. German, January 10, 1981; Hugh M. Cole, The Ardennes: Battle of the Bulge (Washington, D.C.: Office of the Chief of Military History, 1965).

11. Martin van Creveld, Fighting Power: German and U.S. Army Performance, 1939–1945 (Westport, Conn.: Greenwood Press, 1982), 95.

12. See Robert Schneider, "Military Psychiatry in the German Army," in Richard A. Gabriel, ed., Military Psychiatry: A Comparative Perspective (Westport, Conn.:

Greenwood Press, 1986; see also, however, Manfred Messerschmidt, "German Military Law in the Second World War," in Wilhelm Deist, ed., *The German Military in the Age of Total War* (Dover, N.H.: Berg Publishers, Ltd., 1985).

13. See discussions of the replacement system in van Creveld, *Fighting Power*, 74–79; Palmer, Wiley, and Keast, *Ground Combat Troops*; Weigley, *Eisenhower's Lieutenants*, 370–73.

14. T. R. Fehrenbach, *This Kind of War* (New York: Macmillan, 1963), 95–157. North Korean treatment of American prisoners is discussed on pages 172, 199–201; Donald Knox, *The Korean War: Pusan to Chosin, an Oral History* (San Diego, Calif.: Harcourt, Brace, Jovanovich, 1985), 23; Max Hastings, *The Korean War* (New York: Simon and Schuster, 1987), 303–4.

15. Fehrenbach, *This Kind of War*, 144–46. This refers specifically to the experiences of General William F. Dean.

16. Roy E. Appleman, *South to the Naktong, North to the Yalu* (Washington, D.C.: Office of the Chief of Military History, 1961), 205–9; Fehrenbach, *This Kind of War*; Russell A. Gugeler, *Combat Actions in Korea* (Washington, D.C.: Center of Military History, 1954).

17. S. L. A. Marshall, *Pork Chop Hill: The American Fighting Man in Action, Korea, Spring, 1953* (New York: William Morrow and Co., 1956), 272–91.

18. Army figures are 788, congressional testimony indicates 1,016. Richard Gabriel and Paul Savage, *Crisis in Command* (New York: Hill and Wang, 1978), 43–44, 183.

19. Gabriel and Savage, *Crisis in Command*, 47–50, citing *Drug Abuse in the Military: Hearings before the Subcommittee on Drug Abuse in the Military on the Committee on Armed Services* (U.S. Senate, Ninety-second Congress, 1972), 127.

20. This is in some respects an unfair example, as virtually all of the Seventh Army's artillery was incapacitated for about one year after receiving the new fire direction equipment.

21. "Targeting: The Brigade and the battalions expressed a concern that no one at V Corps really knows how or what to target LANCE at. This has been borne out during numerous CPXs and especially REFORGER. The V Corps representative was aware of this, and said he would attempt to fix the problem." Memorandum, Battalion Executive Officer to Commander, August 6, 1985.

22. There is a good discussion of this problem in Andrew F. Krepinevich, *The Army and Vietnam* (Baltimore: The Johns Hopkins University Press, 1986), 205–10.

23. That is not to say that the army does not like bad weather. Rain makes the ground soft, and military vehicles tear up soft ground, causing "maneuver damage." The damaged ground belongs to German civilians and local governments, and it costs money and political popularity to fix it. See Lieutenant General Robert L. Wetzel and the V Corps Staff, "Central Guardian and the Lessons Winter Taught," *Armed Forces Journal International*, December 1985.

24. See Gugeler, *Combat Actions in Korea* (Washington: Center of Military History, 1954), chaps. 3, 5, and 12. The battery defense does not appear to have improved over the years.

25. Figure from Richard Gabriel, *Fighting Armies: NATO and the Warsaw Pact: A Combat Assessment* (Westport, Conn.: Greenwood Press, 1983), 8–9.

26. See John L. Romjue, *From Active Defense to AirLand Battle: The Devel-*

opment of Army Doctrine 1973–1982 (Ft. Monroe, Va.: Historical Office, U.S. Army Training and Doctrine Command, 1984).

27. See General William J. Livsey, "Allied Armies Build as Old Foe Probes and Waits," *ARMY*, October, 1984. Air-Land Battle is, as the name implies, a doctrine for both air and land forces, but the U.S. Air Force has never accepted this army concept as official doctrine. See interview with General William R. Richardson, *Armed Forces Journal International*, May 1986.

28. This figure comes from the first unit exercise in which I participated after arrival in Europe.

29. Meyer, who was Army Chief of Staff from 1979 to 1983, coined this term when faced with the post-Vietnam shambles called VOLAR. By 1983 he thought he had the problem largely fixed, but that was before the army decided to field several additional divisions from the same manpower base. By January 1987, he was resurrecting the term. Quoted by Brigadier General John C. "Doc" Bahnsen, "The Army's in Third Place," *Armed Forces Journal International*, May 1987.

30. See Ninety-eighth Congress, *Adequacy of Marine Corps Security in Beirut* (Washington, D.C.: GPO, 1983). See especially the alleged reasons for concentrating the troops (p. 47), and the discussion of why weapons were unloaded (p. 61).

31. This murder occurred on August 7, 1985. *New York Times*, August 14, 1985, sec. I.

32. "Modified Table of Organization and Equipment."

33. The MAD is concerned only with ERC (Equipment Reporting Code) "A" items, which for some reason are considered top priority by the army's logistical centers. ERC "B" and "C" items are frequently just as important at unit level but are not listed on the MAD Report, and thus do not receive even what little attention the MAD may generate.

34. Soviet special operations forces.

35. Ordering data which worked from 1982–1986 was: Battery, Dry, BA–1567/U, NSN 6135–00–485–7402. It is a class IX item, and works in the AN/PVS 4, AN/PVS 5 and 5A, the AN/TVS 5, and probably others.

36. Even if reinforcing units exist, are passably ready, and can be transported under war conditions—all questionable assumptions—the political circumstances surrounding such reinforcement make it a very dubious proposition. See Richard K. Betts, "Surprise Attack: NATO's Political Vulnerability," *International Security*, Spring 1981, 117–49, and *Surprise Attack: Lessons for Defense Planning* (Washington, D.C.: The Brookings Institute, 1982); Bruce G. Blair, "Alerting in Crisis and Conventional War," in Ashton B. Carter, John D. Steinbrunner, and Charles A. Zraket, eds., *Managing Nuclear Operations* (Washington, D.C.: The Brookings Institute, 1987).

37. Key documents, notably FM 100–5, *Operations* (1982), and FM 25–1, *Training* (1985), are very explicit in demanding preparedness for a no-warning war. For a discussion of the effects of fielding the additional divisions on overall Army readiness, see Lieutenant Colonel John M. Vann, "The Forgotten Forces," *Military Review*, August 1987.

38. Lieutenant General Robert M. Elton (Deputy Chief of Staff for Personnel), writing in the *ARMY* Green Book issue, October 1984. The same point is made in greater detail in David H. Marlowe, ed., *New Manning System Field Evaluation: Technical Report No. 5* (Washington, D.C.: Department of Military Psychiatry,

Walter Reed Army Institute of Research, September 1987), which is a remarkable study of the Seventh Infantry Division's conversion to the light infantry format. This study found that the unit leadership was largely unable to take advantage of the opportunities offered by the COHORT system.

39. See Weigley, *Eisenhower's Lieutenants*, 370–75.

40. USA MILPERCEN, July 21, 1987.

41. Lieutenant Colonel Terrence Murray, USMC, described this sytem in a letter to the editor, *Armed Forces Journal International*, (June 1987). Intrigued, I called him to find out how the marines achieved the personnel stability to maintain a true cycle. He put me in touch with battalion commander Lieutenant Colonel Jim Jones, who expressed great enthusiasm, having just completed a two-year cycle. Just as intriguing, he was unable to provide me with detailed manuals on the system: "I've got to admit, you guys in the Army are much better at that than we are." Figures from Lieutenant Colonel Jones.

42. AR 600–82, *The U.S. Army Regimental System*.

43. John F. Aherne (former Deputy Assistant Secretary of Defense), "Pentagon Strategy: WWNH," *Washington Post National Weekly Edition*, March 16, 1987.

44. Benjamin F. Schemmer, "Army Weighs Unorthodox Approach to Field New Heavy Forces by 1995," *Armed Forces Journal International*, August 1987, 30.

45. Interview with TRADOC commander General William R. Richardson, *Armed Forces Journal International*, May 1986.

46. General John C. Bahnsen (U.S. Army, retired), "The Kaleidoscopic US Army," *Armed Forces Journal International*, November 1985; Colonel John P. Lawton, "Back Off, Bahnsen: The Army Kaleidoscope Is in Focus," *Armed Forces Journal International*, May 1986.

47. At any given time over 15 percent of officers are not assigned to units but are listed under the heading THS (Transient Holding and Student Account). This does not include the large numbers who are assigned to units but are temporarily students at relatively short-term schools. Data from USA MILPERCEN, February 11, 1987.

48. POMCUS: Prepositioning of Material Configured to Unit Sets. Several divisions' worth of equipment are stockpiled in Europe to equip emergency reinforcements. The eventual goal is to have dix division sets prepositioned there.

49. Quoted in Arthur Hadley, *The Straw Giant* (New York: Random House, 1986), 294.

50. The necessity for reliance on such non-specialist personnel was again demonstrated in the Falklands. See Major Gerald R. Akhurst (Royal Artillery), "A Gunner's Tale," *Field Artillery Journal*, March-April 1984. It is worth noting that at the time of the Falklands battle, Akhurst (a major, not a captain as in the U.S. Army) had been in command of his battery for about two years, twice the length of a U.S. command tour, and he remained in command for some time thereafter.

51. Lieutenant General Arthur S. Collins, Jr., *Common Sense Training: A Working Philosophy for Leaders* (Novato, Calif.: Presidio Press, 1978), 5.

52. Former Chief of Staff John A. Wickham, Jr., was very fond of a story told by Creighton Abrams, in which he compared the DOD leadership to a sea captain who liked to demonstrate how maneuverable the ship was, how easily it could take on a new heading. It made the captain feel good, but everybody below decks was constantly seasick. He used the story in his article in the *ARMY* Green Book edition

of October 1983 and in a number of published interviews. After decades of turbulence, the army's senior leadership would like to steer a steady course for a while,
so steady that it will take a full generation to implement a basically very simple
change in personnel policies. What Wickham did not realize is that it is not major
shifts in policy but rather the day-to-day turmoil imposed by absurd bureaucratic
methods that nauseates the crew.

   53. See Martin van Creveld, *Command in War* (Cambridge: Harvard University
Press, 1985).

3

EVALUATION SYSTEMS

Restructuring the army's units so that they are capable of being trained to high standards does not in itself mean that they *will* be highly trained. To make units work, to find out how capable they really are, and to control them requires an effective evaluation system. This chapter will examine the methods that the army uses to evaluate its units and the people in them. These methods do not work and have, in fact, many destructive effects.

SELF-EVALUATION

The army currently has two general methods of evaluating the combat potential of its units. The first of these is the system of reports generated by the units themselves, the second a series of "external evaluations." In peacetime, the self-generated reports are mainly the training and maintenance "report cards" that commanders write on themselves in their monthly Unit Status Reports (USRs). The information contained in the USR then becomes a major input to the individual rating that the subordinate commander receives: his OER (Officer Efficiency Report). This OER is the basis for all future promotion decisions, which are made by centralized boards meeting in Washington.

This may seem to be putting a little too much trust in the integrity of commanders, and it is. Having commanders write their own report cards has the effect of putting them all into competition with each other, not to see whose equipment will be the best maintained or whose troops the best trained, but simply whose report cards will be the most impressive. Good report cards may or may not contribute to a good OER, because there is no reliable connection between unit performance and officer ratings. For officers submitting equally inflated reports on themselves, the difference between a good rating and one not so good depends purely on politics and personal considerations. Good politics also can mitigate or eliminate the effects of those rare events that cannot be concealed within the local rating chain. Bad report cards, that is, accurate reports that reflect the real training and maintenance deficiencies inevitable given the chaotic personnel and logistical situation, are certain to bring bad OERs. This is because they reflect in turn on the senior commander, for the USRs of subordinate units are input to his own efficiency rating. Honest reporting is therefore a sign of disloyalty to one's commander, or at least a lack of concern. It is also seen as just plain stupid. This will be reflected in the rating of any junior officer so naive as to think that the reporting system is meant to identify problems so they can be fixed. Systemic problems are a taboo subject in the officer corps.

The predictable result is that actual training and maintenance operations descend into chaos, because real problems are concealed at every level from squad and platoon on up and the system becomes fatally clogged with false data. In my battalion in Germany, the falsified data being supplied by the battery motor officers and the battalion maintenance technician included non-reporting of inoperable equipment, reporting of work that was our responsibility as higher echelon problems, reporting of non-existent spare parts requisition numbers and job orders, false dating of equipment break-downs, and false reporting that critical communications gear had been re-moved from dead-lined vehicles and reinstalled in usable equipment. The most disturbing results of this flow of disinformation were the destructive effects on our relationship with our maintenance support units, who resented being blamed for our organizational foul-ups. They were therefore extremely difficult to deal with, rigidly enforcing picayune regulations and rejecting work requests because of minor paperwork errors. Because of these diffi-culties with direct support (DS), we had begun doing a very large amount of DS-level work ourselves, installing engines, transmissions, et cetera. This did not result in grave quality-control problems, because our mechanics were no less capable than theirs. It was, however, contrary to Standard Operating Procedures and the army's official instructions, and it made it impossible to do our own organizational repairs and services.

Falsification also had severe effects on the spare parts system, allowing needed parts to go unordered. This made unit NCOs lose all faith in the supply system, leading to an accumulation of excess spare parts through double-ordering, local scrounging, and theft. For instance, one night several jeep wheel-bearing covers disappeared from A Battery's jeeps. Officially, we always blamed the locals for this, but the locals do not need spare parts for jeeps. The only positive effect of this systematic falsification of the Status Report was in improving our reported Operational Readiness (OR) statis-tics. A good report card for the commander.

As a battalion motor officer, I personally got into trouble with this system when I failed to understand that it was not my job to fix the battalion's equipment, only to make sure that the paperwork looked right. Every day

I turned in a maintenance report to the battalion commander, and to the best of my abilities it was accurate. This report was critical to effective management of the battalion's maintenance effort, especially as there was then a severe repair parts budget crunch. Accurate targeting of maintenance dollars was essential, as the unit's equipment was in terrible shape: during my first field problem with the battalion, eight of the nineteen tracked vehicles broke down within twenty-four hours and had to be towed back to post. My assumption was that if we could find out what was wrong we could then proceed to fix it. Unwilling to order me explicitly to falsify the unit's report, the commander nonetheless repeatedly challenged the figures on it. However, I was always able to substantiate my report, often giving him copies of clearly falsified documents submitted by the batteries. My requests for support in getting accurate data from his other subordinates were ignored. Finally, he directly questioned me as to why I was reporting the actual date of breakdown for a five-ton truck that had been inoperable for weeks and about which nothing had been done. Frustrated, I said, "Well, sir, I can fudge it if you'd like." He became very agitated and said, "I'm not telling you to fudge anything." I was then dismissed. Half an hour later I was transferred to B Battery.

The ironic thing about this situation is that I was quite willing to fudge it. I understood the pressures the commander was subjected to from higher. I would have been happy to submit an entirely bogus report to Brigade *if that was what was necessary to give us a cover under which we could actually repair the equipment.* What I would not do was to submit a false report to *him*, and what I could not understand was that this was what he wanted and expected. That I did not do this without subjecting him to the embarrassment of ordering me to was a fatal mark of unprofessionalism on my part. That is the way maintenance is handled in the army. Period. I had ample opportunity to see how things were done in my own and many other units. They all operate the same say, the only real distinction being between commanders who lie for themselves and those who force or permit subordinates to lie for them.[1] Some commanders honestly believe that they are submitting accurate reports, but this is only because they are naive enough actually to believe what their subordinates are telling them.

The sad part of it is that there was absolutely nothing wrong with my commander. He was a decent, caring, but hard-nosed man, and a professional soldier. A former Staff sergeant (E–6), he had been commissioned through Officer Candidate School (OCS) and had commanded a battery in combat in Vietnam. He knew his business. When he arrived in the battalion he quickly won the respect and personal loyalty of the officers and men, and he kept it for the two years of his extended command. He was the kind of man soldiers trust instinctively, and in circumstances where events were under his control he more than justified that trust. He could pat you on the back and kick you in the butt at the same time, and you would take both gestures very seriously. Troops produced for him. Under his leadership the battalion established the best *LANCE* unit record in Europe for two years running. He was almost an ideal officer, but he knew his limitations and he knew the system. He was a super troop leader, but he dared not send an accurate maintenance report to higher headquarters, nor even to have one made up for use by his own staff.

All other reports generated by field units are subject to similar distortions. The annual "Common Tasks Test" (CTT) tests soldiers in seventeen of the eighty skills in which all soldiers are supposed to be proficient, such as map reading, first aid, and firing the claymore mine. Officers and senior NCOs are rarely tested because they are presumed to be experts, which they are not. It is difficult to work the required training and testing into the unit's schedule. To do it all in one block is terribly disruptive, and its timing often conflicts with other, more important events. Some units attempt to minimize the disruption to the work schedule by spreading CTT out over the fiscal year. This does not work because a great percentage of the personnel on hand at year's end were not there when testing started. Many units have a hard time getting the necessary training equipment, because CTT is an army-wide event and scores are due for everybody at the same time. Competition is therefore fierce for what equipment is available, and units that cannot obtain any must somehow make adjustments for the resulting lack of training and actual testing. However, commanders in V Corps were told that the "standard" was 100 percent pass for all assigned soldiers. Such standards are always met. In 1985 B Battery reported 93 percent compliance to the S–3 staff, which was the lowest reported score in the battalion. I knew it to be a greatly inflated figure, since I had just come away from a year as B Battery training officer. Somehow it had become 100 percent by the time it was reported to the Department of the Army (DA).

Other such training results were "adjusted" in more devious ways. All junior soldiers are supposed to be tested once a year in their Military Occupational Specialties (MOS). This is called the Skills Qualification Test (SQT). A statistical abstract of scores is made up for each unit and becomes another minor input for higher headquarters to consider when drawing up the commander's OER. This can be awkward, since many of the test questions are difficult to account for; my mechanics were to be tested on the repair of vehicles many had never seen. We adjusted for this by arranging for them to spend time with another unit that was more properly equipped, time during which they were lost to our own motor pool. In 1984 we enjoyed a real windfall on the *LANCE* crewmen's SQT when the test's writers were reassigned to our battalion as unit NCOs. Our scores were very, very high that year. A more common method of dealing with the uncertainties of SQT testing is to assign an "MOS Manager" to train troops for the test and then to administer it. Many of these managers, who are held responsible for the resulting test scores, have enough integrity not to give soldiers the answers during the test session.

This string of anecdotes is presented in order to demonstrate that the organizational methods that led to disaster in Vietnam, which have been well documented,[2] have in no way been corrected. Management techniques are virtually identical, training and maintenance figures being used the same way "body count" figures were used in Vietnam. For example, in the first half of 1969, the Ninth Infantry Division reported a body count of 10,883 enemy killed. Oddly, however, they suffered only 267 American dead in return and were able to produce only 748 enemy weapons captured. Units blamed the low weapon count on the fact that many Vietcong were killed at night, but if they could find the body, why could they not find the weapon? Some have suggested that the bulk of the enemy dead were in fact unarmed local civilians, but population security statistics show no corresponding impact on the local population. The casualty and weapons-capture ratios were wildly out of sync with those of other units in Vietnam. Nonetheless, the official figures were accepted and the division commander was promoted to command a corps.[3]

The bottom line is that it is absurd to expect a commanding officer to send accurate numbers to the higher commander who writes his OER, since these data have some (admittedly indeterminate) relationship to the efficiency ratings that both he and his rater will be given. Those numbers will be compared to numbers sent by other officers who are competitors for the same future retention and promotions. Considering that maintenance and training statistics reflect phenomena for which the commander is at best only partially responsible, and that they contain errors introduced by subordinates at every level, he would have to be an idiot or a martyr—as well as omniscient—to send correct figures. As a result, inspection, training, and maintenance reports are very often simply lies, and lying is virtually mandated by the system. Officers unwilling to lie for themselves allow their subordinates to do it for them. An officer's promotion, and therefore job security, depends not on his ability to lead his unit in any real-world mission but on fitting into this system.

Obviously, this kind of input is worthless, but it is the source for most of the army's impressive statistics on training and maintenance. In wartime it is used to make crucial tactical and strategic decisions. Good staff officers know from experience that this data is meaningless, and so their actual plans are made on the basis of "guesstimates" that may or may not correspond to reality. To be useful, information intended for tactical or planning purposes must be separated from reports generated to enhance personal careers. Under the current evaluation and promotion systems, this cannot be done.

EXTERNAL EVALUATIONS

The second approach to evaluation used by the army involves the large variety of "external" evaluations to which a unit is subjected in the course of the training cycle. A good example is the annual ARTEP (Army Training

Evaluation Program, pronounced "ar-tep"), during which the unit goes to the field and demonstrates its abilities to a team of evaluators. The evaluators, however, are personnel from sister units and immediately higher headquarters, and they know that they themselves will soon be "ARTEPed" by the same individuals they are presently evaluating. The easily foreseeable result is that artillery units that fire less than half of their rounds within the required time and accuracy limits are certified combat ready.[4] Eighty-man missile batteries that are wiped out in mock attacks by three men with rifles are given passing scores in "battery defense."[5] Such incidents represent, after all, a state of training that no unit can reasonably hope to exceed. A brigade or division commander is not likely to report to his boss that his subordinate battalions are not combat ready. The response inevitably will be "And whose fault is that?" An exception to this rule occurs only when a new commander chances upon a unit being ARTEPed very, very shortly after he has assumed command, a dangerous situation for subordinate commanders.

At various times I served as an ARTEP evaluator for both cannon and missile units. Because my practical expertise was in logistics rather than in artillery, I was usually assigned to judge "Trains Operations." In practice this meant Headquarters and Service Batteries. That was OK with me, first because I am actually interested in logistics and second because it permitted a good overview of the way the entire battalion worked. ARTEPs reveal some strange things about units, especially if one cares to dig beyond first impressions.

For example, it was intriguing to watch the RSOP (Reconnaissance, Selection, and Occupation of a Position, pronounced "ar-sopp") conducted by the commander of the headquarters battery of an eight-inch howitzer battalion. Upon entering a potential battery position, the commander had a group of men fan out with mine sweepers to check out the area. This was impressive. None of my unit's mine detectors were ever used, most were inoperable, and no one knew how to use one. However, the Grafenwoehr training area is littered with a century's worth of Wehrmacht and U.S. Army metallic debris, yet none of the detector operators ever paused in his meticulous coverage of the ground. I unobtrusively dropped an old wheel hub in the grass in the path of one. Listening intently to his earphones, the soldier passed over it and moved on. Later, when he put the detector back in the truck, I opened it. No batteries. I discussed the matter with the supply sergeant. No, nobody had any batteries. He said that he had stocked some once but had gotten in trouble for storing "excess" and had been forced to throw them away.

I mentioned this in passing to the battery's commander, who listened in disbelief. He professed amazement that there were no batteries, but he was really surprised that I had bothered to look. Naturally, I did not bring this issue up at the official outbrief. I got in enough trouble for pointing out that Service Battery had put its sentries on observation posts (OPs) with night vision gear but had not given them any batteries either.

Service Battery had fallen apart completely during a night move. We had informed the battery operations center that they were under artillery attack but there was no response. When I reported this to the ARTEP control center, they suggested that I drop a few hints to the commander that he make an emergency move to escape the enemy fire. I did, but there was still no response. When the Brigade XO showed up he gave me some explosive artillery simulators, thinking that a little realism might spark some enthusiasm. It did: an hour and a half later the battery's vehicles began to pull out of position. Four hours after that they arrived, missing only a few trucks, at the new position four kilometers away.

I felt badly about the report I had to make on this battery, since neither the commander, the XO, nor the first sergeant had been in the battery more than a month, and I thought that they had made a heroic effort. However, I could not avoid giving them a no-go for that event because the Brigade XO had been there with me, hopping mad, during the confusion. The battery commander was furious with me for reporting accurately on his unit's performance. Later, he called to ask me for the stock number for night vision batteries.

These may appear minor matters, and in fact no one was terribly concerned about them. More embarrassing was the performance of the artillery side of the house. The battalion's ammunition officer, an artilleryman as in all field artillery units, had failed to make proper ammunition requests for the ARTEP. He was evidently new at the supply business and did not know exactly what a DODAC is.[6] First of all, he had attempted to use ammunition "borrowed" from another unit's authorization. Although he had the other unit's approval, such "lateral transfers" of ammunition are forbidden in the USAREUR ammo SOP, and the Ammo Supply Point refused to issue the ammo. It looked like the ARTEP would have to be canceled, with red faces all around. (In my battalion, the ammo supply people always delivered what we needed. Our Service Battery commander sometimes delivered the battalion's entire basic load of nuclear warheads in his jeep. We called this "Magic." Of course, we did not suffer from the same inconveniences the eight-inch units did. They had to fire real ammo.)

To save the ARTEP I told the ammo officer to give me his trucks and personnel, then took the paperwork down to the ammo dump claiming to be from the unit that legitimately owned the shells. Since our bumpers had their identifying unit numbers taped over for security reasons, we were able to pull this off. We still had to get a special unit authorization over the phone ("What? I'm not on the signature card? I'll have that file clerk's ass!"). It is quite certain that the ammo people knew what we were doing, but they understood the situation and the blame could be laid on me if someone decided to investigate.

Unfortunately, the original ammo requisition did not list primers, and an eight-inch howitzer cannot be fired by throwing a lit cigarette in the breach and slamming it shut. More negotiations followed, and eventually a deal was cut by which we got primers. In a combat environment, however, it is doubtful that the necessary ammo would have appeared; ammo supply people know ammo but not guns, and they only deliver what is asked for.

Eventually the shells were obtained, but what the gunners did with them was not impressive. Of forty-five graded fire missions, only seventeen fell within the time and accuracy limits specified by DA. That is a score of 38 percent. The brigade commander, a new one whose commitment to combat readiness seemed unusually firm, rated the battalion as combat ready. What else was he going to do? Reporting the unit as unready would bring down an incredible rain of attention from higher headquarters, all wasted since his units are no more unready than anybody else's. The single benefit of the current personnel system is that it has thoroughly homogenized the army. No unit is significantly different from any other, for the people who are here this year were there last year. Commanders can do a lot to affect morale and appearances, but comparatively little about actual competence.

ARTEPs, like other evaluation methods, do a lot to help compartmentalize the army. The battalion S–4 might get in trouble over supply foul-ups like this but the gunners, the high-visibility people in the unit, will not suffer for it. If they are to be tested, ammunition will come from somewhere. If the gunnery people do all right, the supply errors will not be heavily counted against the commander. After all, what does he know about supply? He is an artilleryman. Similarly, infantry units unable to utilize artillery support properly will normally suffer no ill effects; it is an artillery problem. Such compartmentalization has been created throughout DOD, and the results have been disastrous. Edward Luttwak has described in great detail how compartmentalization deranged the American effort in Vietnam.[7] Every arm or "branch" of the army (and of the air force and navy) had its own theory as to how to win the war, and each got its chance. A village would be "pacified" by the Special Forces, "harassed and interdicted" by the artillery, ground into dust by armor, and finally, of course, "communized" by the winners. The political goal of victory was entirely irrelevant to the competitive military bureaus who fought the war. Service "unification" will remain a mirage until the grass-roots causes of this compartmentalization are eliminated.

ARTEPs are supposed to be graded according to a set of criteria developed by DA. In practice, these criteria are always adjusted downwards by field commanders, as were the time and accuracy requirements for the gunners discussed above. This adjustment is necessitated by the debilitating circumstances in which units must train. Failure to pass an ARTEP usually occurs only because of unusually low unit morale, a strong indicator of poor unit leadership. Evaluators will excuse virtually any technical or tactical failure as long as the troops show some real hustle and eagerness to please. Often the criteria becomes a simple, unambitious, but still highly detailed checklist. The result is interesting. Take camouflage, for instance. The Korean and German armies camouflage in order to hide. The United States Army camouflages in order to meet a "camouflage requirement."

In Korea I was often amazed to discover that the view I had just been admiring contained ROK Army tank, cannon, or infantry units. Rice paddies would get up and walk away. I was on my compound for several months before I realized there was an entire ROKA division artillery within 500 meters of my bedroom. The Korean guns were dug in under concrete and nearly invisible, with rounds broken out, ready to fire on pre-set targets. My eighteen howitzers were lined up hub-to-hub in the parking lot, Pearl Harbor style. While visiting a ROK fire direction center with a Korean officer friend, I noticed that my unit was not displayed on the tactical maps. I asked why. He looked embarrassed and tried to change the subject. When I pressed the issue he said that we were not on the map because everybody expected us to disappear in a cloud of smoke with the first North Korean volley.

I was once startled to find myself in the middle of a Bundeswehr gun battery done up in winter camouflage in the snow. My units never once changed their camouflage schemes to match the weather. Camouflage, as any fashion designer knows, is *green*. As an ARTEP evaluator with 3/79th, a fellow *LANCE* unit, I found the Fire Direction Center (FDC) by spotting its camouflage net, bright green "summer" side up. It was November and the net stood out sharply amidst the fallen leaves. I asked the XO, a lieutenant, why he had the summer side up. At first he thought I was spoofing him, playing one of those left-handed monkey wrench jokes to which lieutenants must get inured to. I had to demonstrate that there were in fact two sides to the net, the other being a brownish "autumn" color. He thought that this was pretty clever and pointed it out to his commander. In the next position they occupied they had the troops flip the nets over. I still thought it looked funny, a dull brown net in the middle of a bright green German cow pasture. It was rather the same effect I had seen with my howitzers in Korea. A cannon under a U.S.-issue camouflage net, set in the middle of a dry, red-clay rice paddy, does not look like anything other than a cannon under a camouflage net.

This happens because tactical evaluations are task oriented rather than results oriented. If everybody does everything on the checklist it does not matter whether the bullet lands in the right place. If the camouflage nets are up the unit is "camouflaged," and it does not matter who sees it. The artillery does its artillery tasks, the infantry its infantry tasks, the intelligence people do their tasks, and the supply people keep their files straight. It does not matter whether the whole thing comes together to destroy the enemy.

Usually, in fact, there is no real "enemy" out there to destroy. In my brigade's ARTEPS the live enemy consisted of one military intelligence captain and her driver. She gave the battery defense hell. In my own OPFOR operations I was never permitted to use more than three attackers, and we were required to strike within one hour of a specified time known to the target unit. The results were never reported to higher headquarters, and the attacks were halted once it became clear that defending the batteries would require substantial changes in the way we did things.

For practical purposes, this kind of "external" evaluation suffers from the same pressures and temptations to falsify as the unit's own self-evaluations. They are just as worthless as a gauge of the unit's actual capabilities. The army realizes that this system is somewhat flawed. The technology exists to conduct quite realistic battle exercises, and some exciting training takes place at the National Training Center at Fort Irwin, California. These exercises are fabulously expensive, never exceed a brigade in size, and whatever benefits they bring a unit are quickly eroded by personnel rotation. No such high-tech facilities currently exist in Europe or Korea, and front-line units are the most poorly prepared for combat. This seems backwards, unless we consider these men to be mere sacrificial trip-wires whose massacre will give us an excuse to use nuclear arms.

ARTEP is an army-wide program. Occasionally, a mid-level headquarters will institute an inspection system of its own. This is usually motivated by a need to pass to lower-level commanders the buck for anticipated poor results on other major inspections. In Germany, our brigade commander had instituted a series of surprise inspections conducted by members of his own headquarters. Many of them were not particularly credible in their fields. It is curious how an E–4 can become an expert in weapons maintenance merely by virtue of belonging to a brigade headquarters company.

The brigade commander called these surprise inspections "Swoops," and this term was usually pronounced by subordinate commanders in a strangled falsetto. A "Swoop" could attack any aspect of a subordinate unit, but maintenance was always a prime target. This meant that the battalion's maintenance operation was a major focus of command interest. It did not mean that we were able to fix anything. Maintenance needs to be done in an orderly manner if chaos is not to result in the spare parts, reporting, and periodic servicing systems. The terror inspired by the "Swoop" destroyed all semblance of order in our maintenance program.

On arrival in the battalion I had identified two areas that not only needed fixing but seemed susceptible to reasonably rapid action. The first was the paint job on the battalion's vehicles, the second the portable generators. The first program was reasonably successful. The second failed miserably.

The generators provide a good example of the effects of local inspection programs, which are explicitly tied by their creators to their victims' prospects of promotion. There were about twenty generators in the battalion, several of which worked. Most of them needed to be sent to our DS maintenance unit for extensive rewiring and new engines. DS would not accept them, however, until all of the unit-level deficiencies were worked off. I gathered the battery motor officers together to discuss the matter. I figured that given the needed spare parts, we could do all of our own level equipment inspections and repairs in about ten days without disrupting anybody's training schedule. We had already amassed the parts we would need, mostly spark plugs, cowlings, and canvas covers. Arrangements had already been made with DS to inspect and repair all of the generators as one job order, two weeks later. The battalion commander was aware of the plan and had approved.

The battery motor officers were skeptical. When questioned, they said it would not work but could not say precisely why. Mystified, I said, "Let's give it a go." We would start the next day. That was Wednesday evening.

On Thursday morning we found out why the plan would not work. I arrived at 0600 and found people scurrying everywhere with generators. The enthusiasm was delightful, but this was not part of the plan. It emerged that the battalion commander had received word from a secret source at Brigade that there was to be a surprise inspection that Friday, and that the brigade commander had targeted generators in particular. He had responded to this alarm by directing the battery commanders to fix all the generators "today." Accordingly, all of the generators were repainted, given new spark plugs and cowlings, their burned-out engines filled with new motor oil. By afternoon all of the generators had been officially fixed. There was no "Swoop" that Friday, but I was never again able to mention the generators to the motor officers without being shouted down. I gave up trying to get ahead and turned to the more common army practice of dealing strictly with emergencies.

Other external evaluations are conducted by people who are genuinely outside of the chain of command being evaluated and can be regarded as effectively neutral. Their findings will still be influenced by the interests of the army as a whole. These evaluations are meaningless, and actively harmful to unit readiness, for a set of reasons entirely different from those that affect the evaluations discussed above. As an example, let's look at the external evaluations to which my *LANCE* battalion was subjected annually. Some of these differ in detail from those of other types of unit, but some are identical.

As a nuclear-capable missile artillery unit, we received a number of nuclear inspections and tests in the course of the year. These focused on our missile ammunition handlers and on the launcher crews. We received a visit from a Department of the Army Nuclear Evaluation Team. At another point we were evaluated by FAMSEG, the field artillery branch's Field Artillery Missile Systems Evaluation Group. At yet another point the batteries flew singly to the NATO Missile Firing Installation (NAMFI) on Crete. There they actually fired a live missile into the Mediterranean Sea and were graded in competition with all other U.S. *LANCE* units. Each of these evaluations was based on different—often conflicting—sets of criteria. It was necessary to retrain the crews thoroughly for each evaluation, not only to make up for the inevitable personnel turbulence but also to adjust to the differing inspection criteria. None of these tests was very relevant to any tactical situation, in which many of the procedures necessary for a good test score would have been discarded by the missile handlers. Such a tactical scenario occurred only during the ARTEP, when yet another set of criteria came into play and the very real dangers connected with handling live missiles and warheads were largely absent.

Assuming that the battalion did not embarrass itself too badly on the ARTEP, field training would lapse as the unit prepared itself for the next major event.[8] For most units this would be the Annual General Inspection (AGI), conducted by a team that emanates from a division-level headquarters or higher. The AGI is not concerned with tactical capabilities. It inspects troop morale and facilities; equipment; maintenance, supply, and training records; health, safety, and welfare; and all of the myriad administrative systems that are designed to keep a unit functioning.

Inspections of all these varying sorts are spaced out through the year. The reasons for conducting so many separate inspections are numerous, the most obvious being the convenience of the inspectors. Also, the constant barrage of different events is considered necessary to keep units on their toes and to prevent them from lapsing into inactivity.

The most fundamental reason for spreading the inspections out, however, is the simple fact that no unit can do all of the various things it is supposed to do simultaneously. No unit can conduct serious training and maintenance while at the same time maintaining all of the various administrative records and paperwork systems that are designed to facilitate training and maintenance. That is why AGIs are almost always scheduled long in advance.

One of my favorite such systems is called TMACS ("tee-macs"), which stands for Training Management Accounting Computer System. It was introduced to the Second Infantry Division while I was there, and it caught up to me again in Germany. In 1982, the Second Infantry Division trained one individual from each battalion on how to provide the requisite data, but most of those individuals rotated before the computers became operational. Therefore we all just felt our way along. TMACS is supposed to tell the commander exactly what a given training exercise will cost in terms of fuel, spare parts, and expendable supplies, so that he may distribute his budget dollars wisely. Since every battalion has its own unique training events and operating environment (particularly overseas, where U.S. units are scattered among a large number of small installations), the system requires a tremendous input of unit-specific historical data to begin making its predictions. A detailed monthly report is required. For instance, TMACS wants to know exactly how many miles were traveled and how much diesel fuel was used by how many M548 vehicles during a particular field exercise in May, and again for the same exercise in June. It wants to know the monthly unit expenditures on repair parts and expendable supplies. The figures it produces in return are useless, and we never considered them in planning our training program. The program was constantly being derailed by unexpected requirements anyway.

In Korea, and later in Germany, we did our best to feed this monster. There was considerable command pressure to do so. For some reason, TMACS received a tremendous amount of support everywhere but in the units that were supposed to benefit from it. Feeding it meant, among other things, accounting for every drop of gasoline and diesel fuel. Since we had no meters on our high-speed fuel pumps in Korea, we had to fuel every vehicle by first pumping gas into five-gallon cans and then manually pouring it into the gas tank. Each receiving driver had to sign for every drop. Given that tactical fueling operations call for speed (because no one wants to sit around on the battlefield in a gas truck), this made a joke of the army's oft-repeated slogan "Train the way you fight." Fueling in the TMACS-required manner resulted in battalion-size traffic jams, an inviting target for enemy aircraft or artillery. At the end of the month we were stuck with stacks of illegible fuel receipts, soaked in oil and mud, showing fuel consumption figures that were impossible: jeeps do not burn diesel oil, and the figures never jibed with the known battalion totals. The sources of these errors were numerous and ineradicable, including illiterate soldiers, impatient officers, fuel received from other units in emergencies, fuel picked up for one truck by another, and fuel used in tent stoves and field mess units. It was almost impossible to determine precisely which operation had consumed any particular gallon of fuel.

In the end, despite a real attempt to make the figures fit, we did what every other unit S–4 did. We used the basic fuel-usage estimates appended to the TMACs instruction book, multiplied them by the number of each vehicle-type on hand, threw in a couple of fudge factors to make it look genuine, adjusted the total to fit our known total receipts of gas and diesel fuel, and sent it on up to the TMACS enthusiasts. They were ecstatic. Their system worked.

The data generated by these systems is indeed useful to bureaucrats, not because it is accurate (it is not), but because its collectors (creators) configure it to match the presumed expectations of the agency demanding its collection. If the collector successfully meets the expectations of the relevant bureaucrat, he knows that its accuracy will not be questioned and he can get on with his real job. The system people are happy because the data proves the value of the system, and they can go on foisting it on field units. Possibly TMACS would have some value if it could be made to work, but it could not possibly be worth the price units would have to pay for it. Hard-core bureaucrats refuse to accept such practical limitations as significant, and the army's officers respond to requirement after unsustainable requirement with a hearty "Can do!"

Another paper system that is a favorite among unit personnel is called BTMS. There are many colorful interpretations of this abbreviation, but it really stands for Battalion Training Management System. It is what we may call a cognographic system; that is, a group of systems analysts has considered every possible step in the mental processes an instructor might go through in preparing to teach a lesson. They have then come up with a required form to fill out for each step. BTMS postulates that the army's hundreds of thousands of E–5s and E–6s, most of whom have a public high school education at best, are going to sit down and prepare detailed lesson plans for the training they administer daily. These lessons, which are different every day, are given to the four or five members of the trainer's section, often on some subject that the instructor himself does not understand. In order to make it possible for NCOs (or officers) to teach about subjects they do not comprehend, the army maintains on virtually every installation an extensive library of instructional tapes, films, and printed manuals, with a civilian staff to show soldiers how to use the A-V machines. Such classes usually bring all of the participants to an even level of noncomprehension. Many men have sat through BTMS classes about subjects they thought they understood and come out more ignorant than they were when they went in.

Soldiers rarely use the methods prescribed by BTMS, but they do spend a lot of time in classes *about* BTMS. One might argue that it would be more cost-effective to train NCOs on the subjects they need to teach to others, and then to let them teach it in the relatively informal way in which most effective training is done. The frenetic rate of job-switching forbids that.

Once a year, just before the AGI, a list is drawn up of all the required extra duties to which personnel are supposed to be assigned and of the files they are required to maintain. A partial list of those duties includes:

Unit Safety Officer

Unit Fire Officer

Unit Energy Conservation Officer

Unit Tax Officer

Unit Athletic Officer

Unit Maneuver Damage Officer

Unit Urinalysis Officer

Unit Publications Officer

Unit Non-Combatant Evacuation Officer

Unit Equal Opportunity Officer

Unit Physical Security and Theft Prevention Officer

Unit VD Control Officer
Unit Morale Support Officer
Unit Reenlistment Officer

This is in addition to all of the extra duties that have some year-round relevance, such as Supply Officer, Training Officer, Motor Officer, et cetera. There is one of each at every level of command. At company level they are distributed among the lieutenants, of whom there may be one or several. Each of these duties is also assigned to a unit NCO, so that there is a Unit Education NCO, a Unit Drug Rehabilitation NCO, and so on. The idea behind this cancerous growth of extra duties is Department of the Army's misconception that field units are inexhaustible reservoirs of idle manpower. This manpower can be used to generate large masses of detailed, marginally useful data to be digested somewhere in the bowels of the Pentagon, and to carry out all of the nice-to-have housekeeping functions dreamed up by people who have nothing better to do. All of these tasks take practical priority over military readiness.

The soldiers assigned to these duties spend the weeks before the AGI scrambling around creating or updating files, which have not been touched since the last AGI because they are irrelevant to any real unit activity, cannot be accomplished with unit resources, or are incomprehensible. The soldiers who did the job last year have rotated to another station, have been transferred to another unit, or have been promoted above the particular duties they did before. Odds are they have taken the old files with them or thrown them away.

Units will attempt to schedule a rifle qualification range to meet the annual requirement, which has to be done at least twice annually to keep up with personnel rotation. Should this prove impossible, bogus qualification cards will be drawn up. In the arms room, soldiers will be assigned to crew-served weapons that they have never fired. A false set of DD Forms 314 (Equipment Inspection Record) is filled in. Fire extinguishers are tagged and the monthly inspections for the last eleven months are initialed. Requisitions (often bogus) are made up for missing equipment and publications, because having something on requisition is as good for inspection purposes as actually having it. Better, in fact, because if it is not on hand it cannot be inspected and found deficient. Depending on the information gleaned from other units that have been inspected recently, and on the zeal of newly appointed extra-duty personnel, new requirements can be identified and met. One year we were required to prepare a separate "Commander's Letter of Energy Utilization Authorization" for every electric razor, refrigerator, and hair-dryer in the troops' billets. These were typed on my own electric typewriter, probably consuming more energy than was saved by this army-wide energy conservation requirement. No sensible commander is going to take away his soldiers' blow-dryers to conserve electricity.

Obviously, none of this activity achieves its original purpose, and any inspector who cares to can easily expose the frauds contained in every file. There are always documents signed and dated by personnel who were demonstrably in another country at the time. There is little attempt to do so, however, as inspectors understand the impossibility of maintaining all of these brilliant little administrative devices at the level of real army units. The true function of the AGI is to see how well the unit draws itself together to pull off a collective con job. A successful unit approaches this administrative challenge as the moral equivalent of war, and the AGI is seen as a bureaucratic analogue to the challenge of combat. Certainly it is as close to war as most units ever expect to come.

A SLIGHT DIGRESSION

Periodically we see stories in the press about the large-scale waste or destruction of spare parts or equipment by military units. In 1985 there was a minor scandal when a navy petty officer made public charges that entire aircraft engines and a new computer system had been thrown overboard from his aircraft carrier at the direction of the commander. Naturally, this was pooh-poohed by the chain of command. Horror stories of this sort elicit public alarm, but generally are seen as anomalies because no one outside of the military can conceive of any rational reason for doing such things. In fact, however, it is an entirely rational thing for a military officer to do, and woe to the officer who refuses to do it.

Whenever I was short of equipment or spare parts, I would call around to find out which units in my vicinity were expecting an AGI in the next few weeks. I would then take a truck over to their installation and stock up on "excess" equipment that they were trying desperately to unload. Invariably they had a truck already filled with such gear, which they were preparing either to hide, to burn, or to dump. This could be anything from beds to ammunition. Excess chemical warfare equipment seemed particularly ubiquitous. I frequently saw Eighth Army trucks stopped on the ends of the Han River bridges in Seoul, and troops dumping boxes into the river. Once I stopped and asked what was going on. The E–6 in charge saluted and said matter-of-factly, "Sir, we have an AGI coming up." I looked to see if there was anything I could use, then drove away. Another time I found eight brand-new medics' field bags in a trash can at the 121st Hospital in Seoul. "We have an AGI coming up, sir." I took the bags back to my battalion and completely re-equipped not only my own medics but those of the local engineer and MP units. These are minor examples. The chief of the supply yards at Camp Casey had entire shipping containers full of what he called "frustrated cargo," that is, brand-new supplies and equipment whose owners could not be identified. When I first found out about it he refused even to let me see it, but I obtained several five-ton truckloads in the weeks before his AGI. I took only what my unit could use: mostly tools, communications equipment, athletic gear, and office supplies. I left him the marine corps dress hats and the radar signal generator.

Why did I not report this behavior? Occasionally I did. In Germany I once spotted seventeen olive-drab airtight boxes stacked between a trash dumpster and the scrap metal bin. The local German trash contractor hauled away anything placed in that vicinity, twice a week. At first I assumed that they were old Redeye missile boxes being junked. Out of curiosity, however, I opened one box to see if there was anything that might make an interesting souvenir. Inside, there was what appeared to be a brand-new *Stinger* anti-aircraft missile in perfect condition. Not being an air defense artillery officer, I could not be sure at first that it was not a live missile. I hauled it up to my office and checked out the stock number on my microfiche. It turned out to be a "trainer handling unit." This totally inert plastic and metal toy, which does not *do* anything, was listed at $8,775 a copy. The box alone was an additional $496.[9] The total value of the trash-pile was $157,607.

I took the missile launcher next door to the battalion commander, who from his initial reaction appeared to think I was going to fire it at him. I told him what it was and asked if he knew of any particular reason that it was being thrown away. He gave me the go-ahead to investigate. The missiles turned out to belong to an ordnance company who had left them there "by mistake." They were immediately picked up and taken into a storage area. The last time I saw them, however, several months later, they were stacked between the trash dumpster and the scrap metal bin.

In Korea, other units' "excess" became a major source of new equipment for my battalion. Particularly easy to obtain were tools, office furniture, and chemical warfare gear. The regulation method for acquiring this stuff is called "lateral transfer," and this involves no exchange of money. On the other hand, it requires two or three times as much unit-level paperwork as using unit budget money and simply ordering new supplies from central facilities in the States. For that reason, the division Property Book Officer (PBO) placed so many barriers in the way of our massive scavenging operation that we dropped the legalities entirely. Instead, we added this property which we were legally authorized and required to have by recording it as "equipment found on post." We thus presented PBO with a fait accompli. I do not know how the losing units got it off their books, if indeed it was ever recorded to begin with, but there are ways.

I got into trouble with the battalion XO once when I failed to throw away a two and one-half-ton truck-full of spare parts for weapons, which had been collected from the battalion's five battery arms rooms. I had been given the task of seeing that all the arms rooms passed the AGI. My first task, he said, was to find the excess and get rid of it. I took a liberal interpretation of those instructions. We drove it from battery to battery, making two circuits a day in the week before the AGI. Virtually the entire truckload was consumed in the course of repairing the battalion's weapons. We were left with a single cardboard box full of parts, which was given gratis to the commander of C Battery, 1/38th FA, at Uijongbu. In return he sent a pile of 105mm howitzer spare parts and aiming equipment which we used on the old guns at the division's DMZ fire-base. All the arms rooms passed the AGI with flying colors, but the XO thought I was an idiot for taking chances. He said I lacked "military maturity."

As a battery motor officer in Germany I made a practice of collecting all of the excess spare parts I could find within the unit. From this pile I first met the needs of my own mechanics, then freely handed parts out to anyone who could demonstrate a need. I kept them in several large boxes in my motor bay, and never had any trouble with logistical inspectors. I simply showed them the boxes, identified them as containing excess, and told them that it was being inventoried for turn-in. This is the proper answer, and we did in fact inventory it. We never turned any of it in, however. That would have required a lot of paperwork, and there was no one to do it. We never received in return any budget refunds for expensive items ordered by mistake, and the supply facility people made a regular practice of throwing away any turn-ins. Otherwise it became excess at their level. One day before an AGI, the commander spotted the boxes and asked about them. I told him what they were. He said, "Throw it away. Now." I said, "But...." He said, "Now, Lieutenant." We threw it away. The one box for which we had an accurate inventory was worth $3,200. During the AGI we were unable to make on-the-spot repairs due to the lack of spare parts, and it was months before our vehicle service program recovered. Most of our regular service overstock of air filters, fan belts, et cetera, had been in the boxes. However, the word "excess" did not appear on our AGI report card.

How can we account for such apparently irrational behavior? "Excess" has become a focus of inspectors and a source of terror to commanders because of the methods tacked on to the supply system to enforce efficiency, prevent waste, and control parts and equipment inventories. It is the result of the natural tendency of systems designers to overdesign, to overcentralize, and to apply inappropriate commercial criteria to the very different needs of a combat organization. It is a classic example of what a political scientist would call "Bureaucratic Irrationality."[10]

This system applies to all military equipment, of which there is a truly bewildering variety in every unit. There is very little parts commonality between different types of vehicle, and there may be many different types of vehicle within even a small unit. A *LANCE* battery has at least six major types among its approximately twenty-five vehicles, with a larger number of special modifications. Some are tracked combat vehicles, some are heavy cargo trucks. There are also jeeps and modified civilian-type pickup trucks, both currently being replaced by the new "Humvee." Each vehicle type tows a different kind of trailer. There are several different kinds of generators, numerous radios of several types, a sophisticated computer system, and six different types of small arm. There are many other minor items. Obviously, trying to keep track of authorized spare parts stockage levels, which are constantly shifting, would be an insuperable headache even if parts clerks knew their jobs and the authorized levels corresponded to actual needs. They never do, of course, and parts demand is constantly distorted by weather, the changing pace of field training, and receipt of new equipment, accidents, borrowing, local scrounging, expedient repair methods, and glitches at every point in the system. A just-in-time inventory system should never be applied to military units because requirements are never predictable, and when something is needed unexpectedly, it is needed immediately. It is literally a matter of life and death. To be effective, units must devote a lot of precious cargo capacity to things they may never need, particularly ammunition and spare parts. This is as true in peacetime as in war.

Nonetheless, the system might work passably if the knowledge and experience of the end user were allowed to affect the way it is enforced. Promotion comes more slowly in the support specialties than in combat arms, and most unit motor sergeants have had years of experience working in army motor pools. I had a motor sergeant named Staff Sergeant (SSG) Hodrin who was simply a joy to work with, taciturn, professional, and reliable. Although I was constantly being pressured to interfere in his operation, to inspect this or that, in fact all I ever did was drop by once a day and ask if he needed any assistance from me. He rarely did, but when he wanted something I scrambled to get it. This managment style paid off handsomely. While C Battery sometimes had eight vehicles in various stages of breakdown out in the woods, I rarely even thought about maintenance in the field. All of my OERs compliment me on my maintenance abilities. I loved this man.

If SSG Hodrin had felt that we needed to have 200 Gamma Goat gear-shift control knobs on hand, even though we had no Gamma Goats, I would have believed him. He needed them for something, and any distortion this may have caused in the army's knob inventory was justified. The system does not allow for any expertise at unit level, however. It is designed for idiots, and only blindly obedient idiots at that. Few of the army's soldiers qualify on either count. Many inspectors understand this fact and tend to turn a blind eye toward evidence of excess stockage. Many others take delight in a game of "Find the Excess" and search every nook and cranny looking for the hidden gear. They know it is out there somewhere because no unit can function for long without it. If they fail to find it, they are satisfied that it has either been thrown away or the individual being inspected is one smart son-of-a-bitch and deserves a good report. If it is found, a failing deficiency is noted on the report, a horde of maintenance "experts" descends like a plague upon the unit, and the commander receives a butt-chewing for failing to properly manage his maintenance and supply resources.

Fear of excess has become a neurosis of almost mythic proportions in the army. In reality, being caught with it is not the worst thing that can happen during an inspection, but it is a problem that commanders can understand and a rare one in that it seems susceptible to simple and doable preventive measures. Although I found a lot of ways to avoid this danger and was never personally gigged for excess, most commanders are smarter simply to dump it. So the gear shift knobs and everything else imaginable went into the trash can every year just before the AGI.

This problem is easy to solve, in principle. Simply stop looking for the excess. Some inspection teams do not look now, but this is dependent on the guidance that they receive from their chiefs. The custom of tossing out excess is so ingrained in commanders that it will take years to wither away.

However, only a portion of excess is actually generated on purpose. Most actually is the result of mistakes, accidents, and bad management, and some unknowable amount is purposely created for criminal reasons.[11] Much of the accidental wastage will be cut when units are stabilized and people can learn their jobs. The criminal element cannot be stopped through administrative checks and restraints, simply because the military supply system is so big and complex. Administrative defense measures merely serve to create cracks in the system that can be exploited, while they paralyze its ability to support legitimate users. Only greatly beefed-up police action can stanch the hemorrhage of military supplies into criminal hands.

On the other hand, there is a way to put to practical use the tremendous amount of excess material that is available in the hands of almost every section chief, platoon sergeant, warrant officer, and pack-rat lieutenant in the field army. They have stacks of maps, spare parts, expendable supplies of every description, field gear, training ammunition, and field-rations. They cache it away for emergencies or for trading purposes. Added together, it is a great resource. Turning it in, as per regulation, is pointless and time consuming as well. Much is eventually discarded because of personnel transfers or inspections, and it is difficult to trade because of the general paranoia surrounding it. I never traded such material. I just gave it away to soldiers who could demonstrate a need. I expected—and usually received—the same treatment in return. Let's legitimize this practice and hold regular, local "Excess Fairs" at which people can freely trade this material. Supply unit officers who think that they actually can absorb this stuff and put it to good use, by the book, should be invited to police up the leftovers. It sounds messy, but this approach, and variations on it, will work.

This system cannot apply to ammunition, of course, because there are so many safety problems involved. The "legitimate" internal black market in training ammunition items can be eliminated only by redesigning ammunition supply procedures to meet the needs of using units, which they certainly do not do now. We will deal with this question later.

THE OFFICER EFFICIENCY REPORT

In all respects the most damaging evaluation system used by the army is the one used to promote officers. The Officer Efficiency Report (OER) system could not be better designed to produce a class of timid, dishonest paper shufflers, far more concerned about their individual promotion chances than about producing effective military units. Most of these timid, dishonest, sycophantic bureaucrats in uniform started out wanting to be soldiers, and have the talents and personal qualities to be good ones. However, smart people with extra mouths to feed are good at adopting the qualities that will keep them employed.

Officers receive an OER a minimum of once a year. They also receive OERs when they change jobs or commanders, subject only to the restriction that they have been in the same job and under the same rater for a minimum of ninety days. In certain cases a special OER may be submitted. These records are kept on file throughout an officer's career, and many senior officers worry about the future effects of the ratings they received as second lieutenants. Promotion boards, whose job is almost purely a matter of counting up numbers, are advised to ignore isolated below-par OERs. As the promotion pyramid narrows, however, they inevitably become significant.

The OER (see Figure 3–1) is a complicated document. Parts I and II are basically administrative data. Part III is a brief description of the rated officer's job assignment. Part IV is a checklist of "professional traits" such as "motivates, challenges and develops subordinates," and "displays sound judgment." These are graded on a scale of 1 (high) to 5 (low). Part V is the "performance and potential evaluation," in which the officer's immediate boss, his "rater," chooses from a series of boxes describing his duty performance. He also writes a short comment on that performance. Part VI is for the comments of an "intermediate rater," but this is not very important and is often left blank. Finally there is block VII, where the rated officer's boss's boss puts his comments and locates the officer on a scale of ten. The rater's comments are really for local consumption. The block important for promotion purposes is that filled in by the senior rater. This is far and away the most important block on the form.

Getting the right job assignments is critical in building an ambitious officer's career. Therefore, the contents of block III are more important than many officers realize. There is considerable suspicion among junior officers that choice assignments are based neither on random chance nor on merit, but no one seems to know exactly how assignments are made. However, in October 1984, retired Colonel Gerald K. Griffin wrote a letter to the Army's Chief of Staff concerning that subject.

Figure 3.1
The OER Form

For use of this form, see AR 623-105; proponent
agency is US Army Military Personnel Center.

PART I — ADMINISTRATIVE DATA

a. LAST NAME · FIRST NAME · MIDDLE INITIAL	b. SSN	c. GRADE	d. DATE OF RANK			e. BR	f. DESIGNATED SPECIALTIES	g. PMOS (WO)	h. STA CODE
			Year	Month	Day				

i. UNIT, ORGANIZATION, STATION, ZIP CODE OR APO, MAJOR COMMAND	j. REASON FOR SUBMISSION	k. COMD CODE

l. PERIOD COVERED						m. NO. OF MONTHS	n. MILPO CODE	o. RATED OFFICER COPY (Check one and date)	p. FORWARDING ADDRESS
FROM			THRU					1. GIVEN TO OFFICER	
Year	Month	Day	Year	Month	Day			2. FORWARDED TO OFFICER	

q. EXPLANATION OF NONRATED PERIODS

PART II — AUTHENTICATION (Rated officer signature verifies PART I data and RATING OFFICIALS ONLY)

a. NAME OF RATER (Last, First, MI)	SSN	SIGNATURE	
GRADE, BRANCH, ORGANIZATION, DUTY ASSIGNMENT			DATE

b. NAME OF INTERMEDIATE RATER (Last, First, MI)	SSN	SIGNATURE	
GRADE, BRANCH, ORGANIZATION, DUTY ASSIGNMENT			DATE

c. NAME OF SENIOR RATER (Last, First, MI)	SSN	SIGNATURE	
GRADE, BRANCH, ORGANIZATION, DUTY ASSIGNMENT			DATE

d. SIGNATURE OF RATED OFFICER	DATE	e. DATE ENTERED ON DA FORM 2-1	f. RATED OFFICER MPO INITIALS	g. SR MPO INITIALS	h. NO. OF INCL

PART III — DUTY DESCRIPTION (Rater)

a. PRINCIPAL DUTY TITLE	b. SSI/MOS

c. REFER TO PART IIIa, DA FORM 67–8–1

PART IV — PERFORMANCE EVALUATION — PROFESSIONALISM (Rater)

a. PROFESSIONAL COMPETENCE   (In Items 1 through 14 below, indicate the degree of agreement with the following statements as being descriptive of the rated officer. Any comments will be reflected in b below.)

HIGH DEGREE   LOW DEGREE
1   2   3   4   5

1. Possesses capacity to acquire knowledge/grasp concepts	8. Displays sound judgment	
2. Demonstrates appropriate knowledge and expertise in assigned tasks	9. Seeks self-improvement	
3. Maintains appropriate level of physical fitness	10. Is adaptable to changing situations	
4. Motivates, challenges and develops subordinates	11. Sets and enforces high standards	
5. Performs under physical and mental stress	12. Possesses military bearing and appearance	
6. Encourages candor and frankness in subordinates	13. Supports EO/EEO	
7. Clear and concise in written communication	14. Clear and concise in oral communication	

b. PROFESSIONAL ETHICS (Comment on any area where the rated officer is particularly outstanding or needs improvement)

1. DEDICATION
2. RESPONSIBILITY
3. LOYALTY
4. DISCIPLINE
5. INTEGRITY
6. MORAL COURAGE
7. SELFLESSNESS
8. MORAL STAND-
   ARDS

DA FORM 67–8 1 SEP 79   REPLACES DA FORM 67–7, 1 JAN 73, WHICH IS OBSOLETE, 1 NOV 79.   US ARMY OFFICER EVALUATION REPORT

Figure 3.1 (continued)

PERIOD COVERED		

PART V – PERFORMANCE AND POTENTIAL EVALUATION *(Rater)*

a. RATED OFFICER'S NAME   SSN

RATED OFFICER IS ASSIGNED IN ONE OF HIS/HER DESIGNATED SPECIALTIES/MOS   ☐ YES   ☐ NO

b. PERFORMANCE DURING THIS RATING PERIOD. REFER TO PART III, DA FORM 67–8 AND PART III a, b, AND c, DA FORM 67–8–1

☐ ALWAYS EXCEEDED REQUIREMENTS   ☐ USUALLY EXCEEDED REQUIREMENTS   ☐ MET REQUIREMENTS   ☐ OFTEN FAILED REQUIREMENTS   ☐ USUALLY FAILED REQUIREMENTS

c. COMMENT ON SPECIFIC ASPECTS OF THE PERFORMANCE. REFER TO PART III, DA FORM 67–8 AND PART III a, b, AND c, DA FORM 67–8–1. DO NOT USE FOR COMMENTS ON POTENTIAL!

d. THIS OFFICER'S POTENTIAL FOR PROMOTION TO THE NEXT HIGHER GRADE IS

☐ PROMOTE AHEAD OF CONTEMPORARIES   ☐ PROMOTE WITH CONTEMPORARIES   ☐ DO NOT PROMOTE   ☐ OTHER *(Explain below)*

e. COMMENT ON POTENTIAL

PART VI – INTERMEDIATE RATER

a. COMMENTS

PART VII – SENIOR RATER

a. POTENTIAL EVALUATION *(See Chapter 4, AR 623-105)*

SR   DA USE ONLY

HI

LO

A COMPLETED DA FORM 67–8–1 WAS RECEIVED WITH THIS REPORT AND CONSIDERED IN MY EVALUATION AND REVIEW   ☐ YES   ☐ NO *(Explain in b)*

b. COMMENTS

U.S. GOVERNMENT PRINTING OFFICE : 1983 O – 409-987

I served as the Chief of Infantry Branch, so I have some knowledge of how the [assignments] system really works. I assure you it works considerably different than you imagine or as it was intended to operate. In effect we have institutionalized a dual assignment system. One deals with those officers with senior/general officer backing and the other deals with the rest of the Army. . . . The bottom line is that our system rewards the wrong officer and is creating an officer corps dedicated to personal gain as opposed to service to country. In times of crisis our American soldiers will pay dearly for this oversight.[12]

The most characteristic aspect of the OER is the gross inflation of the language and the numerical scores. This inflation is driven by the fact that most officers are decent men and wish to reward those who serve under them. In ordinary practice only very junior lieutenants are ever given 2s in Part IV, although in some spectacular cases 5s have been recorded. So seldom is any imperfect score given that the army's Military Personnel Center (MIL-PERCEN) has computed no average for Part IV. The average officer is perfect. The same is true in Part V, where the great bulk of officers receive checks in the top box. Therefore, it appears that the average army officer "always exceeded requirements," and should be promoted "ahead of contemporaries." The narrative sections are only moderately important, because they are not quantitative in nature and DA selection boards are notoriously reluctant to make any decision that requires thought. There are a few words that are important, however. The average officer is "outstanding." An "excellent" performance is substandard. Some inexperienced OER writers do not understand these distinctions, with unfortunate results.

Because of this gross grade inflation, any rater who attempts to use the OER as a "developmental tool" or to genuinely describe the strengths and weaknesses of the rated officer will inevitably destroy that officer's career. Honest raters leave no descendants, for any officer not rated as "outstanding" is considered a dud. Eventually he will be booted out of the army either because he is identified as a loser under the "Quality Management Program" or because he is unable to obtain promotion. Under the army's "up-or-out" promotion system, officers not selected for promotion are fired.

However, MILPERCEN has come up with a very clever way of getting around the natural tendency of OER writers to drive scores so high that no useful distinctions can be made between rated officers. The key is the little block in the lower left-hand corner of side 2, with its infamous rows of little men. There are actually nine blocks, but raters have only three real choices. They can recommend the rated officer for Chief of Staff, that he take his chances among the mass of average officers, or that he be thrown out of the army. It really does not matter which blocks the senior rater prefers to use. MILPERCEN, knowing that commanders (for good reasons) prefer not to let their officers know where they really stand, realizes that all ratings are couched in inflated language. Therefore, they create a separate profile for each senior rater and determine the "center of mass" for his ratings. When the OER arrives at MILPERCEN this profile is noted on the form. Regardless of what block the senior rater actually used, the rated officer is clearly placed into one of three categories: "Above center of mass," "center of mass," or "below center of mass."

Unfortunately, while the senior rater profile may adjust for a senior officer's taste in little boxes, it does not adjust for the tremendous differences between senior raters in terms of competence, experience, intelligence, honesty, and understanding of people and of war. There does not appear to be any practical method of compensating for this problem. As far as the OER system is concerned, senior raters are a generic commodity.

Nonetheless, the army is very proud of the current form, for it has made DA selection boards, made up of people who do not pay any price for their mistakes, "very comfortable with their decisions."[13] Unquestionably the senior rater profile is a very clever system, and it accounts for the long life of this particular OER form. While others were inflated into uselessness within months of being printed, this one has lasted eight years.

The inflated language of OERs is often used to disguise bad ratings given for less than honorable reasons. A rater may simply dislike a subordinate or feel threatened by him in psychological or career terms. A subordinate who gets in trouble for insisting on high standards of integrity, pushes too hard for innovation, or defends his subordinates against unfair pressures from above is often given an OER that damns with faint praise. Career-destroying "faint-praise" OERs may take years to have their intended effects. Such delayed action is often preferable to actually confronting an officer with his objectionable features, especially if these include an insistence on filing accurate reports or wasting valuable time and resources training soldiers in military skills irrelevant to the senior rater's own promotion prospects. Sooner or later officers who pursue such policies will incur the wrath of the system.

Although there is an appeals system for bad OERs that can in theory handle complaints based on "substantive issues," it is impossible to justify an appeal on the basis of the use of the word "excellent" in place of "outstanding." Most unfair OERs are merely an accurate statement of the facts; they are damaging only because such honesty is so rare. Only obvious administrative errors or provable misstatements of fact can win an appeal, except possibly in cases of gross abuse where the officer victim has the support of higher-ups.

The OER is often used in this manner as a disciplinary tool. While the offense punished may be too much initiative or too much integrity, the OER is just as often used to punish breaches of military discipline that should be addressed by immediate command intervention or reference to the Universal Code of Military Justice (UCMJ). Officers are rarely brought up for trial under the UCMJ, and when they are it is usually for offenses like drunk driving or pilfering of funds. A commander who charges a subordinate with disobedience to orders or some similar military offense risks opening himself up to charges of weak leadership. UCMJ actions are almost never pressed for actual military reasons like cowardice under fire.[14] Such cases are bad publicity for the armed forces, and it is feared that the public will not understand the rationale behind prosecuting a man who refuses to fly his helicopter into a battle zone. OERs are the way out. "Afraid to fly, eh? Well, you just lost two points on your next OER."

The fact that it is the senior rating that has the most influence on promotions confuses many officers. Often, they hardly know the senior rater, especially if they serve in units that are widely spread out. Many times there is a conflict between loyal service to one's immediate commander and improving one's image with his boss. The senior rater is rarely directly aware of a junior officer's work. This leads to another baneful effect, perhaps as crippling as any already discussed. Although the senior rater may have his own opinion of the junior officer, and will take the immediate rater's assessment into account, there is another source of input. That is the information fed to him by other members of the unit, including the rated officer's subordinates or, if he is a staff officer, people who are subject to his inspection. Many "subordinates," such as senior NCOs, actually have far more prestige and credibility than the rated captain or lieutenant. Many times the senior rating amounts to nothing less than a peer or subordinate rating. While professional jealousy and sheer mean-mindedness may occasionally play a role in shaping this input, more often less malevolent considerations are the determining factor. A staff officer who has a bright idea is invariably seen as causing more work for everybody, when everyone is already running flat out trying to meet requirements imposed from outside the unit. A lieutenant or a company commander who has a bright idea is seen as trying to override his NCOs or to step on what they conceive to be their territory. While the rated officer's immediate boss may appreciate his innovations or unusual accomplishments, the senior rater will hear a lot more from the many wounded parties involved. The senior rating becomes a means of social control. Battles are not won by leaders who have adjusted to this kind of groupthink. This is probably why 49 percent of army officers felt that "the bold, creative officer could not survive" in the army.[15]

The OER system also has the unfortunate effect of focusing all of an officer's attention upward, of making his concern for his raters' opinion completely override consideration of and loyalty to his subordinates. This is not particularly helpful in peacetime, but the impact in combat is disastrous. No soldier is willing to die so that his leader can get promoted. For this reason some reformers have proposed that to the rater's and senior rater's input there should be added a "subordinate rating," a concept the army has played with but never formally adopted. There is merit to the underlying concept, but the idea of letting subordinates fill out paper reports on their commanders is putting a ludicrous faith in paperwork. Soldiers "vote" with their performance; they work well for good leaders, poorly for bad ones. The promotion system ignores this vital input, as shall be demonstrated.

The focus upward has other bad effects. The OER system is intended to enforce a feudalistic personal loyalty to superiors, but since those superiors are constantly changing it creates instead a more generalized loyalty to what are perceived to be the priorities of the army as an institution. However, since all of the army's evaluation and reward processes contradict the overtly stated goals of the army (nowhere, for instance, do army regulations overtly require the trashing of perfectly good spare parts and equipment), this leads to the presumption of a "hidden agenda," the precise contents of which no one can quite nail down. This leads to what appears to be irrational behavior on the grand scale. This is why army, navy, and air force officers buy radios that cannot communicate with each other's, even though few officers today feel any spirit of competition or animosity toward the other services.[16]

Probably the worst individual problem with the OER system is that there is no inescapable tie between a unit's performance and its leader's efficiency rating. An officer's unit may fail significant inspections and graded events without its being reflected in his OERs. In theory, the officer writing the OER takes such factors into account, but in practice they are very often irrelevant.

For example, the biggest event of the year for a LANCE battery is the "Annual Service Practice" (ASP) in Crete, where one of the platoons actually fires a live missile. This is the only chance a battery has actually to demonstrate its crucial technical skills. The ASP is a highly competitive event in which scores are compared between batteries, the six U.S. Army LANCE battalions in Europe, and even other national armies equipped with LANCE. My battalion (and within the battalion, my battery) was the USAREUR champion for two years in a row. Our scores were in the 98 to 99 percent range.

One summer, however, one of our batteries came back with a score of 72. Such a low score was virtually unheard-of. It reflected errors on the part of each of the missile crews that would have prevented successful launch of the missile toward its target. Captain "Smith" was then a few weeks short of completing the standard-length tour as the battery's commander. He received the following comments plus the best possible numerical scores on his last OER:

During the brief period of this report, CPT Smith's performance has continued to be outstanding. He has consistently demonstrated a degree of command presence and professional perceptiveness exceeding that expected of an officer of his grade and experience. His battery is well-trained and highly cohesive, accomplishing all the complex, desperate [sic] day-to-day training and maintenance tasks with pride and precision. Morale in his battery is outstanding, soldiers are well-trained with a strong sense of discipline. CPT Smith is a solid, experienced commander with a keen sense of the psychology of command, strong convictions, and a record of significant accomplishments within this battalion.... [He] has displayed a unique ability to make the right decision in all situations.... [He has] unlimited potential. Strongly recommend repeat command assignments, promotion, and schooling ahead of contemporaries.

How do we reconcile the reported sterling qualities of this commander to the demonstrated performance of his soldiers under stress? This is not a problem, because in fact there is no connection, and the poor performance fades into unpleasant personal memories while the OER marches forward to the promotion board. The system assumes that all raters are honest, equally competent, and that they know what they are talking about. The rater may be an unusually skilled judge of men, able to see real qualities obscured by chance misfortunes. That may well have been true in this case, and there is no suggestion here that the motives behind the writing of this OER were improper, merely that it is—of necessity—unrelated to actual unit performance. On the other hand, the rater may be an incompetent drunk on the verge of being relieved on morals charges. This is of no consequence once the OER is "in the can." Promotion boards see only the words and numbers, and know virtually nothing about the man who wrote them or the facts. An average rating in a superb unit is damaging; a superior score in a substandard unit is not.

This disconnection between demonstrated unit performance and the promotion system is a key failing in our military system. Together with the system of self-administered training and maintenance "report cards" it is a primary cause of the pervasive dishonesty of our officers and of their focus on unit politics to the exclusion of unit capability.

Some would-be reformers have recommended various changes to the OER, to make it more fair or more accurate.[17] These proposals miss the point. The fundamental, annihilating problem with the OER is that it attempts to rate the officer as an individual, to determine his personal potential or worth. The current OER does a pretty poor job of doing that, but this is irrelevant: there are no individuals on the battlefield. Military leaders must be judged by what they have actually accomplished with the units under their control. The subtle moral, technical, and personality aspects of effective leadership absolutely cannot be reduced to a checklist. There can be no meaningful numerical rating of "professional traits," as in Part IV of the current OER. No assessment by any individual, no matter how talented, can have any real significance.

What counts, brutally and simply, is results. Nothing else. Men's lives and the nation's fortunes on the battlefield rest on the practical abilities of our military leaders. None of the various qualities we think we would like to see in them—and think we can measure—means anything next to the demonstrated ability to make soldiers perform. The promotions of army leaders must somehow be rigidly connected to the demonstrated performance of the units they command.

Such an approach could not be fully effective under the current personnel system, because units in constant turmoil cannot reflect accurately the talents or flaws of their commanders. If, however, commanders were actually responsible for building and leading the units they command, as would be the case under the Divisional Rotation System described in chapter 2, there would be empirical methods of determining who is doing the best job, who is doing an adequate job, and who is failing. An effective unit evaluation system should mean, ipso facto, an effective promotion system.

It is clear that the evaluation methods now used by the army mandate a fatal level of dishonesty throughout the army; distort the chain of command; actively destroy unit readiness and morale; cause immense waste of time and material; compartmentalize the army into jealous fragments, incapable of mutual support; reduce the army's leaders to individuals in cutthroat competition with one another; do not measure real capability in any of the areas evaluated; and divorce the promotions of individuals from the performance of their units. They allow leaders to become dependent on administrative methods of enforcing discipline that immediately become irrelevant on the battlefield, causing peacetime command relationships to break down in combat. They fatally disrupt the training process, drive wedges between the various arms, units, and commanders, and cause the falsification of data that the nation's leaders need to make national security decisions. They permit a horde of office workers and obscure departments in the Pentagon to tyrannize the field army.

THE ETHICS OF THE OFFICER CORPS

How do we fix the integrity problems caused by the army's current evaluation system? It cannot be done through the methods of ever closer bureaucratic control and congressional scrutiny that seem to have become the American response to everything. Nor can it be handled by promulgation of an "Ethics Code." That too has been tried and has failed. Official ethics codes are generally written with an eye to meaninglessness to start with and, even if taken seriously, tend to be trivialized into meaninglessness or worse.[18]

The ethical code of the nation's military officers is a subject of much confusion and myth in American society. Among those citizens who do not see military professionals as baby-killers, officers seem to be expected to have some inherent purity and sense of purpose. This is nonsense: we live in a nation with profoundly civilian values, and we would not tolerate an officer corps that was uncompromising in matters of military principle.

Officers who take a firm stand on military principle, rightly or wrongly, are sacked. Generals MacArthur and Singlaub are examples, and regardless of the merits of their individual cases their firings have burned an indelible lesson into the soul of the officer corps. Army officers represent no separate social class, and as a group they have no unique values. The army has grown too rapidly for that. There are as many active-duty officers in the army today as there were soldiers in 1940. Officers have houses and mortgages and wives and kids, and they want to keep their jobs and get a raise. This should not bother us; we truly have a "citizen army."

One hears much talk in the army about the importance of the "word of an officer," but it still requires two IDs and a look at the bad check list for an officer to shop at the PX. Army offices and publications are festooned with high-minded mottoes like "Where principle is involved, be deaf to expediency." This is ridiculous. What principle? Loyalty? A loyal officer is expected to lie for his commander, his unit, his service. Honesty? The word has no meaning in the context of the army's reporting systems. Obedience to regulations and procedures? Such behavior is not principled: it is expedient, because it allows an officer to survive and win promotion without ever accomplishing the mission the nation expects of him, which is producing capable military forces. Unfortunately, even the "principle" of abiding by the book can get an officer into trouble in some areas, particularly maintenance.

I agonized over this problem for a long time, and I finally decided that I was paid to produce military capacity. If following procedure did that, fine, and in many respects I became a stickler for regulations. Otherwise, I followed the motto paraphrased on my office door in Korea: "Had we done for ourselves what we have done for the battalion, we would be the worst of scoundrels." Such an approach is satisfying. It permits real accomplishments. It also leads to events like the Iran-Contra affair.

The army has tried various means of determining officers' performance. All of these methods depend on the integrity of the individual who benefits from being rated or doing the rating. This is an approach that does not work with real human beings. Therefore, like the communist thinkers who came up with the "new socialist man" who would make their system work, the army has promulgated a totally unrealistic image of the officer corps. This image is conjured up so often that many civilian policymakers—and even some in the officer corps itself—appear to believe it:

All officers ... are professional. Officers personally adopt, model, and instill in their subordinates the values that form the basis for a distinct lifestyle and code of behavior. They are worthy of special trust because their character and integrity are above reproach. They command confidence and respect for excellence in their profession; are loyal to the nation and the Army; are self-disciplined to ensure that their own moral and ethical well-being are maintained; and exhibit selfless service to the

Army and the nation in all of their actions, ensuring that they accomplish their responsibilities with no thought of taking unfair advantage and with the least cost in terms of lives and national resources.[19]

Quite aside from the question of whether loyalty to the army can be compatible with loyalty to the nation (it cannot), this kind of pompous bombast obscures a fundamental failing of the army's evaluation systems. Anyone can design a system for supermen. The problem is to design a system that works for real people. In Vietnam, the evaluation system built around the notorious "body count" did not merely distort the public relations image of the war: it destroyed the faith of the nation in its military, of soldiers in their leaders, of leaders in each other and in themselves. Only 2 percent of general officers who served in Vietnam believed that the body count was a valid measure of progress. Sixty-one percent admitted that the system was "often inflated." Some were more specific, saying "A fake—totally worthless" ... "a blot on the honor of the Army" ... "blatant lies" ... "I shudder to think how many of our soldiers were killed on body-count missions—what a waste."[20]

American officers are not a bunch of Mother Theresas with assault rifles, and telling soldiers that they are results in an almost instantaneous loss of faith in their leaders once they see them up close. Soldiers would be satisfied with merely decent leadership, from decent men who know their business, if they were not told to expect so much more. Officers are human beings, and pretending that they are something else is a fatal mistake. The lesson is that officers must not be allowed to write each other's tickets, nor their own. The most facile liar is bound to get ahead, and the morale and integrity of those naturally inclined to tell the truth is rapidly eroded or destroyed.

SOLUTIONS

Officers are not born sycophants, idiots, or liars: they are men of normal intelligence and morals who quickly figure out where the carrots and sticks of the army's personnel system lie. They adjust their behavior accordingly. Change the reward system and they will change their behavior.

The key is to link officers' promotion to the relative performance of their units, to produce a promotion system that forces an officer to concentrate his energies on producing a battle-ready unit. This system must throw him into competition with other officers and units doing the same thing, and yet simultaneously force him to cooperate with them in building the larger all-arms team that actually fights battles and wins wars. Merely changing the promotion system will not do the trick, because the current unit evaluation methods not only do not accurately identify the relative capabilities of units, they actively destroy the ability of commanders to identify and correct problems. They make it impossible to set priorities or to make any but the most insignificant decisions at unit level. Any attempt to correct these evaluation methods will therefore have to deal with the vexing question of the relationship of the field army to the military bureaucracy that created them.

Nearly everyone agrees that the military bureaucracy makes excessive demands upon field units for data and for compliance with an ever-multi-plying number of paper systems, like TMACs and BTMS, intended to in-crease their efficiency. The point of diminishing returns has long since been passed, probably sometime in the 1940s.

A mechanism for reducing this monstrous burden to the point where units can do their actual jobs has been lacking. Bureaucratic leaders can order a reduction of 50 percent in administrative-related reports and duties imposed by their own agencies' directives, as former Secretary of the Navy John Lehman recently did.[21] The immediate result will be another request from the navy's various bureaus to naval field units for data on the administrative load they bear. The next event will be a furious office war to determine just whose influence is going to be reduced. Some required reports will be elim-inated. As a result, some higher headquarters may reduce their requirements for reports from lower headquarters, although this will be resisted at every level because it will eliminate jobs on prestigious staffs. Some reduction in the paper load may eventually be felt at unit level, but it will be nowhere near the 50 percent originally envisioned. Any real reductions made in the immediate future will soon be reversed by the insatiable bureaucratic de-mand for information and influence. This problem is inherent in the current structure, and all of the "fine-tuning" in the world cannot fix it.

The solution is to reduce to a supporting role those elements of the bureaucracy whose true purpose is to support the field units. Their rela-tionship to the field army must become that of a seller to a demanding customer. The only way to cut administrative burdens to a point where units can function is to let the commanders in the field army determine which of these paper systems are contributing to their units' capabilities and which are not. This must be done without undermining the legitimate information-collection and political control functions that the bureaucracy also must exercise. Under the current situation the three functions are hope-lessly intermingled.

Consider the following proposal: Let's take all of the many evaluations a unit is subjected to now and consolidate them into one single massive event, at the level of division-sized units. Call it an "EXEVAL" (External Evaluation). Take the division to a large training area with facilities for weapons firing, vehicle maneuvering, aircraft operations, et cetera. A very large inspection organization will have to be created. Call it the "Tactical Forces Inspectorate." Its field teams, with elements from all the various agencies concerned, will then descend upon the unit and conduct a thorough evaluation of every aspect of its readiness to go to war. Let congressional,

Office of Management and the Budget (OMB), and National Security Council (NSC) staffers participate and observe. Set up stations where company-sized units (including headquarters and headquarters companies at every level from battalion to corps) will be rotated through exhaustive inspections of equipment conducted by real experts, including representatives from the contractors who built it. Rotate all soldiers (including officers and NCOs, where applicable) through their Physical Readiness, CTT, and SQT tests, and any other individual testing desired. While some units are busy there, put others on the weapons ranges, testing soldiers' proficiency with individual and crew-served weapons, and with primary unit equipment like tanks, artillery, ground surveillance radars, et cetera.

Examine unit operational proficiency with detailed command post exercises (CPX) at battalion, brigade, and division level; culminate with live tactical exercises against a large opposing unit, with tactical air support for both sides. Make it clear to units that this is not "training." It is a test that will affect matters of real importance, i.e., promotions and retention for officers and men. The opposing force can be either a simulated Soviet-style aggressor unit, like the one at Fort Irwin, or another combat unit that is not being evaluated. Or, better yet, another unit that is being evaluated in competition. Financial and space constraints militate against live actions much larger than battalion size, and many can be much smaller. Electronic warfare operations should be full scale. The result, of course, until units learn to handle such realism, will be chaos.

There is no reason why the enemy should always utilize Soviet tactics. A major weakness of current army training is that it is always directed against our most dangerous but least likely enemy, and usually portrays him in a straw-man pose. The personnel stability engendered by the new rotation system will permit training aimed at a wide variety of potential foes, which is quite impossible now. Units incapable of adjusting to different tactical situations will not do well, and their leadership personnel will not survive to exercise a baneful influence in the future. It would be interesting and valuable to put the Tenth Light Infantry Division up against the Second Armored, both using their own tactics. Overseas, the host nation and allied armies would be interested in playing, although rigid safety procedures would have to be instituted to insure that South Korean or Turkish troops do not actually behead their captives. U.S. troops also require watching in that regard. Anyone who thinks that American soldiers are boy scouts has never spent a week in the woods with them or talked to them about their images of war. Such testing would have multiple benefits, forcing U.S. units to learn something about their allies and making the military intelligence types and tacticians deal with a genuine and alien threat, instead of the bogus "OPFOR" enemies they create for themselves.

The army virtually never intentionally "tests to failure," that is, subjects a unit to tactical stress to the point where it loses cohesion and can no longer play. Instead, "damaged" equipment and "dead or wounded" soldiers are miraculously restored to health within minutes or hours of their simulated injuries. Minuscule medical, personnel-, and equipment-replacement exercises are used to symbolize the massive operations that will have to accompany serious real-world combat.[22] These exercises are designed to build in the soldiers' minds a self-image as "winners." Sometimes this hope is realized, but the resulting psychological spit-shine is extremely fragile. It cannot be sustained in contact with a truly competent, ruthless enemy. Many army leaders would be horrified at the impact that a realistic test to failure might have on morale. However, real combat is nothing if not a test to failure, and our units have been failing in combat for a long time. If soldiers are made to understand that they *will* be tested until they crack, and that their score depends on how long they can put that off, the impact on morale will be a positive one.

Put the emphasis of all testing exclusively on military results.[23] Call it "Results Limited Evaluation." That is, grade maintenance not by how well the forms are filled out but by whether the equipment works and how well. Score this in comparison not to theoretical specifications but to the actual performance levels of similar equipment in other units. Grade tactical performance not by checking a thousand little subtasks but by whether tactical goals are achieved. Identify artillery targets to maneuver commanders and see how long and how many bullets it takes before they are destroyed. Do not waste time insuring that the forward observers use proper procedures: if their methods don't work, the targets will not be destroyed. If their methods do work but are not consistent with the field manual, so what? Change the field manual to match the methods of the most successful units. Live electronic opponents will ensure that faulty communications procedures will result in tactical failure. Live (non-lethal) chemical attacks will reveal practical flaws in chemical warfare capabilities in ways that will leave an impression. Use of MILES and AGES weapon simulation equipment will insure that casualty assessments are realistic.[24] Safety officers will have to be everywhere to insure that guns do not accidentally fire into nearby shopping centers and that infantry are not run down by overenthusiastic tankers, but these safety personnel must come from outside the evaluated units and their interference must be kept to a minimum.

Translate the results of all this testing into a numerical score for units and staffs at every level from division to company and platoon, such that units' scores reflect not only their own performance but the performance of their battalions, brigades, and divisions in competition with all other battalions, brigades, and divisions. Then base the long-term retention of all unit members, and their near-term promotions and pay-grade increases, on the relative performance of their units. The actual mechanics of the resulting promotion system are discussed in chapter 4.

Also, make this super-inspection the only legal means for the Department of the Army to gain performance and statistical information directly from field units. DA then will be able to extract from these proceedings the detailed, accurate information it needs on equipment, individual, and unit performance, without being able to overload units with demands for information that is beyond their capacity to collect or to utilize at unit level. If some official at the Pentagon afterwards insists that he needs to know exactly how many cups of coffee men in pay grades E–3 and E–4 drink during duty hours, let him send someone down to unit level and record the numbers for himself.

Day-to-day reporting systems will become in-house affairs controlled by military commanders for the exclusive purpose of operational planning. Because officers' promotions will depend on empirically derived and relative performance evaluations, made by observers from outside the chain of command, commanders will no longer have the power to slay the bearers of bad news. No one will have any incentive to falsify reports made within the local reporting chain. Because an officer's promotability will depend not only on the performance of his own specialized unit but on the performance of the larger, all-arms unit of which it is a part, the incentive for mutual cooperation will be high. In practice, there actually will be a strong incentive to uncover rather than conceal both systemic and local problems, and to correct them.

One officer who read this proposal objected that without administrative sanctions to enforce compliance, units would not provide regular reports to higher headquarters. If unit commanders cannot be trusted not to blow off vital information requirements and head for the officers' club, then we must ask why they have been made commanders in the first place. The UCMJ provides the proper means for dealing with uncooperative subordinate commanders.

"Results Limited Evaluation" and the concentration of all evaluations at one mammoth EXEVAL will mean that all training and maintenance evaluation will have to take place more or less simultaneously, and the proliferation of divergent criteria for judging the same task will cease. All evaluation will have to be made in a tactical environment, and the notoriously unrealistic "dog-and-pony shows" demanded by current inspections will end. It will not be possible to force units annually to resurrect unsustainable administrative and maintenance systems. Those that commanders find useful will be retained. Those that are not useful will atrophy. Inspectors simply will find nothing to inspect. Commanders who make the wrong choices will not achieve competitive unit performances and so will not be promoted or even retain their jobs. Units will no longer be tyrannized by irrational application of counterproductive rules like those currently reflected in the game of "Find the Excess." They will not, however, be able to ignore the legitimate requirements of the logistical system, because they will still have to access it for supplies and equipment. If they do not access the logistical system effectively, it will be reflected in performance. No unit moves, trains, fights, or eats without supplies. There will be no loss of accountability, as commanders will still sign for their equipment, and the inventories will be conducted at the beginning and end of each cycle and at the equipment hand-off before rotation overseas. Such an inventory will not be necessary as a part of the EXEVAL itself because a unit that does not have truly vital equipment will do poorly.

EFFECTS ON COMPARTMENTALIZATION

One particularly beneficial effect of this approach is that it should greatly reduce the compartmentalization of fighting units. If we were to give a current commander a counter-insurgency mission, every branch, arm, and specialized unit of the army would try to get in on it in order to garner goodies for its own constituents. Under EXEVAL and Results Limited Evaluation, that is not going to work. The commander who tries to keep all of his subordinates happy by spreading the wealth is going to end up hurting them, because the resulting operation will consume too many resources, take too long, suffer too many casualties, and look too stupid to win a decent score. If he does the sensible thing and sends in his best-trained infantry battalions to conduct a low-key, low-collateral damage pacification operation, the entire division will score points. The division commander will either regain control of his unit from the bureaucratic infighters or he will fail, and somebody will learn from his mistake. This scenario is dependent, of course, on having sensible evaluators and test planners in the Tactical Forces Inspectorate, but this should be possible to arrange. If the other services could somehow be drawn into this program, tactically effective "unification" might be achieved without attempting the political and administrative nightmare of "real" unification. Army, air force, and navy officers would suddenly discover the value of buying radios that can communicate with one another.

This same effect will be visible during normal training periods. For example, the training ammunition supply procedures contained in the USA-REUR/V Corps Ammo SOP clearly are designed for the convenience of the ammo supply people. They make it difficult or impossible for a unit to obtain training ammunition in a hurry, to maintain reserve stocks on hand, or to obtain it from other units. They also make it highly impractical to turn in leftover or excess ammunition items to be restocked and reissued. Although the SOP allegedly is designed to maintain safety and to assure an even distribution of training ammo assets, it actually is designed to cut the workload of ammo supply units and to shift the blame for any accidents onto user units. The result is that units are unable to schedule training effectively, because that (like combat) often requires a very rapid response to fleeting opportunities. It also causes the generation of tremendous amounts of excess ammo, with resulting safety violations and wastage. Another result is that ammo supply units themselves do not receive the personnel and support they need to do their real jobs. Under the current system this happens because logistical units are a commander's constituents just like everybody else, and their desires carry just as much weight. Under EXEVAL, however, a unit that cannot get ammunition for training or for the EXEVAL will lose points. If there is no ammo, there is no weapons firing, and units will get a zero score regardless of whose fault it was. SOPs will be readjusted in a hurry, and logistical units will assume their proper place as customer service organizations.

THE TACTICAL FORCES INSPECTORATE

Moving to this new evaluation system will require the development of a large new body within the army, which we have labeled the Tactical Forces Inspectorate (TFI). The army will have about twenty months to get this organization going (from commitment to the program to the point where the first DRS unit is ready for testing). This inspectorate must be made legally responsible for the provision of all information concerning the field army to all other organizations, including DA, DOD, and Congress. It will operate principally through a few large Field Evaluation Teams whose commanders will report directly to the Commander, Army Field Forces (see chapter 5) or, failing reform of the higher chain of command, the Chief of Staff.

Given that a Divisional EXEVAL will take about three weeks to execute, with the results taking longer to tabulate and absorb, and that there will be about twenty divisions or division-equivalents to evaluate, several TFI Field Evaluation Teams will have to be constructed. These teams will have to be capable of roaming the country or deploying overseas, although at least one could be stationed permanently in Europe. They will have to be large enough to assign well-rounded tactical evaluator teams down to battalion level at least, and preferably to company level. Inspection teams should include congressional watchdogs, military specialists from academia, and military history detachments from the Office of Military History. Special-function inspecting units will establish the stations for standardized testing of individuals. Teams from the combat arms specialty centers (like the Field Artillery School at Fort Sill) will evaluate branch-specific skills on the appropriate ranges and maneuver courses. Equipment will be inspected by teams made up of contractor personnel, military logistics and ordnance experts, and interested outside agencies like OMB and congressional staffs. This should insure the integrity of the process and satisfy civilian leaders that they are in fact getting an accurate picture of what is going on in the field army.

This inspectorate will have a wartime function too, of course. The internal reporting system will have to be the basis for practical decision making, but TFI teams will serve to keep the system honest. They will therefore provide at least a part of the function of what has been called a "directed telescope," a command and control tool used by effective commanders from Napoleon to Patton,[25] and one completely lacking in the modern United States Army.

The EXEVAL scoring system will require careful thought, but there are two critical requirements. The first is that at least 50 to 75 percent of the score for unit proficiency be based on the unit's ability merely to survive in a tactical environment. The portion that is branch-specific must be adjusted in such a way that the score distribution is the same for all branches. Otherwise units will accord too much priority to branch-specific skills, and the scores for units of different branches will be hard to compare. The second is that it be open-ended. That is, there should be no minimum or maximum score for any event, and winners and losers must be identified on a sliding scale. The army's current physical fitness test is an example of what happens when such scores are pre-set. Many soldiers, particularly the most experienced, quit performing once they have hit the minimum. There is no practical benefit to anything above a "pass." Only a rare individual keeps going past the maximum score, although many are able to do so. Since the units being evaluated under EXEVAL will be in actual competition for a concrete reward (retention and promotion), and beyond that for such intangibles as pride and prestige, actual performance objectives will be set by the most capable and motivated participants. Such objectives will thus be both challenging and realistic, and should rise over time.

The frequency of these Division EXEVALs will be dependent on time and money, but it should be more often than annually. It definitely must not be on a twelve-month cycle or we will end up with units that are optimized for operations in June or December. Many current army leaders will be horrified at the idea of a unit drifting along on its own for six to ten months with no harassment from above. If the army picks generals who need constant pressure to stay motivated, this system will not work. Such will not be the case. Capable generals are normally self-starting, and if they need additional motivation the scores they accumulate during the grueling four years they spend in division command will determine both their own futures and that of all their subordinates. The career ambitions and competitiveness of the leadership should be sufficient to prevent any lapse into inactivity.

Where will all the personnel for these inspection teams come from? The answer is that they are already out there. Take all of the personnel who currently serve on AGI teams, or who administer the CTT and SQT systems, or conduct the FAMSEG and the DA Nuclear Evaluations, and all the other roving inspection teams, and add them up. The problem then turns inside out: what are we going to do with all of these excess evaluators? Military personnel requirements will be further cut by insisting that contractors provide expert personnel to help examine the condition of the equipment they have provided. The real problem in constructing the inspection groups will be to find competent, enthusiastic officers to design and control the tactical and operational portions of the EXEVAL. Inspection team commanders and staff will have to be the most widely experienced and knowledgeable officers in the army. Service on such a team should be a vital step on the road to the highest ranks and commands.

Certain necessary aspects of inspection and evaluation cannot be handled by the EXEVAL approach. There are ongoing security functions that will have to be inspected fairly frequently while units are on their regular duty stations. This applies, for instance, to the workings of the Nuclear Release Authentication System (NRAS). Such inspections must be quick and unannounced to be effective and to avoid disruption of routine unit training. TFI should also handle these inspections.

The Tactical Forces Inspectorate will partially absorb but not entirely displace the current Inspector General (IG) system. TFI and EXEVAL are focused on military effectiveness, and over the long haul they will improve the ethics and integrity of the army's leadership. However, there will always be officers who abuse their authority over troops, and desperate or immature leaders may feel driven to extreme methods by the new demand to demonstrate effectiveness. In the long run such leaders will fail because American soldiers react very poorly to such leadership. Meanwhile, soldiers must be able to appeal to the IG for protection from unethical or incompetent leaders.

EXEVAL has only limited applicability to headquarters above division level. Although most of their individual- and unit-level inspections can take place in connection with the regular EXEVAL, their command functions will have to be evaluated in special command exercises by special inspectorate teams. Large exercises like REFORGER and Team Spirit will provide an excellent opportunity to examine these higher level headquarters. The real key to improving the performance of these higher headquarters is to get them out of the peacetime chain of command and to let (make) them focus on their own wartime functions rather than on constantly harassing their subordinate units (see chapter 5).

Outside of the field army and not directly subject to TFI will be installations and installation units (especially food service facilities), administrative units, fixed medical facilities, et cetera. Obviously, these will continue to require supervision, and the current system is generally appropriate for that purpose. Accomplishing this will be largely a matter of coopting agencies already concerned with those functions under a new organization responsible directly to the Army Chief of Staff or to theater commanders.

The principal problems in the army's evaluation system are basically three. One, information needed for operational purposes is hopelessly confused with information intended as input to the promotion system. Two, deskbound bureaucrats and harried commanders persistently seek some quick, convenient analogue for performance—in the soldier's shoe-shine, the maintenance report, or the OER—rather than examining the performance itself. Three, the support, information-gathering, and control functions of the military bureaucracy are hopelessly intertwined, so that agencies whose purpose is to assist or analyze field units have usurped the powers of command. Bureaucrats in Washington refuse to accept that one of their principal purposes is to support the fighting forces, and insist instead on forcing down the throats of field soldiers paperwork "fixes" for problems that either do not exist or were created by the last such attempted fix. Information gatherers have passed their duties on to the soldiers who are supposed to be the subjects of their studies. These bureaucrats are constituents of commanders quite high in the pecking order. The field army is therefore unable either to meet or to resist the demands of the office-workers.

The reforms advocated here deal directly with these problems. The creation of a Tactical Forces Inspectorate, operating through the medium of the Divisional EXEVAL, will permit the collection of masses of relevant, accurate data, without forcing the units to do the bureaucracy's work. Commanders will be able to get accurate information from their subordinates because they no longer will be permitted to slay the bearers of bad tidings. Freed from the current unavoidable necessity to lie, and forced both to genuinely cooperate with their fellow soldiers and to produce meaningful military results, most officers will be as honest on the job as they are in their personal lives. Probably more so. They will actively seek to uncover and correct problems rather than to conceal them. The ironclad connection between unit performance and officers' retention and promotion will ensure that useful administrative techniques are identified and retained, and that counterproductive ones will wither away. The fact that units will still have to use prescribed methods to access the military logistical systems will insure that these systems will not dissolve into chaos, certainly not into a worse form of confusion than at present. The true relationship between "warriors" and "managers" will be clarified, probably much to the surprise of both.[26]

The legitimate control functions of the bureaucracy will also be strengthened, as will the political reliability of the army. EXEVAL will connect officer advancement firmly to achievement of the *overtly* stated goals of the army, which by definition are those that the public finds acceptable. There can be no "hidden agenda" of purely organizational priorities, rational or otherwise. The civilian leadership will be able to obtain the information it requires and to give whatever political direction it wishes. The difference will be that civilian control will be exercised through the military chain of command rather than through a destructive parallel system, and that civilian observation will be made through a microscope that does not destroy the organism being examined.

NOTES

1. This practice has a long history. See Colonel William P. Boyd, "Men of Character, Principles of Honor?" *ARMY*, September 1985.

2. See particularly General Douglas Kinnard, *The War Managers* (Hanover, N.H.: University Press of New England, 1977).

3. Andrew F. Krepinevich, *The Army and Vietnam* (Baltimore: Johns Hopkins University Press, 1986), 254–55.

4. ARTEP outbrief, August 15, 1985.

5. B battery ARTEP report, May 28, 1985.

6. DODAC: Department of Defense Ammunition Code, needed when requisitioning any Class V (ammunition) item.

7. Edward N. Luttwak, *The Pentagon and the Art of War* (New York: Simon and Schuster, 1985), chap. 1.

8. No evaluator wants the unit he is grading to fail, both because he can expect retaliation and because he does not want to be dragged away from his own unit and into the field again for a retake. Occasionally some cocky young officer, confident of his own unit's ability to take the heat, will deliver a no-holds-barred critique. He will not do this twice.

9. Prices from Army Master Data Fiche (AMDF), November 1985; Supply Bulletin (SB) 700–20, September 1985, chap. 2.

10. See Graham T. Allison, *Essence of Decision: Explaining the Cuban Missile Crisis* (Boston: Little, Brown and Company, 1971).

11. "Congressional investigators tell Senate armed services panel that Army is unable to control theft of large amounts of weapons, ammunition, and explosives, which ends up being sold on black market." (Synopsis), *New York Times*, July 24, 1986, sec. I.

12. Letters to the Editor, *Armed Forces Journal International*, August 1985, 10. Griffin, evidently dissatisfied with the chief's response, made portions of his letter public.

13. Evaluation Systems Office, MILPERCEN, February 6, 1987.

14. See Richard Gabriel, *Military Incompetence* (New York: Hill and Wang, 1985), 164–65. Examples from Vietnam are too numerous to mention, but estimates are that unit "combat refusals" were running at a rate of about 245 a year in 1970. See Richard Gabriel and Paul Savage, *Crisis in Command* (New York: Hill and Wang, 1978), 45. The case of the USS *Stark* provides another recent example.

15. Benjamin F. Schemmer, "Internal Army Surveys Suggest Serious Concerns about Army's Senior Leaders," *Armed Forces Journal International*, May 1985, 18–20.

16. A major problem in Grenada was that army, navy, and air force radios were not interoperable. One army officer attempted to coordinate fire support by making a call to his Fort Bragg office from a Grenadian phone booth, using his private credit card. Ninety-ninth Congress, *Defense Organization: The Need for Change: Staff Report* (Washington, D.C.: GPO, 1985), 365.

17. See Lieutenant Colonel Larry H. Ingraham, "The OER Cudgel: Radical Surgery Needed," *ARMY*, November 1985; Lieutenant General Walter F. Ulmer, "Leaders, Managers, and Command Climate," *Armed Forces Journal International*, July 1986.

18. See discussion of the West Point honor code in Gabriel and Savage, *Crisis in Command*, 101–6.

19. Command Information Division, Office of the Chief of Public Affairs *Results of the Professional Development of Officers Study Surveys* (Washington, D.C.: Headquarters, Department of the Army, 1985), 18.

20. Kinnard, *The War Managers*, 74–75.

21. Lieutenant Ralph T. Soule, "The War on Paper," *Proceedings of the U.S. Naval Institute*, January 1987, 34.

22. Had the ratio of dead to wounded in the Beirut disaster been reversed, indications are that the military medical system would have been "overwhelmed." Hearings before the Committee on Armed Services, U.S. Senate, October 16-December 12, 1985, *Reorganization of the Department of Defense* (Washington, D.C.: GPO, 1987), 6.

23. "The functional structure serves to . . . direct vision away from results and towards efforts—DOD is focused on inputs, not outputs." "Overview Analysis," *Defense Organization*, 615. Although concerned with the highest levels of command, the conclusions of this report parallel in many respects the arguments of the present work.

24. MILES stands for Multiple Integrated Laser Engagement System. AGES, Air-Ground Engagement System, is a similar system for airborne and air-defense weapon systems. Essentially, MILES equipment consists of an infrared laser transmitter attached to every variety of direct-fire weapon and a receptor system worn by potential targets (troops, vehicles, aircraft). The receptor can identify an incoming laser beam and determine whether the source weapon has scored a lethal or damaging hit. Through varying frequencies and attenuation systems, a laser can simulate many of the characteristics of the source weapon, such as range and destructive power. It cannot, however, do physical damage or penetrate opaque material. Nor can it simulate trajectories, a minor limitation for direct-fire weapons, but crippling for indirect systems such as artillery. This poses a major problem in simulation, but should be soluble. MILES is extremely effective as a training device, permitting tremendous realism. Unfortunately, soldiers often disable their receptors, either under the influence of their leaders or on their own initiative. They will remove batteries, paint over detector cells, or cut signal wires. This can be detected electronically by evaluators in the field, and strict enforcement measures can deter this practice. MILES can force a unit not only to use weapons and cover correctly, but also to utilize ammunition supplies properly, as the transmitters require the actual firing of a blank round to actuate the laser. Soldiers have discovered ways to defeat this feature, however. This equipment is surprisingly rugged and is on hand in the army in substantial quantities. Minor modifications and additions are required to make MILES fully effective, but the system, even at present, is enormously useful.

25. This refers to organizations like Patton's Army Information Service, usually called his "Household Cavalry." See Russell F. Weigley, *Eisenhower's Lieutenants* (Bloomington: Indiana University Press, 1981), 242. For the term "directed telescope" see Martin van Creveld, *Command in War* (Cambridge: Harvard University Press, 1985).

26. There has been an ongoing debate in the pages of periodicals like *ARMY* and *Armed Forces Journal* over the relative importance of warriors versus managers. See Lt. Ralph Peters, "Leaders and Managers: Rewards out of Balance," *ARMY*, August 1984; Ulmer, "Leaders, Managers, and Command Climate"; General "Yasotay," "Warriors: An Endangered Species," *Armed Forces Journal International*, September 1984.

4

PROMOTIONS

Officers are expected to be patriotic, and to be motivated by ideals of service to the nation. Most officers are in fact patriotic, and feel somewhere in their souls that they are doing the nation a service. On the battlefield they may die for love of country and dedication to its highest ideals. Or merely through a lack of any immediate say in the matter.

In real life, it is a rare individual who gets up at 5:00 A.M. out of patriotism. Soldiers receive their day-to-day inspiration the same way we all do, from the pleasures and pains of the job itself, the need for income and security, and the hope to get ahead. However, while some officers really *want* to be Chief of Staff, most do not. Nonetheless, all are forced into competition for that position by the army's policy of "up or out," in which a soldier must win promotion or face "separation," the army euphemism for getting fired. Only 4.8 percent of the army's officers make it through to the fabled 30-year retirement. Only .8 percent will ever reach the rank of brigadier general.[1]

The up-or-out policy applies to soldiers at every level. "Up-or-out" has its roots, of course, in the old expandable army concept. Every soldier was expected to have the capacity for higher rank, because the emergency creation of actual combat units would place everyone in new ranks and unfamiliar situations. Separated officers remained in the reserves, providing a pool of trained officer material for the projected wartime expansion. Although it would be nice if every soldier were an Audie Murphy, in practice these considerations are irrelevant in today's standing army, with its permanent division, corps, and army-level formations. The up-or-out system has been retained out of inertia and the sense that it breeds in its survivors of being some sort of chosen few. It has the perceived benefit of clearing away deadwood so as to allow superior leadership material to advance and new junior officers to be brought in. The administrative weapon thus granted to the writers of OERs and EERs gives them a comforting illusion of power, but it is a power that evaporates in the presence of the enemy.

This policy is in reality terribly destructive and, like many other counterproductive personnel policies, nearly unique to the American military system. It is one of the major driving forces behind personnel turbulence. It insures that officers place promotability over job competence and breeds a frantic careerism. It prevents anyone from truly learning his job and neutralizes competent leaders through the incompetence of their subordinates. It makes men who have to trust each other in combat into cutthroat competitors for an ever-decreasing number of key assignments and promotions. It makes people who lack the innate drive and talents for high command pursue it in spite of any self-doubts, and the winners are not necessarily the right men for the job. It discards those merely competent in a quixotic search for supermen.

The army understands in its leadership theory that battlefield leaders must be motivated by a spirit of selflessness, because concern for personal gain is incompatible with the risks and responsibilities such men must assume: getting killed is a poor career move. The present promotion process, however, systematically eliminates soldiers who do not energetically pursue the prestige, power, and money that come with higher rank. The resulting naked pursuit of self-gain destroys the respect of soldiers for their leaders.

To appreciate just how absurd this policy is, try applying it to any other business. Fire any machine tool operator, no matter how expert, who lacks the talent to be shop foreman. Strip the retirement benefits from any teacher who fails to become a school principal. Give notice to the mechanic who does not wish to be a car designer. Fire the service station manager who does not aspire to be an oil sheikh. Recall the congressman who is not nominated for president.

However, up-or-out may be necessary under the current OER system, because it is virtually impossible to identify capable officers. All are outstanding. Under the senior rater profile system the vast majority fall by definition into the "center of mass," and even this status is unrelated to military achievement. Since there is no way to determine actual relative performance, some means must be found to force officers to compete for retention and promotion, decisions which are made by anonymous boards with no stake in the effectiveness of the system. Without the constant threat of being fired, unambitious officers might be able to stake out a hold on low-level jobs and prevent the accession of new officers needed to feed the promotion machine.

Using EXEVAL and Results Limited Evaluation as the basis for all retention and promotion will adjust for these and other problems and allow us to replace "up-or-out" with "perform-or-out," a very different concept. The relative performance of all units, at every level from company to corps, will be known in great and reliable detail. By proper manipulation of EX-

EVAL data for the purposes of retention and promotion we can force unit leaders to cooperate while they compete. We can give officers and men a great sense of shared purpose and mutual dependence. We can identify capable leaders at every level and allow them to retain their jobs or seek promotion, without forcing them (or permitting them) to lie. We can do it without inducing a promotions logjam that will reduce us to the situation of the army at the close of the Indian Wars, when officers could stagnate for decades in the same rank and retire as lieutenants. Likewise, we can identify and remove commanders who, for whatever peculiar combination of reasons, cannot elicit a good performance from their subordinates. By taking the paper sword out of officers' hands we can force them to use *military* leadership techniques, backed if need be by the cudgel of the UCMJ, to motivate their men. By tying promotion to the *overtly* stated goals of the military organization, we can insure that actual military considerations will take priority over irrational or organizationally derived goals. The promotion system will thus become a tool for stimulating the entire organization to the pursuit of legitimate, collective, military goals.

After a division's first EXEVAL, its performance can be compared to that of other new divisions at that point in their cycles. Depending on its relative standing, the unit will then be allocated a certain number of promotions at every pay-grade. Almost all will be in the most junior grades. These promotion authorizations will then be distributed through brigade, battalion, and company commanders in varying numbers depending on their units' rank order. Thus the overall number of promotions will depend on the division's performance as a unit, and the relative number of promotions in a brigade, battalion, and company will depend on the relative performance, within the division, at each level. The best company in a battalion will be able to promote more E–1s to E–2, more E–4s to E5, et cetera. The best companies in the best divisions should be able to promote virtually all of their junior troops. A brigade commander will have no option but to pass the specified number of authorizations on to subordinate commanders, but will retain a certain number to distribute among his own headquarter's troops. Each soldier will depend for his promotion on the opinion of his own immediate commander, who must, however, distribute his entire allocation.

Thus, no unit can benefit from the failure of another in its own chain of command, and each is dependent on the other's performance while still benefiting from maximizing its own. The greatest immediate incentive goes to the junior soldiers, and their commanders hold the immediate power of selection of promotees. Both selfish and collective motivations will be tapped, as everyone wants to be paid better and everyone wants to be part of a winning team.

In the course of thirty-six months as an active unit, each divisional command package will accumulate several sets of EXEVAL scoring data. When it comes time for the division to stand down at the end of the cycle, it will have an overall performance-based rank order among the six divisions that will complete their cycles in that particular year. Army personnel people, doing what they do best, will determine what overall percentage of people in each rank need to be taken off of active duty in order to maintain the authorized rank structure. The overall shape of the performance curve may also be useful in helping to determine this number. Those numbers will specify ranks but not branch. Separations will be distributed much the same way as promotions were earlier, with a few critical differences. First of all, the differential between top-scoring units and losers should be much steeper. Let's say it is determined that in fiscal year 1992 natural attrition (people quitting, retiring, being discharged for health reasons, UCMJ violations, et cetera) will cut the number of lieutenant colonels (pay grade 0–5) by 5 percent. In order to meet authorized levels, an additional 5 percent must be cut.[2] Of this number, 2 percent will come from the top-scoring division. Division number two will lose 8 percent, number three 15 percent, number four 20 percent, number five 25 percent, and number six will absorb 30 percent of the yearly attrition in lieutenant colonels. Some separating battalion commanders in division number six will actually have higher unit scores than some being retained in other divisions. That is the penalty paid by subordinates in a division that does not hang together very well. Clearly, the division commander will not be hanging around either.

At company level the system will differ somewhat, because COHORT companies will not remain within the same division structure throughout the unit cycle. A company may serve under several different DCPs in the course of three years. Ideally, the system for rating COHORT units should be linked to that of the command packages for which they work. However, this is probably a mathematical fantasy, because such a complex piece of number-crunching would prove confusing to units and impossible to execute fairly. In that case, company-level units must simply be ranked against all other such units on the basis of their company-level performances, which will to some extent include their ability to function as part of the higher unit. This is why it was stressed in chapter 3 that 75 percent of a unit's score must be based on directly comparable battlefield survival skills. In the 25 percent that is branch-specific, company scores must be weighted in such a manner that companies of different branches compete on a level playing field. The burden of getting company-level units to worry about combined arms cooperation will then fall with disproportionate weight on battalion commanders and staffs, but then, that is a major reason for creating higher-level command packages in the first place.

Commanders will be selected for retention or separation based purely on the numerical standing of their units in the last unit cycle. However, only a certain percentage of the lieutenant colonels in a division will be commanders, and the percentage of 0–5 commanders who will be forcibly separated must match. Others will be in staff positions. *All* of the separated staff 0–5s will come from the staffs of commanders who are themselves relieved. The same will hold true for other officers, warrants, and senior NCOs. There must be no incentive for subordinates to sabotage or fail to support their bosses. Individuals whose performance is markedly substandard can, of course, be relieved for cause without waiting for the end of the unit cycle.

Junior enlisted men will once again be dependent on the choice of their immediate commanders, with the exception that no officer being separated will be given the opportunity to choose who to take with him. Each unit will face a number of cuts in each pay-grade fixed by the inexorable mathematics of EXEVAL scores and personnel projections, but the selection of specific enlisted personnel will be made by the first commander in the chain of command who actually will be remaining in the army. He therefore will have some incentive to choose wisely, and he will have the individuals' test scores and personnel records files on which to base his choice. In the great majority of units, the number of personnel to be cut will be small, unless there is some overall reduction in the size of the army.

Many officers will be concerned that their loss of direct administrative power, through abolition of the OER/EER system, will greatly diminish their influence over their subordinates. In military terms, however, this administrative power is illusory to begin with, and the legal powers of commanders will in no way be decreased. In practice, a commander's position will be enhanced considerably because he will now be the natural focus of his unit's attention. He will no longer have to struggle to gain the genuine, active cooperation of subordinates, for they will now have an automatic interest in his success. This system will serve to subordinate NCOs and warrant officers to their commanders, for no form of political maneuvering will be effective if the unit does not perform well. Capable subordinates unfortunate enough to be placed under an incapable commander will have to try to make good his failings, and if the unit fails anyway they will have to fall back on their individual records and accomplishments.

Is it fair that some commanders who are personally duds will be carried through to retention not by their own efforts but by those of capable subordinates? Is it fair that officers who are personally good guys will be shafted by worthless underlings? Simply put, a commander who is capable of recognizing competent subordinates and of letting them carry the ball is not a bad commander at all. The *Army Officer's Guide* used to carry a quote from a German general to the effect that there are two sets of opposing qualities to look for in an officer: he is either stupid or clever, and he is either industrious or lazy. If he is clever and industrious, great! Make him a staff officer. If he is lazy and stupid, no problem. Send him to the infantry (not a viable solution today). If he is clever and lazy, that is outstanding. Make him a commander. But if he is stupid and industrious, he must be shot.[3] The very best officers are those who excel at *getting other people to do the work*, and to do it well. That skill is the very essence of command. An officer who is unable to get troops to perform, even when a good performance serves their own interests in terms of pay, promotion, and retention, is a bad officer. There is no way to tell the difference other than by the hard facts of unit performance. Some poor soldiers undoubtedly will be retained by this system, but at least they will be members of capable units that have found ways to work around their weaknesses. In the long run, such individuals will be identified and removed through the efforts of superiors and subordinates concerned with their negative impact on unit performance.

The discussion above has concerned the negative side, who will be separated. Let's turn to the positive matter of assignments and promotions. Currently, assignments and promotions are in large measure determined by the individual branches, a circumstance that contributes heavily to compartmentalization. Because of the workload and the anonymity of the officers whose records they examine, promotion boards base their actions on quantifiable data. Career development accordingly has become a numbers game. Boards may be impressed by an officer who has held six wildly divergent jobs in the last five years, whereas a commander whose own future depended on the competence of his subordinates would be much more skeptical. Assignment officers and promotion boards do not suffer any of the evil consequences of their decisions. This system, as one assignments officer put it, is "proof that socialism doesn't work." What we want to do instead is essentially to "privatize" the promotion and assignments system. That is, to put power in the hands of people who stand to benefit from good choices and to suffer from poor ones.

The division command package has now been deactivated, and those who are going to quit or be separated are gone. Others, whose units' performance has won them retention, will wish to move on to other stations. A fair number of officers and NCOs will desire to stay on in the division or company for the next cycle. The new commander will be appointed by higher authorities, but he may be the same man who commanded during the last cycle. A successful unit commander should have first call on retaining his job, although many will wish to go on to a higher staff or command. A new leader may be a man from outside the old unit or a successful subordinate who has applied for the job. In the unlikely event that no one has asked to command the unit, someone with an impressive record will be appointed.

From among his subordinates, applicants from elsewhere, and newly assigned personnel, the new commander will pick his staff and his immediately subordinate commanders. They, in turn, will pick theirs. Everyone's future depends on making the right choices, because commanders who consistently pick incompetent staffers are not going to have the opportunity to make the same mistake again. Individual or drastic mistakes can, of course, be corrected when discovered, although actually throwing an unsatisfactory subordinate out of the army will have to be based on EXEVAL data or UCMJ action.

Therefore, if a brigade commander knows an officer that he wishes to make a battalion commander, let him do it. Commanders probably cannot be trusted with the authority to bump a subordinate up by pay-grade, but they must be allowed to give him whatever rank insignia his actual duty position calls for. If a captain, for instance, was appointed to command a battalion, he would wear the rank of a lieutenant colonel. If after three years his unit's performance wins him retention in that role, give him permanent possession of both the rank and the pay his job deserves. Or perhaps it would be better to advance him one pay-grade, regardless of how many ranks he jumps. Such jumps probably will be rare, but they must be made possible.

To receive end-of-cycle promotion, all officers desirous of higher rank will have to submit an application, to be examined by a board headed by the next higher commander of a rank superior to the highest granted by the board.[4] The army's number-crunchers will determine the numbers of promotions to be granted at each rank. Higher commands will monitor to ensure that promotion is indeed based on unit performance, not anyone's personal judgment. In the case of a tie, of course, commanders should make the call. In the unlikely event that there is a shortage of applicants for promotion, members of the highest-scoring units should be promoted without application. Individuals should be permitted to decline. In wartime, forced promotion may be necessary.

There may well be many officers who will not desire promotion, for any number of reasons. For example, being a company commander can be extremely satisfying as well as a lot of fun, while higher command can be a headache. Some officers will feel that they just barely made it the last time and had better stick to a job they know. Let these people keep their positions and pay-grades. Some provision eventually will have to be made to give substantial periodic pay-boosts at some point to career captains, majors, and colonels. A decision on this can be put off until such people begin raising the issue. Clearly, pay-grade and rank frequently are going to require a divorce, and this poses no real problems. Some valuable subordinates are going to end up making more than their bosses, a situation that should prove satisfactory to both. Rank on the collar can be a very satisfying substitute for money to people who are really goal driven. We might even see the amazing spectacle of senior officers competing to prove who is the lowest paid, since a lower pay-grade would indicate faster promotion.

The compartmentalization of the army into competing specialty branches (field artillery, infantry, military intelligence) will be reduced greatly because branch offices now will be serving a new customer: the field army. Their old customers, the branch officers themselves, now will depend for their career development on the performance of the combined arms team, not on the ability of the branch manager to wrangle a few extra slots for his wall charts. Field artillery (FA) commanders who are less effective than officers from other branches at producing combat-ready units, and in playing on the combined arms team, will get fired. The FA branch will then receive a mission to obtain and train some more FA officers.[5]

Not all officers will be in the field army, and so this system cannot apply to everyone. For office-workers in the depths of the Pentagon, the current system may be appropriate. However, for officers who run operations that directly service the field army (finance, personnel, and installation services), a dual system is needed. Within their own chain of command, an administrative tool like the OER will help insure that procedures and policies are adhered to. Such officers should receive another rating as well, which should be given equal weight. This should come from the commanders of the units they exist to support. Thus commanders of such service agencies will have to meet the demands of both policymakers and their customers.

How will we implement the new promotion system? The new system takes off from a standing start, that is, no one is being demoted from his current rank and pay-grade, and no effort is being made to get rid of officers from the old regime. Implementation of "local hiring and promotion" undoubtedly will require a substantial amount of legislation, since officer authorizations and pay are closely controlled by Congress. Personnel who enter the new DRS divisions will automatically be drawn into it, although we probably will be into the second cycle before it becomes fully effective. If they win retention and wish promotion, they can show their personnel records to the commanders and boards who are making the decisions. At first, those files will contain the old OERs, and commanders can take them for what they are worth in addition to whatever other pitch the applicant wishes to make. Later, as EXEVAL becomes standard, they can show the printouts that list their units' performance ratings and copies of their orders showing their duty assignments. Negative information like courts martial records, et cetera, will be available from MILPERCEN.

In sum, these proposed reforms call for a radical redistribution of authority. The army's personnel offices will be used to do what they do best: number crunching. They will no longer be permitted to do what they do worst, which is determining who should be retained, promoted, or assigned to key positions. Under the proposed new system, hiring, firing, and assignment decisions will be based on empirical performance data and made by people who have a personal stake in the performance of the people they promote and assign. If a commander consistently makes the wrong personnel decisions, he can complain about the system later as a private citizen.

This immense change in promotion policy will have a number of positive side effects. Job stability for people who do not want to be Chief of Staff will reduce their antagonism to people who do, and this will permit the development of an elite corps of high command officers. Capable, hard-driving officers will find that promotion prospects will be much better in the field army than in the anthills of the Pentagon. Unit performance will benefit from their presence. Easing and speeding the promotion of talented individuals will attract such people into the army and serve eventually to broaden the organization's social base.

As a result, uniformed service will become much more attractive to bright, self-confident young people of the middle and upper classes, who currently avoid the military like the plague. This is not because they are anti-military on principle but because they know it will take a minimum of twenty years to achieve a position of any real significance. College campuses are full of civilian war-gamers and amateur strategists, but they know that real influence can be won more quickly in politics, in the civilian national security hierarchy, on congressional staffs, or even in journalism or private industry than in the army. Unfortunately, the influence so won is too often held by people with little practical understanding of the military instruments actually at the nation's disposal.

Within a fairly short period, these changes will secure for the field army the institutional independence required by its post–1953 status as a standing military formation. Personnel who do not enter the new units eventually will find themselves frozen out of the field army because they will lack the experience to make them attractive to field commanders. They will continue to be rated under the old OER system, or whatever takes its place, and to do the various housekeeping jobs assigned them by DOD. Their promotions will depend on whatever percentage of authorizations is left over after field army slots have been filled. They will become career military bureaucrats with no prospects of attaining command or high rank. If it becomes necessary to pay these people better to retain them, they should receive pay-grade promotions that do not change their rank or military authority. The field army will be effectively walled off from the bureaucracy that supports it and to which it reports. It will be professionalized.

NOTES

1. Figures from USA MILPERCEN, February 11, 1987.
2. These figures are examples only.
3. The officer quoted was General Freiherr von Hammerstein-Equord. *The Army Officer's Guide* (Harrisburg, Pa.: The Stackpole Company, 1981), 211.
4. Colonel Dandridge Malone suggested such an application procedure, but suggested it be tied to evaluations of three kinds: superior- , peer- , and subordinate-ratings. General Walter Ulmer, an officer noted for his own innovative approach to leadership, thought that this "outrageous concept" should be given serious consideration. See Ulmer, "Leaders, Managers, and Command Climate," *Armed Forces Journal International*, July 1986. The concept of requiring an application fits in well

with the demise of up-or-out and the idea of job stability. The concept of peer- and subordinate-ratings is a poor one, however, as Ulmer appears to recognize.

5. For this reason, if for no other, EXEVAL war-games will have to be designed carefully for realism. Otherwise, certain of the combat arms will gradually be edged out of MTO&Es. This applies particularly to field artillery and other indirect-fire systems, for they are very difficult to simulate effectively even with MILES.

5

THE CHAIN OF COMMAND

The changes wrought in the army by DRS, EXEVAL, and the new promotion system will be radical, and from the same human and material resources as the current system they will produce far more effective units. It may appear to be striving for utopia to press on with further reforms, but serious problems still will remain in army organization. The first is that the army is all chiefs and no Indians. The second is that all the chiefs are wearing war bonnets, but only a few carry tomahawks. Third, the chiefs are all busy inspecting each other's teepees while their own teepees are burning down. Fourth, no one seems to have the authority to make the Indians put out the fires if they fail to do so voluntarily.

THE RANK STRUCTURE

As a battery executive officer, I often wondered why it was so difficult to get someone to dig the latrines. Very often they were not dug at all, and it is at considerable risk to one's shoe-shine that one wanders through German forests habitually occupied by U.S. units in their field training. A look at the rank structure of the U.S. Army quickly reveals why. Of 781,609 active duty personnel, 93,558 are commissioned officers.[1] That is 12 percent, or somewhat better than one for every nine in lesser ranks. Add warrant officers, and the percentage creeps up slightly to 14 percent, about one for every six soldiers. Add non-commissioned officers and you reach 49.5 percent, one "leader" for every mere "soldier" in the army. When you consider that a certain small percentage of E–4s are "acting jacks" wearing sergeant's stripes, and that the bulk of E–1s are new recruits in basic or advanced individual training, this leaves substantially under 50 percent to do all of the dirty jobs thought up by the top 49.5 percent. There were fewer than sixty-five privates in my battalion in Germany, totaling less than 15 percent of authorized personnel. Digging latrines is unquestionably bottom-of-the-

totem-pole work, and ordering an NCO to do it will have negative reper-
cussions throughout the chain of command. The surprising thing is not that
the latrines were not dug, but that once in a while they were.

The rank structure is further distorted by gross disparities in the prestige,
abilities, and effective power of the various groups who make up the rank
pyramid. It is an intrepid lieutenant who tangles with anyone above the
rank of staff sergeant (E–6), for the lowest-ranking sergeant in the army
has years of experience, the lieutenant usually none.[2] This disparity between
officers and NCOs disappears only very slowly as one moves up the rank
structure, and it is a very foolish battalion commander who angers his own
or a higher commander's sergeant major. Warrant officers are in many ways
outside of the chain of command. They have a technical expertise unique
in the army, particularly in the areas of supply, personnel, food service, and
the maintenance system. These areas are mysterious but vital to the commander, as they may cost him his job. Warrant officers make up a large
proportion of any inspection team, and this, plus their usual long experience
in the army and the common perception of a "Warrant Officers' Protective
Association," leaves them a lot of room for intrigue and maneuver. A commander is therefore heavily dependent on his key warrants, and his sense
of dependence often makes him easy to manipulate. The multiplication of
swollen staffs at every level causes a fragmentation of responsibility that
often places very junior people in a position to harass higher-ranking people
who have lower-ranking bosses.

Possibly the very worst violation of the concept of a chain of command
is the presence at every level from battalion to Chief of Staff of a command
sergeant major (CSM). This individual exists solely to violate the chain of
command and to usurp the influence of the commander over his NCOs and
enlisted soldiers. He has become necessary because most officers are so
ignorant about enlisted men. At battalion level the sergeant major serves a
useful unifying function, assisting the commander in dealing with troops
and serving as a trainer for the unit's first sergeants. Above battalion, command sergeants major interfere with subordinate units, contradict local
command guidance, and provide a disruptive back-channel for political
maneuvering by NCOs dissatisfied with their commanders or their positions
in life. At the Chief of Staff level there is a "Command Sergeant Major of
the Army" with prestige exceeding that of many generals.

These "super NCOs" are particularly dangerous because they are very
often enormously impressive individuals with twenty or thirty years of practical experience. They tend to ride rough-shod over junior officers, to operate
directly on the NCOs and troops of subordinate units, and to ignore the
prerogatives of intervening commanders. Twice I have seen sergeants major
lock horns with lieutenant colonels, and the result each time has been the
relief of both commander and subordinate.

Those soldiers who have made it to the rank of sergeant major (pay-grade

E–9) by virtue of their ability, as opposed to the substantial number who have made it through sheer persistence and longevity, are indeed among the most valuable people in the army. They are the best living repositories of the army's "institutional memory." Soldiers do what they say, with no argument. They are troop leadership incarnate. Unfortunately, they are improperly utilized by the army because of vestigial class considerations and because the army really is not concerned about the disastrously poor officer leadership at platoon and company level. As always, the eyes of the officer corps are fixed on the office of the Chief of Staff, and the army is far more interested in producing Eisenhowers than it is in producing effective platoon leaders and company commanders. Therefore it shunts these tremendously capable—but, in civilian terms, often somewhat undereducated—men off into a parallel chain of command, where they proceed to wreak havoc.

Many analyses of the U.S. Army fault the huge proportion of officers to enlisted men. Ideas as to what constitutes an ideal ratio vary, but the German army (1914–1945) had about 3 percent to 4 percent officers, usually a lower ratio in war than in peace. The German attitude was that it is better to have an officer shortage than adequate numbers of poor officers, and they were right. This was reversed in the American Army, which in 1940 had about 5.75 percent officers, a figure that swelled to 9.6 percent by 1945. So numerous did U.S. officers become that some company-sized units consisted entirely of lieutenants.[3] Today, the figure stands at 12 percent.

Much of the excess in officers occurs at the highest levels: there are now 10 percent more three- and four-star officers in the American armed forces than there were at the end of World War II, when those forces were 600 percent larger. However, a great many of these "officers" are not actually in the chain of command, and the ratio of commanding officers to soldiers in fighting units is not all that bad. The principal danger in having hordes of officers standing in the wings is the pressure they generate to rotate commands at a mind-numbing pace. DRS eliminates this problem by fixing commanders in place for the length of the unit cycle and by giving successful commanders first call on their old jobs in the next cycle. That leaves us with the question of what to do with all of the officers left over, who are not in DRS units or higher command headquarters, or are in units but not as commanders.

THE COMMAND SUPERSTRUCTURE

What is really curious about the army's command system is that there are so many commanders in the pyramid, and yet no one is at the apex. There is no Commander, U.S. Army, much less a unified or specified commander of all U.S. forces worldwide.[4] In theory the president is the commander in chief, but that is a pretty thin fiction. No one is in charge. In wartime a president might create some military command structure that actually would exercise command of worldwide multi-service field operations, but none exists at present. In the absence of a wartime emergency to keep it gainfully occupied, such a structure would become just another layer in the cake, interfering with subordinate commanders in every dimension of their duties. It might conceivably pose a political threat to the republic.

The army has unconsciously created an organizational structure that cannot help but paralyze the chain of command. In order to be ready for instant conversion to a war-fighting force (something for which peacetime MTO&Es and actual unit dispositions are not designed) all of the various headquarters layers from brigade to division to corps to army to theater command are kept plugged into one another, as if a division commander required the constant supervision and assistance of multiple higher headquarters to do his peacetime job. If such oversupervision was limited to commanders, the system would still be awkward, annoying, and destructive, but it is not so limited. Every staff officer, with his minions, works directly on the staff sections of lower echelons, bypassing the commanders. A certain amount of this is inevitable, but staffs have grown so massive that subordinate units are completely hamstrung by their constant demands for information and compliance with pet schemes, and by intrusive inspections that have no result but the creation of fear and confusion. The V Corps staff, located in Frankfurt, West Germany, is supposedly a tactical headquarters unit. In World War II, such a corps headquarters would contain perhaps 200 officers and enlisted men.[5] Today, V Corps occupies the entire building that once housed the international headquarters of I. G. Farben, with some 2,800 people who represent only a portion of V Corps staff personnel. They are constantly shuttling up and down on the building's curious little elevators with no doors, which never stop moving. These elevators probably represent the greatest danger to life and limb that many of these soldiers, bureaucrats, and local nationals ever expect to face. All of the personnel and equipment turbulence that afflicts field units is present in such higher commands, often in more intense form.

Meanwhile, there is no evidence that this or any other of the army's higher headquarters are capable of performing their own unique wartime missions. They are too busy trying to straighten out their subordinate units. For example, the role of LANCE missile units is to serve as the corps commander's "hip-pocket artillery." All targeting for LANCE comes from him. Yet none of the responsible actors at V Corps understood the capabilities and limitations of this missile, the most powerful of corps artillery weapons. This is not atypical. Studies of the Grenada operation show that responsible commanders had no idea of the capabilities or proper functions of the units used in that operation.[6]

This top-heavy superstructure is still not a war-fighting organization, and the transition to war would trigger many changes in command relationships.

After all, in the event of a European war U.S. commanders will be working for a *German* general.[7] There is nothing for much of this chain of command to do but to interfere with itself. Joint commanders are not really a problem in this regard, for they have no idea how to run units of another service. The army's generals, however, have a natural fixation on fighting forces. Deprived of the opportunity to deal with real decisions of a nature compatible with their status, they meddle unmercifully with troop commanders. Merely attending all of the annual change-of-command ceremonies for senior leaders can disrupt lower units beyond belief. This meddling is mitigated only by higher commanders' need to deal with the confusion at home and with harassment from the next higher command.

This multiplication of staffs and commanders has produced an army whose leaders, however effective they may be as individuals, cannot significantly influence the organizations they "command." A leader cannot effectively inspire his subordinates, as they know that however brilliant his concepts he cannot put them into action. I remember being terribly impressed by a presentation made to my unit by the V Corps artillery commander. Finally, after two years in the unit, I had been told by a superior how he planned to use us in the event of combat. He stressed realistic combat training, told us we had to avoid getting mired down in the day-to-day garbage the army threw at us, and that he would support our efforts. We gave him a standing ovation. As soon as he had left the room, the battalion commander turned to the executive officer and said, "What bullshit."

He was right. The fact is that no matter what one commander or faceless bureaucrat wants, another of equal or greater authority will contradict it. It is impossible to know in advance which commander or faceless bureaucrat is going to go after you for not toeing his particular line. My battalion commander was subordinate to at least two unrelated commanders: the brigade commander located about 50 kilometers away and the "Community Commander"[8] just across town. We also received visits from the V Corps commander (and sometimes the V Corps artillery commander), who lived about 30 kilometers away. Additionally, we had to contend with the virtually independent "NCO chain of command," for a command sergeant major has his own ideas, priorities, and ego, and he is frequently taken more seriously than his boss. For each of these characters, and for miscellaneous visiting U.S. and German VIPs, the grass was cut, the floors waxed, the weapons stripped of every speck of potentially embarrassing lubricants (and fired that way on the range), and the training schedule thrown out the window. This is not to mention the hordes of file clerks and paper shufflers on the massive staffs of those various commanders between battalion and the Joint Chiefs of Staff, each of whom, regardless of his rank, speaks with the authority of General so-and-so. All of these individuals have the power to jump the whole battalion through the hoop over the most obscure issues.

Meanwhile, the business of training for war is reduced to a farce. The evolution of the army's web of command—it cannot properly be called a chain—has created an organizational nervous system analogous to that of a rich, immensely fat man with an advanced case of Alzheimer's disease.

As a result of all this self-inflicted damage, it is impossible for commanders to set any kind of priorities. It is true that getting a large number of troops killed through monstrous tactical stupidity may cause an officer some career problems (although in practice this does not often appear to be the case). A commander can get into equally hot water if a couple of his subordinates get arrested off-duty for drunk driving. Or if the toilets habitually back up in the barracks. Because commanders are theoretically responsible for everything, and because they are responsible to so many different higher commanders, agencies, and mysterious offices, no one can properly be held responsible for anything. If someone does end up holding the bag, it is due to an accident or bad politics.

Some career officers, with their twenty- or thirty-year retirements dangling before them, like this arrangement. It means that no one need ever pay the price for resounding disasters like those in Vietnam, Iran, and Beirut. It means also, however, that a commander is not really in charge in any meaningful way of the people under him. He may visit a subordinate unit and raise hell because the grass has not been cut, but in all likelihood he knows nothing about the unit's primary weapon system or the tactics it requires, nor does anyone on his staff.

Another result of this web of non-related authorities is that front-line units do not initiate anything, do not do anything unless ordered, still don't do it until convinced that there will be dire consequences, and then attempt to satisfy the demand through falsifying the paperwork if possible. Unit officers do not take this attitude because they are lazy; they are usually working sixty- to seventy-hour weeks merely to keep routine operations going. They don't do it because they are inherently dishonest; I do not recall ever being lied to by an officer regarding any but official business. They do it because those who do not do it do not survive, and after awhile they do not even realize that they are not performing their duty to the nation. They are doing what they have been told they are paid to do.

Over beers in the club, some of the junior officers in my unit once tried to imagine the reason why 350 marines were put into a dormitory in a war zone in Beirut. The most credible theory (and I stress that this was just drunken speculation, albeit based on experience) was that some Morale Support NCO in Norfolk, having determined that regulations required that certain minimum housing standards be maintained for the peacekeeping troops, sent a directive to the Beirut commander over the signature of some senior officer, who at the time was out giving testimony to Congress about $600 toilet seat covers. Who are you going to hold responsible, the president? We were torn between wanting someone to get burned for this humiliating tragedy and our conviction that the wrong person would take the fall. We were disappointed on both counts.[9]

So who was responsible for the failure of six out of seven "special operations" in Grenada?[10] No one. Who was responsible for putting 350 men in a "dormitory" in the middle of Beirut? No one. Why were the guards forbidden to carry loaded weapons? No one knows.[11] What happened to the commander responsible for putting the Iran Raid together? He was promoted. Why wasn't he reprimanded for this military debacle? Well, he was not responsible. Truly, he was not. Who was? No one.

Let's simply admit that it is not possible to maintain a wartime command structure, or any approximation thereof, in times of relative peace.

SOLUTIONS

The first problem is what to do about rank inflation among the enlisted soldiers. This rank inflation is driven by two factors. One is the up-or-out system which forces commanders to promote to leadership ranks good, reliable, trustworthy soldiers, including those who have no leadership potential. Not to promote them is the equivalent of firing them. This motivation will be removed by the demise of the up-or-out policy. Second, good soldiers deserve pay boosts, and the only way to arrange this is to promote them to the limited number of junior enlisted ranks. Eventually, and fairly quickly at that, any decent soldier will be promoted into the leadership in a classic example of the Peter Principle at work.[12] The solution once again is to divorce rank and pay-grade, and also to make some changes to the rank structure itself.

There are currently nine enlisted pay-grades and thus nine ranks. These translate, in effect, into nine additional layers in the chain of command. No military rule is more strictly enforced than the one that says "Shit rolls downhill." It keeps on rolling after it has left the leadership ranks, down to the bottom of the relatively tiny class of "soldiers." Unfortunately, as we have seen, there is often no one there to make the final catch. It makes sense to have nine pay-grades, but not to have nine ranks. Why not make pay-grades E-1 to E-5 a generic soldier rank? Entitle these soldiers "Soldier," and give them no visible indicator of their pay-grade. Pay-grade will continue to have social significance among soldiers, but will no longer be a crippling factor on the job. Let superiors give junior leadership rank to any such soldier, of whatever pay-grade, who occupies a leadership position, i.e., section chief. Call such junior leaders corporals, with corporal stripes and an additional pay increment. Then we can reward good soldiers for being good soldiers, and put capable junior leaders in appropriate jobs with appropriate rank and a pay boost, without confusing good leaders with good followers. Leaders with real promotion potential will be identified at the end of the unit cycle and fed into NCO- and officer-producing programs (see chapter 6). Reliable soldiers with no leadership potential will linger in the E–5 zone until they get tired and quit, or get in trouble and get thrown out. A certain number will remain as career soldiers, satisfied with regular longevity and cost-of-living raises. A fund of experience in the most junior ranks will not hurt the army as long as these men are not allowed to develop bad habits and to pass them along to new men.

While we are fixing the bottom end of the chain of command, there is one other critical change that should be made to army policies in this area. The army traditionally has made a practice of sending the least intelligent or least educated soldiers into the combat arms. Being ignorant should not be a capital offense, at least not in the junior ranks, and yet that is often the effect of this policy. Quite apart from the unfairness of this practice, it produces poor soldiers and poor units, and it reduces the prestige of the combat arms. Category IV soldiers (the lowest mental category the army can accept) were concentrated in jobs where mere survival calls for quick wits and the ability to learn. In very recent years, however, this policy has been reversed. Today it is the service units which are starved of capable soldiers, with equally disastrous results. There is no question that mental categorization has a profound effect, one of which is to concentrate talent beyond the ability of beneficiary units to utilize it while making junior leadership in other units desperately scarce. For example, LANCE crewmen are a conspicuously bright group, but a missile crew needs only so many junior whizzes.

This practice has complex roots, and is only partially traceable to the traditional American contempt for the fighting man. In World War II recruiting and job classification was done by the Army Service Forces, and they naturally tended to skim off the cream for their own use. In units hastily being created as in World War II, or purposely kept in constant turmoil like today, it is necessary to put the brightest soldiers into certain jobs. In stable units, however, it should be possible to work with a more representative mix of soldiers. Attempts to produce psychological profiles, to match classes of men to categories of job, have been conspicuously unsuccessful.[13] Given the time to learn their jobs, most soldiers will manage. Most effective on-the-job learning is transferred not in formal training by superiors but by informal peer-group contact. Having a reasonable percentage of bright young junior soldiers in every unit will speed this process. Also, junior soldiers provide the basis for future NCO leadership in every area. Therefore, distribution of new soldiers by mental category should not be aimed at concentrating the most capable in any unit or specialty, but rather at achieving a uniform mix throughout the force, including the service units.

Moving up the rank structure, the next question is what to do with overly powerful and prestigious NCOs? These men constitute one of the most underutilized resources in the army, and they are wasted because the jobs of platoon leader and company commander are regarded not as being vitally important in themselves but as steps in the training of more senior officers. Therefore the cutting edge of army combat forces, the very reason-for-being of the entire military structure, is in the hands of the most inexperienced element of the army's personnel. These are the junior lieutenants and captains. Men whose only qualification for leadership is recent graduation from college chemistry and business departments simply cannot, with the necessary consistency, lead American soldiers in combat. Soldiers are not stupid. They quickly perceive that they are being short-changed and, as a number of military critics have put it, are being "managed to their deaths."

The next chapter discusses the selection and training of new officers in more detail, but this point needs to be made here. The best source of leaders that soldiers will willingly follow is in the senior members of the NCO corps. Obviously, not all or even a majority of small-unit commanders can come from this source, because that would denude the army of its vital NCOs and plug up the promotion pathways with men who, because of their age and often their educational limitations, cannot be expected to go on to higher rank. On the other hand, many very capable men have risen from the ranks, including General John Vessey, former Chairman of the Joint Chiefs of Staff. A very large proportion of company-grade officers, perhaps 30 percent, should be derived from the NCO corps. Simultaneously, the position of command sergeant major should be eliminated from all echelons above battalion.

Translating substantial numbers of NCOs into the junior officer ranks will have many benefits. The biggest benefits will be in increasing the legitimacy of small-unit commanders in the eyes of their troops, putting strong, experienced, credible leadership at the cutting edge of the fighting forces. This legitimacy and the practical knowledge and ability of these men will rub off to some extent on their new peers, the majority of junior officers coming from more traditional officer-producing programs. Just as important, it will place these talented men at a level in the chain of command where they can achieve their high potential without subverting the chain. A few of them will show great practical ability and win the rapid promotion that will be possible under the new promotion procedures. Most, however, will be prevented by age and education from being a great threat to the existing officer corps.

One major reason that there are so many officers in the army is the assumption that in order to attract the large numbers of well-educated people who are needed to run our technology-intensive forces, it is necessary to offer not only officer-sized paychecks but also officer rank, prestige, and authority. It is assumed that pay must equal prestige, as in mercantile, middle-class society. Given the nature of American culture, it is unquestionably true that high pay and a certain prestige must go to skilled people, but it does not follow that high military rank should accompany it. Certainly it would not be fair or reasonable to give officers in any one branch or group of branches (i.e., the combat arms) a disproportionate shot at the high-paying jobs. On the other hand, there is simply no reason that chaplains, finance officers, or officers' club managers should wear the same rank and carry the same visible military authority as unit commanders. The existence of hordes of these "officers" milling in their masses behind the lines does much to convince combat soldiers that their leaders prefer to congregate out of the reach of enemy fire. Their equality of rank with combat commanders convinces everyone, including the combat commanders, that they should have an equal say in the conduct of military operations. Something must be done to trim this vast command body without losing the skilled, capable, and indispensable people in it, who wear commanders' rank but are not and have no prospect of becoming commanders.

Personnel who never have a command function, that is, who will never command or issue orders to field units, have no need to wear insignia that serves to identify immediately their place in the pecking order. Office personnel in stable bureaucratic positions know their superiors and their subordinates. Military lawyers, doctors, money-handlers, and ministers all fit into this category. Certainly they deserve the respect and pay due professionals, but essentially they exist to provide services that are connected only very indirectly to military operations. Officers who command field medical units are legitimately military commanders, but usually these soldiers are not themselves medical personnel. Specialty personnel should constitute a separate category of officers. Call them "Specialty Officers," with a single rank insignia and a specialty emblem on the uniform. Keep them in the same officer pay-grades as at present, entitle them to a salute, but place them clearly outside the chain of command.

The same principle should be applied in a somewhat different way to officers who serve in positions outside the field army, or even inside it but in positions without command authority. Many of these men may find themselves in positions where they may inherit command, or they may go from staff positions to field units. The principle followed should be the old one that "staff officers are invisible," which is not heard often in today's army. Officers who are neither commanders (down to platoon leader), executive officers, or primary staff (i.e., S–1, G–2, et cetera), should wear specialty officer rank. There are a number of benefits to the "invisiblity" thus induced. Invisible staff officers can come down to units to observe without causing the panic and hasty disguises provoked by high-ranking visitors. Staff officers without rank on their collars will be more dependent for their influence on the commander they serve. A specialty officer will wear sufficient rank to issue on-the-spot directives or corrections to enlisted soldiers but will not be able to interfere directly with commanders of subordinate units. Should these officers inherit or be appointed to command or primary staff jobs, they will don the appropriate rank insignia.

This does not mean that high rank will only be available to combat arms officers. Military intelligence, communications, and logistical officers, among others, are part of the fighting organization. They play a crucial role in command. This is something the army's self-professed "warriors" do not appear to understand.

It may appear that such changes are more cosmetic than real, and they are. The aphorism that the clothes make the man is nowhere more true than in the military. Battlefield leaders must be made sharply distinguishable from technical and administrative personnel, and the currency of command power must not be cheapened by the current proliferation of brass. No doubt this proposal, if adopted, will be undercut by the renaming of jobs. Dentists will find themselves in slots entitled "Commander, Tenth Cavity Prevention Platoon." There is nothing that can be done about such persistent pettiness, but the creation of the specialty officer category is just one piece in a process designed to reorient the huge, complex, institutional machine that is the army.

Turning to the problem of high command and staff multiplication, basically, we need to get all commanders and staffs above division out of the peacetime chain of command. Higher staffs are subject to all of the turmoil that the current personnel system inflicts on field units, and they are so obsessed with obtaining a respectable performance from inherently incapable subordinate units that they neglect their own specialized functions. If a division commander is incapable of training and maintaining his division, he should be replaced. If the division's design makes it inherently impossible to command from division headquarters then change the design, for in wartime neither corps commanders nor the Department of the Army are going to be able to do the division commander's job for him.

Leave the current plans for wartime organization intact. In peacetime, we must take into account the dangers that idleness brings to any organization. We must create a peacetime chain of command that will permit (and compel) the various pieces of the war machine to focus on healing themselves, so that when called into action they can mesh together into a balanced, coherent force. Additionally, by taking peacetime administrative elements away from powerful commanders we can force them to assume their proper customer-service role.

In brief, the idea is this: take the entire field army, that is, all corps headquarters, divisions, separate brigades and regiments, et cetera, and make each of their commanders directly responsible to a "Commander, Army Field Forces" (CAFF). He should have equal standing with the Chief of Staff, or be his top subordinate. For wartime purposes or exercises, attach these separate units to the appropriate headquarters, but otherwise leave their commanders directly responsible to CAFF. Place all administrative and installation operations (finance units, fixed hospitals, military courts, et cetera) under the current appropriate geographic or functional commands, but let the promotions of officers in charge of those operations (except military courts) be dependent on a dual system of regular ratings by both customer units and their own chain of command. No unit commander should be simultaneously an installation commander: the requirements are utterly different, and practical peacetime worries about plumbing, union contracts, and new construction will always crowd out military concerns. Theater assets like fixed communications, radar, and air defense installations; non-divisional logistical support units; border troops; and intelligence-gathering organizations with a real-world, day-to-day mission should also be directly subordinate to existing geographical and functional joint commands, but will come under the control of appropriate lower tactical headquarters for exercise or wartime purposes. Such units will be subject to evaluation by the Tactical Forces Inspectorate in conjunction with divisional EXEVALs.

Corps headquarters units should be restricted to the command, control, and communications elements needed to assume direction of corps assets in wartime operations. Like the DRS divisions they will have a four-year life cycle, and there can be more of them than at present. Corps headquarters can be created to deal with different contingencies, or competing headquarters units could even be created to deal with similar contingencies, making enemy intelligence-gathering and prediction of U.S. operational responses more complicated and uncertain. This may, incidentally, soak up some of the officer surplus in units which may even prove useful in war. In an emergency the best existing command organization would be plugged into the chain of command. This is not as radical an idea as it may seem. Many U.S. units are double-tasked and may fall under different commands depending on the nature of the operation. In World War II the same ships constituted the Third Fleet under Nimitz and the Fifth Fleet under Admiral Spruance. While one commander and his staff planned future operations, the other conducted missions. Then they switched. Peacetime corps commanders can get to know their wartime subordinates during exercises and planning meetings, in military schools, and through informal contacts. Given a new unit stability, their working relationships still will be closer than at present.

This arrangement has many benefits. First of all, it puts an actual commander at the apex of the pyramid, of the field forces at least. He will also command the Tactical Forces Inspectorate, and so his powers as a peacetime commander will be much more real than those of the Chief of Staff. This will give him the practical ability to limit the institutional infighting that plagues the army. He can pose no political threat to the nation because he does not control the multi-service units needed to conduct real-world operations, and he relinquishes control in the event of war. Nonetheless, he can serve as the chief advisor to the Chief of Staff, and his limited focus on the tactical forces should make his advice worthwhile. The power relationship of joint commanders to their army subordinates will remain unclear, but problems can now be laid on the desk of one man.

The benefits at corps level will be that corps commanders and staffs will be able to concentrate on understanding their jobs and each other. They can hone their own skills as a unit, studying their military problems in a quiet detachment that is both vital to serious contemplation and impossible now. The downside of it, for the corps commander, will be a drastic reduction in the number of people hurrying to light his cigarette and the lack of opportunities to inflict damage, destruction, and parades on subordinate units. There is the countervailing consideration that, should war come, he will be considerably less likely to go down in history as a bumbling idiot.

The benefits at the level of field units will be immediate. The peacetime chain of command will have been radically simplified, and the administrative organizations that previously have tyrannized them will have been converted into eager-to-please services. The division may now train itself without the unhelpful interference of many redundant layers of command. The EXEVAL system will ensure that units do not lose sight of their reason for existence. Care will have to be taken that commanders share common doctrinal concepts, but this is a problem for the military schools. Since most training material will continue to come from TRADOC, the Army's Training and Doctrine Command, this should not be a problem. TRADOC produces excellent training guidance: it simply cannot be utilized by currently existing units.

DISCIPLINE

One last major problem remains, and in some ways it is the most vexing of all. American leadership doctrine stresses positive leadership in building discipline.[14] Many commanders, however, frustrated with the chaotic environment engendered by the army's blend-o-matic personnel system and by subordinates who understand the system better than they do, dream of crucifying powers. Fear can be a great motivator if the sanctions available include flogging, KGB death squads, and the knout. The monetary, administrative, and generally mickey-mouse sanctions available to the American commander may suffice to maintain order in garrison, but on the battlefield they become entirely irrelevant. The more effective kinds are quite properly unavailable in our society. The army's leadership doctrine is the correct answer, but even under the favorable circumstances produced by the reforms already discussed, some negative sanctions must remain.

What disciplinary powers should American military leaders be given over their subordinates? It may appear that this question was answered in 1949 by promulgation of the Uniform Code of Military Justice (UCMJ), but this is not the case. Commanders have proven to be very reluctant to use the

UCMJ in cases involving purely military offenses like cowardice under fire. They have also been reluctant to use the UCMJ to enforce barracks discipline, because the system does not provide for quick, one-step punishment that can be administered as a corrective admonishment while having no other lingering effects. The army always tries to connect present punishment to future progress, so punishment, once begun, never stops. Official punishment records for even minor offenses can block promotions and retention, particularly for officers. Commanders therefore are reluctant to use such methods on men who could benefit from them.

On the other hand, this system is designed to protect enlisted men against arbitrary action by their leaders, and there can be no question that such protection is necessary. Very frankly, given the irrational pressures to which they currently are subjected, the army's officers really cannot be trusted with any sort of draconian power over their men, certainly not in peacetime. Permitting commanders to administer substantial punishments off the record would be disastrous. A start has been made in this area, however, by allowing commanders to specify that certain damaging data be placed in a restricted portion of the personnel record.

There is a lot of confusion within the army about exactly what immediate enforcement powers an officer really has. Usually a sharp word will suffice to correct offenses like the wearing of hats indoors, et cetera. Beyond that, however, there should be some step short of legal action. I personally liked to drop offending soldiers for push-ups, customarily ten of them, but outside of basic training camps this is a questionable procedure. That is, while there is no question that it is effective in bringing an error to a soldier's (and bystanders') attention in an immediate, effective, harmless, and even humorous way, the practice is not always approved by higher authorities. Often when I ordered a new soldier to "give me ten" he would pause and ask me why I was not getting down and doing push-ups with him. Somewhere these soldiers were being told that leaders were responsible for their soldiers' actions, and therefore should share their punishment. Others would question the order on the grounds that it was "degrading," although they usually complied when I explained how much less degrading it was than an Article 15 (legal action) for disobeying an order. (Usually this was a hollow threat, since such punishment can be initiated only by a unit commander, who is understandably reluctant to let outsiders interfere with unit discipline.) In Germany we received a command letter explaining the application of such measures, demanding that the punishment fit the crime. As an example, it went on, a soldier who repeatedly showed up in formation wearing his rank upside down should not be dropped for push-ups, but rather compelled to attend after-duty classes on the proper wear of the uniform.[15] This may be good textbook psychology, but the one being punished is the NCO who has to give the classes. The theory is that it is the NCO's responsibility to train his soldiers, so he should do the teaching and thereby share the punishment. The effect of this approach is that soldiers quickly learn that they will not be held solely accountable for things that any reasonable person would consider personal responsibilities. The end result often is that the NCO, with a pleading look in his eyes, quietly turns the rank insignia right-side-up.

Such refusal to place official responsibility where it actually lies is characteristic of the army. Responsibility for vehicle accidents rests not on the driver but on the vehicle's senior occupant. Often there is a message to that effect stenciled on the dashboard, and the senior occupant (whatever his rank) is considered to be the "assistant driver." During REFORGER our brigade commander sent down notice that any "assistant driver" caught sleeping, reading, or studying maps while the vehicle was in motion would be replaced in that capacity by his battalion commander. This had far-reaching effects, none of them positive. The specific reason for this threat was the large number of accidents caused by poorly trained drivers, and their poor training is the result of personnel turbulence and systematic falsification of training and maintenance records. My own military driver's license shows that I am qualified by many hours of training to drive vehicles I have rarely seen, much less driven, and it was falsified by the issuing authorities not because I asked them to (I had no need to drive a ten-ton Goer) but as a matter of routine.

In essence, the commander's punitive powers have devolved into three categories. Soldiers can be punished for offenses that do not differ from civilian crimes, by methods that are the same as civilian methods. They can be punished for fairly minor civil offenses like bouncing checks, or military crimes such as cursing at a superior, with administrative punishments like losing a pay-grade, bars to reenlistment or promotion, extra duty, et cetera. Most of these punishments are effective only against soldiers who are concerned about their career prospects within the army, and particularly those with families. In the latter case, the real punishment will be imposed by the spouse, one reason why the army is so eager to promote the "military family." Irate husbands and wives have partially taken the place of irate first sergeants.

In most cases of serious military indiscipline, however, the army has forsaken actual punishment and taken simply to throwing out misfits and poor soldiers with no other penalty. This feature of army discipline has been much criticized by hard-core believers in punitive measures, for the threat of being thrown out of the army is no great deterrent to someone who did not want to be in it in the first place, like the draftee. Nor is it a useful sanction against the sunshine soldier who suddenly recognizes the more awkward features of his profession, as when bands of unpleasant, foreign-looking people try to kill him.

However, it is a pretty sensible policy for the army. It is the inevitable result of civilian mistrust of military justice, and this mistrust has been

earned by past abuses. Actually getting a soldier punished is such a bureaucratic and legal headache that most commanders are happy just to get
rid of the miscreant. The less-than-honorable discharge has lost much of its
sting in recent years, and commanders suspect that any soldier given one
will eventually be able to get it upgraded by some understanding agency of
the federal government. There are a number of other, fairly simple, painless
ways to separate the soldier from the service. The army's drug-detecting
urinalysis program, the chief sanction of which is discharge, has been remarkably effective in destroying the barracks drug culture of the 1960s and
1970s.

Given the realities of American society, this is probably the best solution
we are likely to produce.[16] The building of firm interpersonal relationships
in stable units will make this sanction more effective in keeping most soldiers
in line. It is still, however, a little extreme for most of the disciplinary
problems a unit commander faces. The army should clarify its policy regarding instant sanctions like push-ups and give military leaders wide lat-
itude in their use. Above the push-up level, but below legal action,
commanders should be allowed to instigate the immediate transfer of any
subordinate (except subordinate commanders) without having to justify it
to anybody.

Instant transfer as a disciplinary method offers many good features. It
cannot be considered a punishment in the legal sense, and it will be effective
in solving a wide variety of unit problems. It will be useful when a commander and a subordinate just cannot get along, or when a subordinate has
done something to lose the commander's confidence in a way not susceptible
to legal action (as in mentioning the virtues of "fragging" in a private
conversation, which will not hold up as evidence in court). The commander
will be required to write a letter stating his reasons for instigating the
transfer, to be sealed and placed in the transferring individual's MILPER-
CEN file. The subordinate will go back to the army personnel pool, there
to be sent to a newly forming unit. New commanders will not be made
aware of the presence of any existing letters. If a certain number of them
accumulate, say three, a board will be convened to examine the soldier's
record. If the letters from three different commanders seem to indicate a
dangerous pattern, separation proceedings may begin. If, on the other hand,
they appear unconnected or frivolous, they can be resealed or removed at
the board's discretion. This system will permit instant action, will serve to
identify misfits and poor soldiers, and yet will be difficult to abuse. It is
doubtful that commanders will use this power too frequently, since under
DRS they will receive no replacements. A commander who cannot resolve
most problems in more constructive ways will soon find himself without a
unit to command. The value of instant action in disciplinary matters, even
when it involves no "real" penalty, cannot be overestimated.

This sanction will not be terribly useful on the battlefield, but commanders can use it to insure that they do not take into combat individuals they do not trust. For battlefield discipline they will have to rely on the UCMJ and the leadership doctrine of FM 22–100, *Military Leadership*. Soldiers in cohesive units that experience prolonged combat will probably be the first to demand stronger disciplinary sanctions for those who do not pull their load.

Beyond this, some attempt should be made to establish a zone of responsibility for the individual soldier, an area in which his mistakes will redound upon him alone, not on his chain of command. If we are to expect soldiers to act like men on the battlefield, we must stop treating them like little boys in garrison.

Producing an effective officer corps that actually can control the organization of which it is in "command" requires four things. First, separation of technical and administrative personnel from the command net. Second, elimination of intra-organizational competition to command personnel from other elements, either by effective subordination or by absorption. Third, improving the competence and perceived legitimacy of commissioned officers through more sensible selection, training, and promotion methods. Fourth, protecting the field forces from both the internal and external military bureaucracies.

The various measures advocated in the past four chapters, together with changes in the selection and training of future officers discussed in chapter 6, will allow us to rationalize the rank structure without changing the pay-grade structure, with all of the problems the latter action would entail. Given that no one will lose money on the deal, that promotion possibilities for those who seek them will be greater than at present, and that job stability and security will increase, this should not lead to a crippling exodus of officers.

Clarifying and simplifying the chain of command will ease the practical problems of formulating and transmitting military directives. Coupled with the stability provided by DRS, the existence of clear collective goals provided by EXEVAL and the related promotion system, and improvements in the perceived legitimacy of the officer corps, the reforms described in this chapter will strengthen greatly the likelihood that such directives will result in positive action.

NOTES

1. Figures from *Defense 86*, September-October 1986, published by DOD, American Forces Information Service. As of March 31, 1986, there were 386,860 NCOs and officers in the active army, and 390,321 E–4 and below. This imbalance extends to field units. In my artillery battalion in Germany, for example, there were 34 officers, 161 NCOs, and 198 junior enlisted soldiers assigned (figures for August 1985). 1987 figures show an even greater preponderance of leaders, with the officer

and NCO ranks accounting for slightly over 50 percent of the army's uniformed manpower. However, this is probably a transient result of budget cutbacks rather than an indication of any trend. *Defense 87*, September-October 1987.

2. As of early 1986, it took a soldier four years, one month, to reach the rank of sergeant, E–5. It took three years, eight months, for an officer to reach the rank of captain. USA MILPERCEN, "System Update," April 3, 1986.

3. Martin van Creveld, *Fighting Power* (Westport, Conn.: Greenwood Press, 1982), 151–53.

4. So powerless are high military commanders that one of the major provisions of the Goldwater-Nichols DOD Reorganization Act (Public Law 99–433), signed into law on October 1, 1986, was to give commanders of the ten major geographic and functional commands some input to the assignment and removal of officers on their own staffs. *New York Times*, September 12, 1986, sec. I; Michael Ganley, "DOD Reorganization Awaits Reagan's Pen after Compromise Bill Clears," *Armed Forces Journal International*, October 1986.

5. Kent R. Greenfield, Robert R. Palmer, and Bell I. Wiley, *The Organization of Ground Combat Troops* (Washington, D.C.: Office of the Chief of Military History, 1947), 361.

6. V Corps' knowledge of *LANCE* is discussed in chapter 2. On Grenada, see Richard Gabriel, *Military Incompetence: Why the American Military Doesn't Win* (New York: Hill and Wang, 1985), 149–86; John Fialka, "In Battle for Grenada Commando Missions Didn't Go as Planned," *Wall Street Journal*, November 15, 1983.

7. U.S. Fifth and Seventh Corps (forming U.S. Seventh Army) will fall under the orders of Commander, Allied Forces Central Europe (COMAFCENT), a *Bundeswehr* general.

8. U.S. units in Germany are scattered in small installations, often several in the same town. Many local functions such as security and civil-military relations have been consolidated into the hands of a local Military Community (MILCOM) commander, who may or may not be a unit and/or installation commander as well.

9. The president actually ended up taking responsibility for this one, saying that marine commanders had "suffered enough." *New York Times*, December 28, 1983, sec. I.

10. Gabriel, *Military Incompetence*, 156–62.

11. See Ninety-eighth Congress, *Adequacy of Marine Corps Security in Beirut* (Washington, D.C.: GPO, 1983).

12. Laurence F. Peter and Raymond Hull, *The Peter Principle* (New York: William Morrow and Co., 1969).

13. Problems with job classification of soldiers by psychological tests are discussed in van Creveld, *Fighting Power*, 68–70; Robert R. Palmer, Bell I. Wiley, and William R. Keast, *The Procurement and Training of Ground Combat Troops* (Washington, D.C.: Office of the Chief of Military History, 1948), 1–13.

14. See FM 22–100, *Military Leadership* (Washington, D.C.: Headquarters, Department of the Army, October 1983) and DA Pam 600–50, the Chief of Staff's *White Paper on Leadership* (Washington, D.C.: Headquarters, Department of the Army, 1985).

15. I would cite the source of this letter, but my commander took it out of my

hands and made a short, solemn ceremony of tearing it up and putting it in the trash can.

16. There is nothing unusual about such a reluctance to use coercive measures in a democracy. This has always been a problem in American armies, and the solution to it has usually been about the same. See Fred Anderson, *A People's Army: Massachusetts Soldiers and Society in the Seven Years' War* (New York: W. W. Norton and Co., 1984), particularly 111–41. A similar situation prevailed in ancient Athens, which nonetheless was able to field effective armies. See Hans Delbrück, *History of the Art of War within the Framework of Political History,* trans. Walter J. Renfroe, Jr. (Westport, Conn.: Greenwood Press, 1975), 286.

6

SELECTION AND TRAINING OF
OFFICERS

Commissioned officers make up about 12 percent of the army's active-duty strength. The bulk of these officers receive their commissions through ROTC. In fiscal year 1985, ROTC commissioned about 8,300 officers, the majority of whom received active-duty assignments. By contrast, West Point produced just over 1,000, and another 769 came from Officer Candidate School. There are other routes to an army commission, mainly for people with advanced and specialized skills such as medical doctors. Most new officers are commissioned as second lieutenants. Almost all are in their early twenties, a few still in their teens. Almost all have college degrees. About half of army officers are assigned to branches of the combat arms, i.e., infantry, armor, field artillery, engineers, et cetera. About 20 percent are in the health service area and the rest are in various support or "service support" fields.[1]

Probably the most damaging single feature of the American military system is its manner of choosing and training junior officers. These are the men who stand at the critical interface between the command structure and the soldiers who do the fighting. Although there has been much criticism of these men from the standpoint of their class background and personal qualities, there is nothing much wrong with them as individuals. The problem is that for reasons that are quite easy to understand they lack credibility in the eyes of their soldiers, and especially in the eyes of their NCOs. They are simply too young, too inexperienced, and too poorly prepared for their great responsibilities.

THE SELECTION OF OFFICERS

Consider the following statement: "Leaders must know what they are doing. Their primary leadership tool cannot be fear, but rather the ability to inspire confidence in their subordinates." Most of us would agree with this statement, whether we were talking about military leaders, union leaders, business executives, teachers, whatever. The army's leadership doctrine is based explicitly on this theory.

How then can we explain the phenomenon known in military parlance as the "Second Lieutenant"? No one believes that this person knows anything about leading men in battle, yet he is legally in a position of authority, and in combat he is frequently the only member of the officer corps in sight. This young man may be a natural-born leader, although the odds are against it and there is nothing in the officer selection process to increase the chances of this being so. His NCOs, with many years of experience between them, have no illusions on this score. His junior soldiers will quickly be disabused of any misconceptions they may have brought with them into the ranks.

Yet this lieutenant has been told that he is in charge, that he bears responsibility for both the lives of his men and the success of their mission. If he has any character at all he takes these responsibilities seriously, and if he is career-oriented he assumes (incorrectly) that his promotion will depend on his accomplishments. He has the confidence in himself and in his training that is the special privilege of the young, earnest, and ignorant. In practice, however, he lacks real-world experience, and probably lacks even academic knowledge of the battlefield. He also lacks the routine familiarity with military life and with the characteristics of his soldiers which might cause them to give him their confidence anyway. His only source of real influence in any emergency is the fear he can inspire with his presidentially granted legal powers. Frustrated by the seeming intractability of his subordinates and of the situation, he will sooner or later attempt to use it. This does not work very well even in peacetime. On the battlefield, it can be fatal.

Many officers, despite the fact that they have virtually no coercive powers effective on the battlefield, continue to labor under the illusion that they can get cooperation by "kicking ass." Thrown into deadly combat, the American soldier promptly disregards any threat to his paycheck or future promotion, and these are the practical threats he faces. Given the anomie induced by the present personnel system, more positive motivations like group identification and a desire for the approval of leaders or fellow soldiers are absent.

Therefore, if the soldiers of this young lieutenant take his threats seriously at all, their response is not at all certain to be obedience. They will definitely think twice before exposing themselves to enemy fire, if in their view such exposure is militarily unnecessary, in order to evade a mere court-martial. Instead, in a statistically significant number of instances, they will decide simply to kill the officer in question. This was a solution resorted to literally hundreds of times in Vietnam. It does not take many such occurrences to weaken dangerously the confidence of unit-level leaders. Even the rumor of such an occurrence can prove paralyzing to officers who do not know their troops well. There are many men who will risk death in battle, but being murdered by one's own troops is a different matter. Today's soldiers still tell "fragging" stories about Vietnam, whether they were there or not.

Frankly, given the nature of the army's small-unit leadership the decision to frag an officer or to mutiny is a decision with which it is difficult to quarrel. The soldiers are not consciously resisting their obligations to their country. They are resisting a dangerously inexperienced kid, who is motivated not by any fundamental goal of national policy—which he is ill-equipped to understand—but by the carrots and sticks of the army's promotion system. An officer is reminded of these motivators daily, but they apply only to him, not to his men. Men do not risk their lives for such leaders.

The lieutenant does have a second option, however. He can place himself under the tutelage of his senior NCOs and act, in effect, as his platoon sergeant's subordinate and as the unit's mascot. This is what the wise lieutenant does, but that leaves us with several problems. First, we must wonder why he is in charge. Why is he wearing the rank and drawing the pay? And who is really answerable for the unit's actions? The senior commander knows that the platoon sergeant is calling the shots, but he must pretend that the young lieutenant bears the blame for faulty decisions. He cannot hold the NCO legally responsible for serious foul-ups, but he is reluctant to punish an officer for actions that in practice were out of his control. Where does responsibility lie?

Second, the officer does possess from his training and education important military knowledge the NCO lacks. He is trained in tactics and doctrine, and his role in the chain of command is to integrate the actions of his small unit into the overall mission of the larger force. His NCOs, on the other hand, are not so trained and bear no such responsibility. Their quite proper aim is almost invariably going to be the preservation of the unit, to which the officer, if he attempts to place the combat mission first, poses the greatest threat. The young, inexperienced officer does not possess sufficient prestige or credibility to reorder the unit's priorities.

These conflicts between the education, responsibilities, competence, and credibility of the members of the small unit's leadership will in many cases render the unit either ineffective or actively mutinous in combat. Not always. Perhaps not even most of the time. But it will happen often enough to destroy the bond of faith between officers and men, and between different units and different levels of command, that is the basis for unified, goal-driven military action.

Even in peacetime, the frequent reduction of junior officers to the role of mascot leaves a permanent stamp on them. A great many of them never gain a sure feel for soldiers, and they remain far more dependent on NCOs than is healthy. This has led to the creation of the parallel NCO chain of command. The effect is to erode further officers' security and authority, while driving another wedge between commanders and their men.

In theory, NCOs are subordinated to their commanders by the UCMJ and by the fact that their officers write their EERs (Enlisted Efficiency Reports). This does serve to make NCOs cautious. In practice, however, NCOs do not derive their power from that of their immediate superior but rather from their ability to influence junior soldiers on his behalf. Officers are mystified by the actual mechanics of ARTEPs, Annual General Inspections, and the supply, maintenance, and personnel systems. Accordingly, they are most frequently dependent on their NCOs' and warrant officers' expertise and ability to motivate troops. A dedicated, responsible NCO who respects the chain of command and the traditions of the army will seek to educate the young officer, to protect him from his own mistakes, and to feed him real authority as fast as he can handle it. A merely clever NCO will feed his ignorance and sense of helplessness. The relationship between these experienced NCOs and their inexperienced immediate commanders is thus an extremely ambiguous one, characterized by a mixture of dependence, overfamiliarity, and mistrust, open to all sorts of intrigues and abuses. Because both the officer corps and the NCO corps have a strong sense of corporate identity, with divergent goals, interests, and capabilities, the chain of command often becomes hopelessly muddled right down at unit level. It does not improve as it wends its way back to the Joint Chiefs of Staff, who are not in charge either.

Given the contrast between the sanctions available and the dangers of the battlefield, it is clear that American combat leaders can gain legitimacy only by virtue of their evident superior maturity, dedication, and capability, the confidence they can inspire in troops. The U.S. Army's junior officers, the lieutenants and captains who actually lead troops, are notoriously lacking in this regard, purely through youth and lack of experience. They face virtually unbeatable competition from the NCO corps. Any young sergeant has more experience both in the army in general and in working with soldiers than does the new lieutenant or even the junior captain. Senior NCOs, who frequently do gain the confidence of the soldiers, usually lack the general and military education necessary to utilize them effectively in pursuit of larger military goals.

Why do we select officers the way we do? In part, it is another holdover from the emergency expansions for World War II and Korea. Perhaps it is more fundamentally a holdover from a period in which a college education of any sort had a real significance in identifying people as members of the social elite, an elite that could retain respect despite bloody failures on the battlefield. There is no longer any such class, and in Western society as a whole there has not been one since the disasters of World War I.[2] Perhaps Americans took a little longer than most to grow disillusioned, but the

Vietnam debacle seems to have completed the process. Officers certainly require a higher education, but a college degree is no longer taken to imply membership in a natural leadership group. The social and educational distance between today's officers, NCOs, and junior enlisted men is no longer the yawning gulf it once was. Officers should also be gentlemen, but these young men who graduate from college and suddenly find themselves in strange places, with money in their pockets and authority on their collars, often fail to meet any reasonable definition of that term. Ask any waitress in any officers' club.[3]

The first part of the solution to the problem of poor officer leadership at small-unit level is that advocated in chapter 2: to produce stable units in which officers and men can gain a reliable measure of simple human familiarity with one another, and in which decent officers can win the respect of their subordinates. The second part is to create some common interest binding officers and men in pursuit of a common goal. The current individual race for promotion is terribly divisive, but the EXEVAL system discussed in chapters 3 and 4 will do much in this regard. Everyone's promotion will depend on unit achievement, and the commander's success will benefit everybody in the unit. Hopefully, the attitudes thus generated in peacetime will live on in combat. The third component in the solution is to produce officers who can, by virtue of their selection and training, command the respect of their NCOs and soldiers.

This cannot be done by taking young philosophy majors fresh from their college graduations and making them platoon leaders. There is no social class in America today that can claim a right to military leadership. Such leadership must be found in the ranks. Rather than taking people with irrelevant B.A.s and trying to turn them into leaders and soldiers, we must find soldiers who have shown themselves to be leaders, give them an appropriate education, see them through to emotional maturity, and commission them.

The fly in the ointment is that current enlisted promotion practices do not do a very good job of identifying natural leaders. Even if the present leadership was itself made up entirely of experienced, capable combat leaders, there is no reason to suppose that it would naturally seek to identify and promote the most promising natural leaders from among the rank and file. Many factors lead them to focus instead on those who are the most pliable, the best dressed, or simply the most ambitious.[4] In many cases, these characteristics are explicitly considered the mark of leadership.

THE SPIT-SHINE SYNDROME

Individual appearance is one feature in which the U.S. Army really shines, literally. An incredible emphasis is placed on the "spit-shining" of the combat boot, which produces a mirror-like shine very difficult to maintain once achieved. I do not know how many times I have heard the following exchange: "Well, is he a good troop?" "Sir, he has the best-looking boots in the platoon." This is a source of despair to soldier-mechanics, whose oil-soaked boots will not take a spit-shine. Some become quick-change artists in order to look "military" at morning and afternoon formations. Others say to hell with it and accept their designation as dirt-bags.

Soldiers exercise a lot of ingenuity trying to achieve a perfect shine, preferably one that is permanent. This leads to all sorts of experiments with new waxes. Particularly intriguing to experimenters is acrylic floor wax. This can preserve a shine practically forever, at considerable expense to the feet. Another answer is patent leather, which some officers buy not only for their low-quarter dress shoes but for their combat boots as well. I always promised myself that if I ever caught a subordinate officer wearing patent leather combat boots I would do something drastic, but in retrospect I have come to see the practice as a kind of Dadaist protest of the absurd symbolism embodied in the army's spit-shine syndrome. The soldier's shoe-shine has become so important as a symbol of "leadership" that officers will go to ridiculous lengths to avoid mud or dust. Because officers rarely get to know their quickly rotating troops well, and because nearly everything in the field army is based on appearances (in the absence of any viable method of determining actual capability), the spit-shined boot has become the living symbol of the "Army of Excellence." It is probably true that the shoe-shine is a better tip-off to a soldier's qualities than the other ornaments that he may wear, for medals and decorations are a joke. They are awarded for actions beyond the call of duty, such as passing inspections or graduating from schools that have a 100 percent pass rate. One lieutenant in my unit in Germany got a medal for organizing a battalion party. It was a great party, and for the next twenty years she can look at the ribbons on her chest to remind her of it. On the other hand, I was unable to get so much as a letter of commendation for a group of junior officers and soldiers who volunteered for (and very successfully carried out) a difficult and possibly dangerous piece of combat training for our soldiers. For Operation URGENT FURY (Grenada), somewhere between 8,000 and 19,000 medals were awarded even though there were never more than 7,000 U.S. soldiers on the island.[5]

A major impediment to the goal of looking "military" in the ornamental sense is the new Battledress Uniform (BDU), which has upset a lot of people in the army by its inherently unkempt appearance. Many attempts are made to spruce it up. Some soldiers insert cardboard tubes in the trouser legs above the boot to achieve the perfect "blousing" effect. This produces an appearance similar to that of the Tin Man in the *Wizard of Oz*. Bizarre things are done to uniform hats to give them whatever shape appeals to local sartorial tastes. Starching and ironing the BDU is also common, although this destroys its infrared-reflective properties. A soldier in heavily starched BDUs shows up in an infrared scope as a neatly man-shaped black figure against an amorphous green background. Starching it, and until recently even ironing it, is against regulations. Nonetheless, it is done, often under explicit direction from the local chain of command. The G–5 officer of the Second Infantry Division once gave us a briefing in BDUs that had not only been starched and ironed but had had the creases sewn in. So heavy was the demand for neater tailoring that the uniform was recently redesigned with a sleeker look, including tabs on the sides to give it a waistline. These added several more buttons, each of which seems to be drawn like a magnet into the tangles of the camouflage netting that drapes all army equipment in the field. Presumably, the BDU will continue to evolve until we reach the point of requiring a new Battle *Undress* Uniform.

In late 1985 there appeared in the European edition of *Stars and Stripes* a letter from a young sergeant, twenty-one, who was disturbed deeply by what he perceived as sloppy wear of the BDU by some people who were supposed to be military leaders. He was disturbed by those in the leading ranks who did not participate in this fashion competition, who obeyed regulations and treated the BDU as what it is, a tactical uniform. Some of these characters sported boots that were not spit-shined.

The line that really angered me was the thesis sentence: "The appearance of the soldier is the soldier," a philosophy in which soldiers are diligently instructed by the army's leaders. I could not resist the urge to reply. My letter was a broad-gauge criticism of the spit-shine syndrome. Needless to say, the moment this appeared in print I was called into the commander's office for an explanation. After some discussion, he relaxed and said he actually agreed with the substance of my letter.

More enthusiastic was the response I received from about 300 soldiers over the next week, troops I did not know, who stopped me and talked about the letter. *Stars and Stripes* printed an entire page of replies, 75 percent of which were written in emphatic agreement. However, the most interesting reply I received came in the mail.

Dear Sir,   10 DEC 85

We would like to express our gratitude for the article you wrote in which you stated that the appearance of the soldier is the "icing on the cake, not the cake itself."

I don't know what paper or magazine the article was printed in. I found a copy stapled to a bulletin board in my work area with a note addressing it to officers and NCOs.

It seems to be the attitude here that it is alright if nothing gets accomplished as long as you look sharp while you're not doing it. Too many times we have seen the stripes go to the E–4 with the battery-powered boots. Or the A.J.[6] that goes to the person who takes the time to learn the AR's[7] during work hours while someone else is out in the rain doing two people's jobs.

Of course, forget about the soldier with the mud on his boots and the wrench in his hand. Put him aside with "that slug" who gets locked out of the hangar on a daily basis because he's a half-mile down the flight line working on an aircraft and doesn't want to quit until he knows it's ready. Don't stop to think that these are the people who spend two hours a night on their boots so that in formation the next morning they will look as good as the individual whose boots haven't been anywhere in weeks but the nearest coffee machine.

This is our first tour in the Army and now, coming up on our re-up time we are giving serious thought to staying in or getting out. We love the army and the idea of being soldiers. But in a unit where there is no organized leadership, unrecognized achievement, misplaced credit and where such FM's as FM 22–100, 22–101, and 25–3[8] are virtually non-existent it's hard to tell what the Army really is. Thank you for letting some of us unseen people know that there is more to the Army than starch and pot-bellies. Some of us might have gotten out as first-termers thinking the Army is a joke. We might have ruined our chance for an outstanding career. But thanks to your letter we know we won't be getting out until we are E–8's with berets on our heads.

Thank you Sir![9]

I did not know whether to laugh or cry over that one. Soldiers like this man are the only reason anything works in the army, but I am afraid he is doomed to further disillusionment.

It *appears* that enlisted soldiers do not think highly of the leadership they receive, nor of the enlisted promotion system.[10] If you are one who believes that appearances are reality, as do many in the army's unit-level NCO and officer leadership, this should provide food for thought. Perhaps you can come up with some sort of program that will convince these soldiers of their error without actually doing anything about the system. Perhaps there is some new form they can fill out.

All this is not to say that there are no good junior NCOs in the army. There are, lots of them. And there are many good senior NCOs, so many that they should be absorbed into the officer corps to improve it. The problem is that there are just too many NCOs to start with, particularly in the grade of E–5, and many of them have been promoted for the wrong reasons. Some are good, reliable soldiers with little leadership ability. These soldiers are valuable to unit leaders because they do what they are told, never compete with their bosses, and never stir up trouble by proposing better ways to do things. It may sound contrary to the American national myth, but the army needs people like that, and their leaders feel that they owe them a promotion. Promoting them merely puts off the problem, however, since they are not likely to win another promotion from this, their level of incompetence. On the other hand, many E–5 "sergeants" are in units that are so overloaded with NCOs that they are never placed in an actual leadership position. In my unit in Germany, as an example, there was one E–5 for every 2.3 soldiers of lower rank. In such a situation, junior NCOs unable to handle a leadership role can continue to accumulate promotion points toward the next pay-grade.

Other promotees are the ubiquitous "soldiers with the battery-powered boots" referred to above, who win approval because, while they do not actually do anything, they manage to "look sharp while they're not doing it." There is a lot of this, because officers who do not really understand what it is that their men are supposed to be doing appreciate soldiers who create a good impression for visiting higher-ups, who are even more ignorant. This factor holds true at higher ranks. The focus on appearance over reality is amply demonstrated by the fact that in 1985 only three officers (all very junior lieutenants) were eliminated from the army because of failure to pass a training course. Nineteen were thrown out for being too fat. In 1986 the figures were eight and fourteen, respectively.[11] Staff Sergeant Hodrin, the outstanding maintenance NCO described in chapter 3, was eventually thrown out of the army for being "overweight" even though he never failed a physical fitness test. A demonstrably good performance in both his job and physical ability counted for nothing in comparison to the dictates of appearance (and Staff Sergeant Hodrin looked fat only on paper). Grades in military schools are not even included in the data given to officer promotion boards, but the file must include a photograph.

There are a great number of soldiers who are promoted to leadership ranks because they deserve it. The system is simply not consistent enough to be the basis for identifying potential officers and senior NCOs.

A WORKABLE SELECTION PROCESS

The best way to identify the natural leaders who should be developed as command-track officers and as NCOs is to let the soldiers point them out. This cannot be done by formal elections or by paper "peer-ratings."[12] Asked to rate their fellows on paper, soldiers' answers will be distorted by all sorts of unknowable considerations. Most people simply do not understand their own value systems well enough to make such theoretical judgments.

Instead, periodically take the unit to the field and strip it of its normal leadership. Remove the soldiers' rank insignia. Provide them with a competitive tactical problem that requires them to break themselves down into small groups. Offer winning units a meaningful reward (not money, please). This reward must go not to the leaders but to the unit as a whole. After a couple of days of playing military games, find out who is in charge of the various sections. Mark down the leaders for later reference.

This could best be done as part of the EXEVAL. When the unit reaches the end of its life cycle, look at the lists to identify soldiers consistently chosen as leaders. Offer a percentage of these select soldiers career status as NCOs or officers, the number selected to be determined by projected requirements. The rank order will be based on specific details in each soldier's individual record, particularly those that reflect on his academic potential. Allow their commanders a veto in order to weed out undesirables, but give them no positive input. Those that show promise as NCOs should be sent to NCO academies and advanced training schools, to emerge as E–6s. The rest should be financed through the best universities to which they can obtain admission. There they will become command-track ROTC cadets with a lengthy military obligation after graduation.

While this program will provide insufficient numbers to replace entirely the current sources of ROTC cadets, it will alter substantially the nature of the ROTC product. Command-track officers, when they emerge from their education and training, will be older, more mature characters who understand enlisted soldiers and the nature of military life. They will be people who have already proven themselves as natural leaders, who were selected by their fellow soldiers to lead them in military operations in the success of which all shared a common interest. Their college programs will have been designed to be relevant to their vocation as soldiers. These people will form the basis of an effective, professional officer corps.

The possibility of winning selection to this sort of educational program should help attract good people into enlisted service, although it must be made clear that these scholarships are not the usual GI Bill–type benefits but prizes obtainable through high achievement and a commitment to further military service. It may become a moderately expensive program, but it will apply to only a portion of the cadet corps, those destined to be unit commanders and primary staff officers. Tuition at most schools, plus a subsistence living allowance, will not exceed the pay of a very junior officer.

Potential technical types, warrant officers, and specialty officers can be identified from among junior soldiers fairly easily through centralized assessment of standardized tests. Current unit techniques for subverting these measuring devices will be ineffective under the EXEVAL approach to evaluation. Such soldiers can be urged to use their regular GI benefits to go to college and to join ROTC units. Like non-prior-service cadets, these men will enter the army as specialty officers, not as potential commanders.

Officer Candidate School (OCS) will be another option for individuals who have already completed their college educations and have been identified as leaders during the unit cycle. Contrary to the popular impression, a substantial number of enlisted personnel do have college degrees or some education beyond high school, a total of some 17 percent.[13] As for putting recent college graduates into uniform for basic training and then straight into OCS, this can be useful only as an emergency measure. Such officers should go to COHORT replacement companies and activated reserve cadres. Frankly, it would be much better to commission troops who show leadership potential and ignore their academic shortcomings until the emergency is over.

There will also be a certain number of soldiers entering the officer ranks directly from the NCO corps. Some of these, those with technical or administrative specialties, will become warrant officers. Others, with the same specialties plus college degrees, will become specialty officers. NCOs who have reached the pay-grade E–8 and served successfully for one unit cycle as senior troop-leaders (principally as company first sergeants) should be given a set of options. First, they can remain as career first sergeants, being frozen in that rank, although being eligible for pay-grade promotion to E–9. Second, they can elect to try for promotion to sergeant major, but this path will be rather narrow since all sergeant major slots above battalion-level will be eliminated as constituting a violation of the concept of a chain of command. Third, they can go to school (a concentrated version of the Officer Basic Course which focuses on doctrine and tactics and skips the "Introduction to Leadership, 101" phase) and emerge as "1st Lieutenants, permanent grade," pay-grade O–2. They will come back to their units as professional platoon leaders. At that point they will have a single promotion possibility, to captain, permanent grade, company commander. Fourth, if they have the educational potential or have already earned higher degrees in appropriate subject areas, they can apply for regular commissions with no promotion ceiling. Upon selection, they can be sent to the appropriate military or civilian schools.

Personnel currently in pay-grade E–9 should be given these options when it comes time to enter the new DRS units. NCOs applying for translation to officer status should, if selected, be guaranteed tenure in their new permanent ranks and positions, assuming of course that their units perform to standard. The guarantee is necessary because the army has an ugly history of commissioning capable NCOs when it needs capable battlefield officers, then cashiering them when the emergency subsides.

The only real problem is that some of these men will be unable to adapt to their radically changed status. Some have a deeply ingrained hostility or contempt for officers. They will get along poorly with their new peers and oppress subordinate officers. A crusty old Sergeant major is not going to accept the indignity of becoming a "butterbar" second lieutenant. Most E–9s seeking translation to officer status will have to go directly to captain or higher, and be carefully socialized as officers.

As for West Point, which currently produces about 10 percent of each year's new officers, this appears to be another political non-issue. Nonetheless, there are severe problems with the West Point curriculum. Military Ethics is taught by the English department. Visiting scholars have complained that they have been admonished not to use the word "kill" in instructing cadets; the proper verb is "to service targets."[14] Military history requirements are minimal. The isolation in which West Point officers develop cannot be healthy, but the academy system would offer some potentially great advantages if the curriculum could be changed and if the training of cadets could be altered along the lines described in this chapter. If West Point does not alter its training to meet the challenge of the new breed of officer, academy grads will lose out in the competition engendered by EX-EVAL. Some say this is already happening, arguing that West Pointers are not achieving high rank in proportion to their numbers in the officer corps.[15]

New officers should never enter the active army as second lieutenants, a rank that should be abolished. Soldiers with extensive prior service in the army should enter simply as lieutenants, or higher in the case of translated senior NCOs. Those who come from other backgrounds, hopefully a tiny minority, should not enter as officers at all but as cadets with a functional rank equivalent to E–6. The realities of recruiting college graduates being what they are, these people would have to be paid on a scale similar to that of the present second lieutenant. These cadets should not be entitled to a salute and should be clearly subordinate to the senior NCOs to whom they are assigned. After successful completion of a year in this position, they should be commissioned as lieutenants and transferred to a newly forming DRS or COHORT unit. Officers with no experience in live army units should never be placed in charge of experienced soldiers.

ACADEMIC TRAINING

Although junior officers receive more training in tactics and doctrine than do their subordinates, a great many of them are not intellectually equipped to understand that training. The single distinction required of young Americans to make them eligible for a commission is a college education, but this distinction is often nullified by the irrelevant nature of their academic background. Officers share no common base of knowledge preparing them for their professions. Take armor officers as an example. As of 1986, we find tankers with a hopeless hodgepodge of academic specialties. Four-hundred and one majored in business administration. Ten had degrees in theology or religious education. Fifty-seven were in marketing, thirteen in philosophy, fifty-three in agriculture, and one-hundred and fifteen in biology. Thirty-five had legal backgrounds, twelve were in wildlife resources. Two were aerospace engineers. One was a nurse.[16] The military education of officers at the entry level is limited to narrow technical and administrative subjects, and more advanced professional training often comes too late in a soldier's career to influence his operational worldview. Many see attendance at the Command and Staff school as a formality, a mere ticket to be punched. About 40 percent take it as a correspondence course.

The eclectic background of the current officer corps is seen by the army as a source of strength and prestige, since many officers have degrees in fields that, however irrelevant to their business as military men, are the same as those of professions that are held in higher esteem by American society. The real reason for the eclecticism is that the army has had to take officers where it can get them, and because the army leadership has so little appreciation of the unique requirements of its own profession. The inclusion in the officer corps of many technical and administrative specialists has compounded the problem. The subjects pursued by army officers in seeking higher degrees often represent nothing of value in a military sense, and they are not expected to.[17] They are merely a career fall-back should the next promotion be denied. "Up or Out" compounds this problem, for it is a foolish student who prepares himself exclusively for a military career.

Nonetheless, to be true military professionals the army's officers need a relevant intellectual background. To a soldier, weapons are tools. He does not need to know their scientific or engineering details or their cost, just how they operate, what they can do, and what logistical support they require. He does not need to understand business management techniques and, in any case, traditional American management does not appear to be any more effective in business than it has been on the battlefield.[18] Why should we send a biology major into the infantry? The idea that twentieth-century soldiering is something to pick up on the job is ludicrous, and the idea that only senior officers need to know what a vertical envelopment is, or whose side France is on, even more so.

The basis for any academic program intended to produce military leaders must be the study of military history. Professional armies have always emphasized the study of military history, not only because of its often inspirational character or its factual content but also because of its impact on the collective mind-set of the officer corps. Successful armies throughout history, particularly the Roman and the German armies, have been able to act as a coordinated team even in the absence of sophisticated communications systems because their leadership shared a common understanding of military problems and of military doctrine.[19] Military doctrine is largely the product of historical research, with the past being reconsidered in the light of modern technology and practical experience. Even to understand basic tactical terms like "refused flank" or "oblique attack" requires historical study. Social issues, tremendously important to military leaders in a democracy, also require a historical perspective. As limited as historical truth may be, military history is the only available military counterpart to the scientist's laboratory, the businessman's market research. Historical study combined with bloodless military exercises is the only source of military experience, however vicarious, for peacetime soldiers, for even practical experience on one battlefield may prove irrelevant to the next; the American command system in the Indochinese War was no model for anything.[20]

A good general knowledge of the world's history, geography, and international relations is also a vital leadership tool. This is especially necessary to the American officer, since he may expect to be sent virtually anywhere in the world and to fight almost any enemy, for any of a wide variety of reasons. Given the political nature of war and the physical circumstances in which it is carried out, this is the only conceivable intellectual background for someone expected to lead armies to victory. He must understand the situations in which he finds himself, to know the reasons why he is fighting and why he must order his men into bloody combat.

Some armies do not have this problem. Some armies fight under the lash of totalitarianism, some out of ideological or religious fervor, and some simply because they are professional killers. American soldiers (and their parents, spouses, and friends) are citizens and voters. They cannot, therefore, be considered as a mere tool of policy. They are instead a double-edged sword, and it is an illusion to believe that they will sustain the will to fight when their leaders cannot explain the cause for which they may die.

History and related disciplines such as political science are, in fact, well represented among combat arms officers. The largest single group of armor officers with academic majors[21] got their degrees in history: 731. Political science, including international relations, is not too far behind with 532. Overall, however, the American officer corps lacks any common academic base. It is therefore quite unable to utilize its own doctrine. Officers simply do not think in a common language. This lack makes a mockery of any claim to military professionalism.[22]

Even among readers of military history, many officers are "buffs" rather than serious students of their profession.[23] Much of their reading reflects an adolescent fascination with battlefield heroism, and there is a disturbing amount of adulation for the German army of the Kaisers and Hitler. There seems to be much less interest in the West German army of today, still a formidable organization and one imbued with a democratic ethos. An interest in the old German army is understandable given its accomplishments, and reform-minded people inside the army and out have a tendency to reject American experience and turn rather crudely to the old German model. Unfortunately, few officers understand the radical differences between German and American society or the impact of those differences on military organization. Something of a backlash to this Germanophilia seems to be developing within the army,[24] but it appears to be rooted more deeply in chauvinism than in a desire to search for a native inspiration for effective military reform.

Perhaps one underlying reason for the lack of a deep grounding in these subjects is political: many people fear that a "thinking" officer corps would question orders or pose a threat to civilian control. This is also quite likely the reason why military recruiters stress self-interest over patriotic motives when attempting to attract recruits, for bureaucratic methods require personnel who can reliably be manipulated through administrative carrots and sticks, not those who have strong inner motivations.[25] It is not necessary, however, that a commander agree with government policy. Soldiers understand the argument that goes "I don't like it, but we are soldiers and that's the job we are here to do." Military leaders ignorant of political concerns cannot give credible advice to political leaders. Nor can officers who themselves do not know why they are risking their lives expect to inspire troops willingly to do the same. Soldiers may not understand the explanation, but they will quickly detect the fact if their leaders do not understand it either. Such an understanding can be gained only through the study of sophisticated military history.

The historical record, however, is not something the army pays much attention to. ROTC cadets are required to take only one class in history, and West Point requires only six credit hours in "History of the Military Art." The following is the official unit history of one of the artillery battalions in Korea. It is read solemnly at important unit functions. In form and content it is representative of all such unit histories in the U.S. Army.

Constituted on 1 July 1916 in the Regular Army as Battery B, 17th Field Artillery. Organized 6 June 1917 at Camp Robinson, Wisconsin. (17th Field Artillery assigned 21 September 1917 to the 2nd Division; relieved 18 December 1920 from assignment to the 2nd Division; assigned 22 July 1929 to the 1st Division; relieved 1 January 1930 from assignment to the 1st Division and assigned to the 2nd Division; relieved 16 October 1939 from assignment to the 2nd Division.)

Reorganized and redesignated 1 March 1944 as Battery B, 17th Field Artillery Battalion. Inactivated 16 April 1946 at Camp Kilmer, New Jersey. Activated 1 August 1946 at Ft. Sill, Oklahoma. Inactivated 24 January 1948 at Ft. Sill, Oklahoma: concurrently, redesignated as Battery C, 17th Field Artillery Battalion. Activated 15 December 1948 at Ft. Sill, Oklahoma. Inactivated 1 June 1958 in Korea.

Redesignated 2 June 1958 as Headquarters and Headquarters Battery, 2nd Howitzer Battalion, 17th Artillery (organic elements concurrently constituted). Battalion activated 25 June 1958 at Ft. Sill, Oklahoma. Redesignated 1 April 1968 as the 2nd Battalion, 17th Artillery. Inactivated 26 April 1971 at Fort Sill, Oklahoma. Redesignated 1 September 1971 as the 2nd Battalion, 17th Field Artillery. Assigned 13 September 1972 to the 2nd Infantry Division and activated in Korea.[26]

This might be inspirational to an archivist or a national park administrator, but it is of no interest to soldiers. One day in Korea, after a unit change-of-command ceremony in which our own unit's history had been recited to the troops, several soldiers asked me the purpose of reading "that bullshit" while they had to stand out in the cold, freezing. I replied that it was because it was important for military units to have a sense of their own history, of tradition. The response to this was markedly negative. So I told them about the *battlefield* history of the Second Infantry Division: Second battle of the Marne; Battle of the Bulge ("Wow! Really?"); the Korean War. I hesitated, then told them of the battle of Kunu-ri, some miles north of the battalion's present location. In this action the division's artillery was virtually wiped out in a Chinese ambush, with the loss of some 4,000 men. I thought the troops' response would be something to the effect of "Yeah, well, you know how screwed up the Army is." To my surprise, however, I found the troops to be very excited by this story. They got all puffed up and strutted around saying "Hey, my unit got exterminated once not far from here." I was asked to retell the story to other groups several times that day. I had similar experiences with my soldiers in Germany.

That may seem irrational, but then, in battle, anyone with the standard suburban sense of rationality runs away as fast as possible. The fact is that this kind of unit history is a big motivator for soldiers. Later, I visited Bastogne and saw the Second Infantry's patch on the Ardennes monument. It moved me deeply. The army as an institution has a very different attitude. Real military history is an embarrassment, because the army is not run by soldiers. The U.S. Army is basically a uniformed bureaucracy, and its primary purpose is to process paper and produce paychecks, promotions, and twenty-year retirements. Combat is an unpleasant interruption, the price to be paid for the fringe benefits. Give the men an idea of what war is really like and they might not re-enlist. It is certainly nothing with which to inspire anybody. Officers who believe otherwise do not survive.

Should circumstances require a massive expansion of the army, or a drawn-out conflict require large numbers of command-track officer replacements, officers will have to be found wherever possible. In the meantime, command-track officers need a military education, not an M.B.A. or a degree in homiletics. This means a liberal education, accompanied by practical military experience *in real army units*. A structured curriculum is needed to impose coherence upon cadets' fantasies of battlefield heroism. A good general background in history, geography, and international politics must be required. Majors in any of these areas should be acceptable, with other fields of concentration carefully scrutinized for content. Such general academic work must be unified and built upon by specific course-work taught in ROTC departments. Otherwise we will have an officer corps that is expert only in "Women's 19th Century Labor Movements" or the Marxist interpretation of American imperialism. Students must understand the official doctrine and diplomatic positions of the United States as taught by government representatives.

Officers who have gained experience in one DRS cycle should be put into higher-level command and staff schools as early in their careers as possible, and officers from the same classes should be sent on to the same units afterwards. Unit cadres should attend training as a unit, especially adventure training like the Ranger school. Scattering graduates also badly dilutes the value of command and staff training. The fact that students have learned the same doctrine, techniques, and concepts from the same instructors is just as important as the factual content of their studies.

INTELLECTUALS IN THE ARMY

Unit-level command does not call for intellectuals, and there is little role for the deep thinker in fighting organizations below the level of corps. An exception exists in the areas of special operations and counterinsurgency, where leadership with a profound grasp of complex issues is required if we are to be more successful than we have been to date. While unit commanders certainly require an educated intelligence, no one needs to grasp the writings of Clausewitz to command a tank company, a missile battalion, or an infantry brigade. An introspective, probing mentality is probably a hindrance to commanders at that level.

On the other hand, the army does need to have some genuinely intellectual elements in its leadership. When we move beyond tactics to the operational, strategic, and organizational levels of military activity, we begin to require deep intellect above leadership charisma. High command requires an intellectual component entirely separate from that required to lead troops in combat.[27] Modern history is full of talented troop commanders who failed at leading armies, because the requirements are utterly different. A fair number have adequately bridged the gap, an extraordinary few have leaped it. While the army should not attempt to transform itself into a community of scholars, it must somehow restrain itself from suppressing on principle any that may appear.

They are, however, systematically weeded out, suppressed, or diverted from the paths to influence, resulting in an organization that has no collective capacity for higher thought. Accordingly, the nation's military leadership lacks the credibility to exercise any positive influence on the making of national military policy.[28] There were many historical precedents for the military-political problems posed by Vietnam in the 1950s and 1960s. In some cases these problems had been dealt with successfully by other nations' military leaders, most notably Great Britain's, but the American Army in Vietnam operated in an intellectual vacuum. The words of Thucydides most surely apply to today's America: "A nation that draws too broad a distinction between its scholars and its warriors will have its thinking done by cowards and its fighting [or at least its military policy-making] done by fools."

Unfortunately, the United States Army is a fundamentally anti-intellectual organization. In some ways this is surprising, since all of the other great Western armies have a distinct intellectual tradition. In the American context, however, it is understandable. The American officer corps is a monolithic body with a marked intolerance for any kind of an elite within itself. Its deep historical roots are on the American frontier, a better breeding ground for alcoholism than for scholarly introspection. American intellectuals are unattracted to uniformed service, not because they are anti-military on principle but because they correctly perceive the army, in particular, as being hostile to their kind. Real influence is much easier to acquire outside the services, in organizations where deep thought and creative analyses are more often greeted with an enthusiastic reception. There, the fact can easily be overlooked that many of the conceptions and conclusions of political and bureaucratic leaders are formed in ignorance of military realities. Soldiers are quite correct in feeling that a lot of their problems stem from the bright ideas imposed on them by civilian deep-thinkers in the anthills of the Washington bureaucracy.

The weeding out of intellectuals is not, however, merely the result of reflex anti-intellectualism. Commanders often have little choice. Intellectual activity always implies criticism and experimentation, but the grossly inflated OER system has made all U.S. officers extremely sensitive to any kind of criticism. The merest hint of disapproval or hesitance on the OER can be a career-killer, and the resultant distaste for criticism carries over into other areas. Also, criticism of army methods is generally perceived at unit level as pointless whining, which it is. No commander can do much about the tactics he uses, the training methods he employs, or the organization of his resources.

As for experimentation, from the viewpoint of harried unit commanders this is a dangerous waste of scarce resources, a waste of time even if it works, because trained units are broken up so quickly. There is no point to it, because improved methods are irrelevant under the army's "Task, Condition, and Standard" methods of evaluation. So negative is the army's attitude toward experimentation that even those who claim to be in favor of it call it "freedom to fail." Since failure of any kind—except, it would seem, on the battlefield—can be fatal to an officer's career, the scope of activity is progressively narrowed to what can safely be predicted as a sure thing. Creative, goal-driven, mission-oriented people are notoriously difficult to lead or manage, but in serious organizations dealing with real-world problems, they are indispensable. In the artificial universe created by the army's evaluation systems, such people have no value. The OER system provides the means by which they can be repressed or eliminated.

Under EXEVAL, however, this will cease to be the case. Commanders will be able to vary their methods, for no one will be inspecting their adherence to a checklist. It will become very difficult to silence progress-minded officers through administrative means, although genuine indiscipline will still be subject to the UCMJ. In stable units experimentation will be possible, and, under EXEVAL, successful experimenters will set the performance standards for the rest of the field army. Those officers inclined to experiment should be given the time, resources, and opportunity to do so. Left to plan and execute exercises on their own, they will learn a lot of lessons the hard way, particularly the lessons of logistics and coordination that seem to escape so many young officers now. It is only through trial and error that leaders can learn the more subtle aspects of their craft, and only in an evaluation-free environment will officers do the experimentation needed if we are to "push the envelope" of unit capability. This is not "freedom to fail": it is freedom to learn the job. On the other hand, the army will not become a paradise for hare-brained schemers, because only concrete results will count. There will be no "weenie points" merely for being creative, and traditional methods will not be abandoned where they are effective. Therefore the practical obstacles to thinking will be removed, and commanders who prove unable to utilize the creative energies of their bright young subordinates will fall behind. Creative young citizens will be able to find an outlet for their ambitions in the army, to everyone's benefit.

THE ROTC ENVIRONMENT

Future commanders' psychological capacity to lead troops suffers some severe blows even before they reach the field army. ROTC cadets are socialized in a non-military environment where the officer corps is depicted as a variation on the college fraternity. "Leadership training" is conducted in such a manner as to enforce a run-with-the-pack mentality. The new cadet rarely even meets a private soldier until after he has already been granted leadership rank.

Most ROTC cadets obtain their commissions through the four-year college program. Students from community colleges without ROTC programs can usually arrange to join one at a nearby university. Students with prior military service get credit for the first two years. Latecomers to ROTC can catch up by attending a short summer boot camp between their sophomore and junior years. This is called ROTC Basic, and it is conducted by real army drill sergeants at Fort Knox. It was by far the best training I ever received in the army. All cadets attend a summer camp called "Advanced Camp" the summer before their commissioning, an experience that most officers regard in retrospect as worthless. For most cadets this is the first experience of life in a genuine military environment, but they are kept carefully segregated from regular troops. The following June, they receive their commissions in whatever branch the army has selected for them. The new lieutenants then report to their various branch Officer Basic Courses. In the field artillery this lasts about twenty weeks. Only then is the officer introduced to the real army, most often as some sort of a platoon leader.

TRUE!

The worst feature of ROTC training is that cadets are used as substitutes for soldiers. Most of the time cadets play a pseudo-subordinate role to other cadets. They are rotated through "leadership" posts on a daily basis. The cadet quickly learns that his temporary role as a military leader is meaningless and that his authority is based on the consent of his fellow cadets. Spending most of their time as "troops," cadets pick up all of the bad habits of the army's junior soldiers. This is not leadership training. Training military officers on the American college campus is like training race horses in an aquarium. It is difficult to account for the army's reluctance to expose future leaders to real soldiers. It is wrong, and it must be corrected.

ROTC classes should be limited to technical, administrative, and professional background subjects. Tactics and doctrine should be taught as theory only, the purpose being to impose some order on the broader background gained by regular academic studies. There should be no cadet rank structure. Command-track cadets should never be allowed to play the role of private soldiers, and no training unit should ever consist of concentrated cadets. Ideally, all cadets should be prior-service enlisted personnel, and those who are not should go through a regular-style basic training course, with regular drill sergeants, among normal trainees. They should receive their active leadership training during the summer, serving as un-commissioned instructors and junior NCOs in live units or military schools, or as "gophers" on TFI inspection teams.

These changes in the selection and training of the army's incoming junior officers are designed to produce an older, more mature company-grade officer, one who already has some military experience and the academic training to understand his profession, military doctrine, and the political/strategic rationale—if any—behind the missions he has to execute. They do away with the vestigial class considerations that have divorced the army officer corps from the mainstream of American society and from the practical experience necessary to producing hard-nosed field commanders. These measures are not designed to produce an officer corps of intellectuals, merely to prevent the army from suppressing capable intellectuals who find their way into the service.

Their purpose is to produce troop leaders who will have legitimacy in the eyes of the soldiers and especially of the NCOs they command. These troop leaders will have the intellectual background to understand and explain their missions, and sufficient prestige to revise the natural priorities of their soldiers.

The bulk of these officers will rise fairly slowly in rank, and many will settle into low- or mid-level positions in which they are competent and comfortable. There they will capably execute the directives of more senior leaders. Competition for the top slots will be reduced to people who really want them and who have demonstrated their effectiveness along the way. Some will rise with meteoric speed, providing the army with the dynamic young leadership needed to take chances and to win. Their example will attract capable, ambitious young Americans into the service. Others will rise slowly and methodically, providing the stability and the fund of expertise needed to sustain the force.

These officers will have the breadth and depth of knowledge and experience to provide the leadership the army will need over the long haul to resist the relentless pressure of the nation's bureaucratizing tendencies. Bureaucrats and politicians will always seek to centralize functions that must be delegated and to compartmentalize people who must cooperate. We must have capable, professional, tough-minded *soldiers* on hand in positions where they can resist this self-destructive drive.

NOTES

1. Data from USA MILPERCEN, February 11, 1987; Armed Forces Information Service, *Defense 86*, DOD, September-October 1986.

2. The domestic prestige of the post–World War I German officer corps is often overestimated. One important and popular feature of the National Socialist program was the subjugation of the old German officer corps. This was a natural outgrowth of the experience of Adolf Hitler and other *frontsoldaten* in World War I. The officers of Hitler's new army came from very different sources. The old leadership went down to destruction after the coup attempt of July 20, 1944. See Harold C. Deutsch, "The Rise of the Military Opposition in the Nazi Reich," in William Geffen, ed. *Command and Commanders in Modern Warfare: The Proceedings of the Second Military History Symposium, U.S. Air Force Academy, 2–3 May, 1968* (Office of Air Force History, 1971); Peter Hoffman, *The History of the German Resistance*, trans. Richard Barry (Cambridge: MIT Press, 1970); John Tolund, *Adolf Hitler* (New York: Ballantine Books, 1976).

3. On the night of my arrival at my unit in Korea, I was taken out on a road trip by several of the senior lieutenants in the unit. We got into serious problems when they irritated the Korean bus driver by rowdy behavior, including the shouting of obscenities and racial epithets from the windows. He threw us off the bus, which was awkward because it was half an hour before curfew, after which personnel on the streets out of uniform are liable to be shot. It took an armed Korean policeman's threat to shoot to quiet one of the young officers, who was not drunk. This was not atypical behavior for young American officers set loose in a foreign land. Most junior officers are not juvenile jerks, but far too high a proportion are.

4. Walter Ulmer discusses the problem of determining junior leaders' actual effects on subordinates. Lieutanant General Walter F. Ulmer, "Leaders, Managers, and Command Climate," *Armed Forces Journal International*, July 1986.

5. Richard A. Gabriel, *Military Incompetence* (New York: Hill and Wang, 1985), 184–85; "Grenada and Lebanon Bring a Rush of Medals," *New York Times*, December 5, 1983, sec. II. Sun Tzu says, "Too frequent rewards indicate that the general is at the end of his resources." Sun Tzu, *The Art of War*, trans. Samuel B. Griffith (London: Oxford University Press, 1963), 122.

6. "Acting Jack," an E–4 in an NCO slot who is permitted to wear sergeant's stripes.

7. Army Regulations.

8. Leadership and Unit Training manuals.

9. Letter, SP/4 A. L. Hite, December 10, 1985.

10. A 1979 study showed that only 39 percent of enlisted soldiers believed that their units would perform well in combat. Fewer than 45 percent believed that their officers were competent. These and other similar statistics are cited in Richard Gabriel, ed., *Fighting Armies: NATO and the Warsaw Pact, A Combat Assessment* (Westport, Conn.: Greenwood Press, 1983). They are excerpted from John Fialka,

"The Report No One Wants to Talk About," *Washington Post*, December 15, 1980, and Stephen D. Westbrook, "The Alienated Soldier: Legacy of Our Society," *ARMY*, December 1979. I do not quote these figures in the text because the quality of army enlisted men has risen dramatically in the 1980s, and because such opinions are so highly subjective. Many of the negative attitudes of early VOLAR soldiers were brought with them into the army and did not reflect the leadership they received. A similar survey today probably would reveal better attitudes, but would be similarly difficult to interpret.

11. USA MILPERCEN, "Officer Eliminations Initiated (By Calendar Year)," August 21, 1987.

12. Such ratings are discussed in Lieutenant Colonel Larry H. Ingraham, "The OER Cudgel: Radical Surgery Needed," *ARMY*, November 1985; Ulmer, "Command Climate."

13. Army data, USA MILPERCEN, May 28, 1987. The DOD-wide figure is only 1 percent higher. *Defense 86*, DOD, Armed Forces Information Service, September-October 1986. In 1976, only 4.1 percent of enlisted accessions had "some college." Peter Karsten, ed., *The Military in America* (New York: The Free Press, 1980), 485.

14. See Fred Downs, "It's Time West Point Stopped Sugarcoating Combat," *Washington Post Weekly Edition*, August 31, 1987.

15. Benjamin F. Schemmer, "Is It Time to Abolish West Point?" *Armed Forces Journal International*, September 1985. An Academy graduate himself, Schemmer may not have been entirely serious, but some of the statistics he cites are intriguing. Each West Point graduate costs the taxpayers somewhere between $175,000 and $226,190, six to nine times more than an ROTC officer. (West Point gives figures that indicate that USMA graduates cost only three to four times more than the ROTC product.) Academy students are required to take only six credit hours in "History of the Military Art." Of eight battalion commanders relieved for cause in 1984, six were West Pointers. The meaning of these statistics is unclear, but it is certain that West Point no longer dominates the army leadership. This article engendered considerable debate in the ensuing months, carried on in the pages of *AFJ* and elsewhere.

16. "Armor Branch Breakdown by Bachelor's Degree Discipline," USA MILPERCEN, February 11, 1987.

17. The army has even set targets for officer recruiting by general academic areas, i.e., Engineering, social science, etc., including 10 percent from "Other." MILPERCEN, "OPMS Update," February 11, 1987.

18. The origin of the term "Army of excellence" is obscure, but it was evidently related to the brilliant "art of business" book by Thomas J. Peters and Robert H. Waterman, Jr., *In Search of Excellence: Lessons from America's Best-Run Companies* (New York: Harper and Row, 1982), and its sequel by Tom Peters and Nancy Austin, *A Passion for Excellence* (New York: Warner Books, 1985). The army put *In Search of Excellence* on its list of required reading at the Command and General Staff College. "Excellence" is a code word for a specific management style, but most of the army took it in its generic sense: being "excellent" is no great challenge when everybody is already "outstanding." Some products of this management/leadership philosophy did surface, such as the "skunkworks" that produced unorthodox equipment for the Ninth Infantry Division at Fort Lewis. For the most part, "excellence" was just another buzzword.

19. The value of military history is argued most authoritatively by Clausewitz: see Carl von Clausewitz, *On War*, trans. Michael Howard and Peter Paret (Princeton, N.J.: Princeton University Press, 1976), book II. The argument is made best in John Keegan, *The Face of Battle* (New York: Viking Press, 1976), 13–72. See also Hew Strachan, *European Armies and the Conduct of War* (London: George Allen and Unwin, 1983), 1–7. The most comprehensive statement is in John E. Jessup, Jr. and Robert W. Coakley, *A Guide to the Study and Use of Military History* (Washington, D.C.: Center of Military History, 1978).

20. "To study command as it operated in Vietnam is, indeed, almost enough to make one despair of human reason: We have seen the future, and it does not work." Martin van Creveld, *Command in War*, (Cambridge, Mass.: Harvard University Press, 1985) 260.

21. West Point officers graduate with a degree in "Military Science." Since 1982, West Pointers have had the option of choosing an academic major. In 1986, 1,386 armor officers were West Pointers. USA MILPERCEN, February 11, 1987.

22. For a critique of military professionalism see Sam C. Sarkesian, *Beyond the Battlefield: The New Military Professionalism* (New York: Pergamon Press, 1982).

23. This seems to be the key point in an interesting article by Captain Ralph Peters, "The Dangerous Romance: The U.S. Army's Fascination with the Wehrmacht," *Military Intelligence*, October–December 1986.

24. For example, Keith E. Bond, an army captain pursuing his Ph.D., has proposed a dissertation entitled "When the Odds Were Even" concerning U.S.-German combat in Lorraine, 1944–1945. Bond appears to be intensely hostile to the work of van Creveld and focuses on tactical rather than organizational issues. Keith E. Bond, "When the Odds Were Even: A Doctoral Dissertation Proposal," University of Chicago, May 8, 1987.

25. See James Burk, "Patriotism and the All-Volunteer Force," *Journal of Political and Military Sociology*, Fall 1984.

26. Janice E. McKenny, comp. *Army Lineage Series: Field Artillery, Regular Army and Reserve* (Washington, D.C.: Center of Military History, U.S. Army, 1985), 271.

27. This is well discussed in Russell Weigley, "American Strategy from its Beginnings through the First World War," in Peter Paret, ed., *Makers of Modern Society: From Machiavelli to the Nuclear Age* (Princeton: Princeton University Press, 1986), 420–421.

28. For fruitless attempts by American military men to influence Washington's military perspective on the Indochina commitment, in a manner that hindsight indicates was correct, see Bob Buzzanco, "The American Military's Rationale against the Vietnam War," *Political Science Quarterly*, issue no. 4, 1986.

7

GETTING THERE

THE PARAMETERS OF PRACTICAL REFORM

Despite repeated military failures over the past thirty-five years, and despite a plethora of suggested reform prescriptions, meaningful reform has not occurred. Some proposed reforms have been aimed at social, political, and ethical factors that, while they may contribute to American military ineptitude, are neither fundamental nor susceptible to practical efforts at reform. Other suggested measures are hardware oriented, and therefore call for great expense while missing fundamental organizational problems. Whatever the innate value of such proposals, they are irrelevant in the face of the hardware commitments of the Reagan build-up. Some proposals with great theoretical promise, i.e., creation of a true General Staff or a return to the draft, expend the energies of their proponents in a frontal assault on impregnable political barriers. All reformers assail the convoluted military bureaucracy and the paralyzing personnel system it has spawned, but practical systemic prescriptions have been lacking. No political constituency exists to push the cause of military reform upon a Congress whose own military decision-making processes are gravely flawed.

As a result, we have seen politically motivated changes like VOLAR, but these were not aimed at improving effectiveness. We have paid for a lot of quite necessary hardware modernization, which enhances American firepower without enhancing our ability to use it. There have been a few toe-in-the-water experiments like COHORT, which addresses fundamental problems but only in a very unambitious manner. COHORT cannot be sustained in combat and is being implemented at a snail's pace. Other than this, efforts to produce a capable, professional army have consisted of layer upon layer of traditional bureaucratic programs that have progressively buried field units in paperwork, destroyed all initiative, and deprived field commanders of both the ability and the responsibility to produce capable military units.

This book has proposed specific prescriptions for curing the ills of the United States Army. They address fundamental problems in the nation's military system. Specifically, they address fundamental flaws in the internal organization of the army without attacking directly the many related social and political problems often discussed in the literature on military reform. These reform measures do not address the pro- or anti-military biases in American society as a whole, and only indirectly address matters concerning the class or social origins of army officers and men. The incapacity of the American Army is not caused by widespread, deeply rooted pacifism among the most capable elements in our society, although an appreciable level of such pacifism does exist. The true relationship is the other way around: the nation's will to use its military power has been weakened by frustration induced through repeated military failure, and the most capable elements of society avoid military service because the armed forces themselves have proven to be incapable of utilizing and rewarding their talents. We may hope that by creating an organization that can utilize and reward capable, creative leadership the social base of the army may be broadened. We may hope further that by creating a force that can perform its mission without humiliating the nation through its incompetence we can restore the nation's will to defend itself and its interests.

The proposed reforms do not include a return to the draft because past abuses have made that politically impossible and because it would not affect the fundamental problem of an inadequate leadership body. They do not include creation of a General Staff, even in disguised form, because this is unacceptable to the nation's political and bureaucratic leaders and because such a body would be resisted furiously within the officer corps itself, as presently constituted. They do not include any form of "Ethics Code" for military personnel because the pervasive dishonesty of our military leaders is rooted in organizational absurdities, not personal immorality or turpitude.

Nor are these reforms concerned with "unification" of the services, because unification is an illusion. "Inter-service rivalry" is essentially no different from the rivalries between different bureaucratic entities at every level in every DOD organization. Army-Navy competition is no more destructive to combat-arms effectiveness on the battlefield than is the lack of trust between the field artillery and the infantry, or between supply units and tactical units within organizations of the same arm. The problem here is not so much structural as it is a matter of training and motivation, factors tremendously influenced by the army's defective evaluation systems. There is a tremendous difference between cooperation and compromise, and between the drive to achieve a goal and the drive to achieve consensus. The army's organizational methods consistently emphasize the wrong values.

No particular leadership style is suggested here, although certain politically imposed limitations are acknowledged, as in the matter of discipline. The stabilization of units and commanders will, however, permit the development of different leadership styles, and the new evaluation and promotion systems will ensure that unsuccessful leaders do not persist in their errors or in command. The changed relationship between commanders at different levels and between the field forces and the military bureaucracy will ensure the end of the current style of "leadership through administrative terror."

Lastly, these reforms are neutral regarding questions of arms procurement, force structure, doctrine, and the scope of American military commitments, all of which are accepted as given. They do not address decision making at the highest levels, only the forces that must carry out the decisions. Although these other areas require attention, in the absence of effective field units to use the arms, doctrine, and higher command guidance they are peripheral issues. As officers experienced in the new model units rise to higher rank, trained in a system that demands and rewards collective achievement, many of the problems of procurement, doctrine, and the high command will be solved through internally initiated action.

In historical perspective, the fundamental flaws in the army's organization derive from two related anachronisms. First, the army's leadership has never completed the conceptual jump from the venerable American tradition of the expandable army to the post–Korean War policy of preparing for the "come as you are war." Second, the entire defense structure has never adjusted to the existence of large, permanently organized fighting formations. The defense establishment is geared to producing and maintaining the fighting forces in much the same way as a movie projector produces images on the screen: turn off the projector and the image disappears. Until 1950 that was the way America's fighting forces were created, with a few experts at the center desperately trying to educate the new, temporary field units. Today, for the first time in American history, a field army exists as a living institution. The DOD bureaucracy, like an overly dominating parent, refuses to stand aside and let Junior take over the family business. There is general agreement that the bureaucracy interferes excessively with the field army and that units themselves are imbued with a spirit of bureaucratic compartmentalism and competition that prohibits the pursuit of collective goals. The field army is kept in this infantile state of dependence and confusion by its creators, who continue to regard it as an expression of themselves rather than as a truly professional army-in-being.

What has been lacking is a mechanism whereby field units can be allowed (and obliged) to focus on their mission without destroying the ability of the bureaucracy to perform its legitimate and necessary functions. The proposed reforms will create such a mechanism. They will free commanders to train large-scale, cohesive, effective, combined-arms units, and force the "supporting" elements of the bureaucracy to support rather than tyrannize them.

The field army will be able to emerge from its fetal subordination and take its proper place as a standing military organization. Meanwhile, reform will improve the power of the nation's civilian and military leadership to obtain accurate information on the one hand and to exert meaningful political and military control on the other, for promotion and job security will now depend on fulfilling the *overtly* stated goals of the army. These are inherently consistent with the political and strategic goals of the nation, as opposed to the unarticulated and often irrational goals of the organizational "hidden agenda," which itself has not consciously been created by anyone.

While the expandable army concept may have some continuing validity, it will no longer be allowed to affect adversely the units supposedly designed to "win the first battle" of the "come as you are war." Commanders of stable units will be empowered to configure available resources into combat-ready organizations. The cadres for an additional six-plus divisions will always be formed or forming, providing the basis for an emergency expansion should that be called for. National Guard and Army Reserve units will have the clear, politically acceptable, and achievable mission of providing company- and battalion-sized replacement units for divisions that have suffered losses in large-scale combat, while higher-level reserve headquarters and training cadres will provide the mobilization base for longer-term emergency expansion. This will permit the consolidation and rebuilding of American units that have been committed to action, using cohesive replacement units instead of anomic individuals. It will also prevent the cannibalization of trained but as-yet-uncommitted units that proved so disastrous in World War II.

Superimposed on the present system, these measures will create pressures and opportunities for the production of effective military forces, sustainable in wartime. Instead of constant upheaval, evenly distributed throughout the force structure, there will be a continuous ripple of orderly evolution sweeping through the field forces on a four-year cycle. The forces so produced will meet current military commitments, and highly trained, flexible headquarters at corps-level and higher will stand ready to assume operational control of tactical units in order to deal with contingencies. Forces of such quality do not currently exist, but there is no reason why they cannot be produced from the people and material now on hand and projected in the active army.

Contrast this with the current situation in which eighteen divisions and assorted fragments never reach anything approaching their readiness potential, all active units remain in a homogenized state of confusion, higher commands and staffs are so overwhelmed by peacetime administrative concerns that they have no time to prepare for their own wartime tasks, the great bulk of reserve units have no credible wartime mission, and the individual replacement system will be the only viable option should war occur.

MOVING TOWARD REFORM

The reforms advocated in this book have not been created out of whole cloth. They are based to some extent on an understanding of the evolution of modern armies throughout the world and of the peculiarities of that evolution as it has proceeded in the United States. They are also based on the practices of more successful and professional military organizations belonging to the other Western democracies. They have been most profoundly influenced by seven years' close-range observation of the United States Army. Many of the underlying ideas have been adapted from other armies and from the writings of other would-be reformers, but they have been retailored to deal with the realities of American society, American governmental organization, American commitments, and most of all, American soldiers. These reforms are complex but concrete, doable, and confined largely to organizational structures that are under the control of DOD or the Department of the Army.

However, it is extremely doubtful that the army will ever develop on its own initiative a system like the one described. Current army leaders grew up under the present system, and it is unreasonable to expect them to initiate sweeping changes. Although many senior officers will welcome a system that demands that they produce results, other will be horrified, and bureaucrats at every level will be appalled at the impact of sweeping practical reform on their complex, inflexible administrative systems. Given the corporate manner in which all significant organizational decisions are made, the latter would be able to stifle any positive change. No one within the military establishment itself possesses the power to set rapid, fundamental change into motion, nor even to find out what is really going on down at unit level. For many of the same reasons, agencies of the Executive (meaning particularly DOD's civilian hierarchy) also will not act.

On the other hand, the great bulk of the army's officers will welcome the opportunity for job security at a level of responsibility that suits their individual needs and talents. Job stability will permit them to develop a genuine professionalism and expertise in their chosen or assigned fields. They will be more than happy at the opportunity and demand to justify this new security by producing units that actually can perform their designated missions. The army's officers and professional soldiers are, in fact, the natural constituency for the proposed reforms. Unlike many other proposed reform programs, this one is not designed to cut the pay or retirement prospects of current personnel, to punish them for inadequacies imposed upon them by a fatally flawed national military system, or to replace them with some mythical better element of society. Given the nature of the military hierarchy, however, these officers can agitate for reform only by lobbying very cautiously within their organizations and by bringing indirect pressure to bear via their elected representatives.

It is therefore probable that only Congress can serve as a motor for serious military reform. With good reason, most people with military experience come naturally to fear and loathe the idea of further congressional interference in internal army matters. Congressional meddling has been a major aggravating factor in—and perhaps one of many underlying causes for—the army's current sorry state. Nonetheless, if fundamental reforms are to be made to the American military system they probably will have to originate in Congress. If effective steps can be taken, however, the resultant strengthening of military institutions will eliminate much of the need and much of the opportunity for further congressional micromanagement.

Left unstated here is now the proposed reforms should be packaged and imposed on the army. Congressional reformers must identify experienced military personnel who are genuinely enthusiastic about the kind of army such reforms would produce and work with them to generate legislation that would bring about their implementation. Two concepts critical to effective reform of the field army are changeover to a Divisional Rotation System and creation of the Tactical Forces Inspectorate. The army will have to be forced to do away with its traditional individual rotation and evaluation methods, the up-or-out promotion policy, and the distorting concept of "loyalty to the army." If these proposals are implemented, much of the rest of the program will fall fairly readily into place.

The time frame for army implementation of these requirements is not critical, but it should be a crash program with no more than twelve months between legislation and the activation of the first of the new divisional command packages. The army must be compelled to execute these reforms as rapidly as possible, even at the cost of considerable initial confusion. Left to plan an "orderly" conversion process, the army would attempt to create a whole new layer of bureaucracy to manage it, and expenses would mushroom. It would seek to "grandfather" current personnel, call for reams of "studies," and try to proceed toward reform by timid steps that would destroy momentum and permit subversion of the new institutions. It would want to have new suburban subdivisions, pawnshops, and massage parlors in place before the first soldier reports to his new unit.

Such rapid implementation of military reform is justified by the same dangers that have led us to create large forces in the first place. The only difference is that now we will be getting something for our money. A modicum of chaos in the process of achieving military capability is preferable to "an orderly approach," the only purpose of which is to maintain the current institutionalized incompetence. In any case, military organizations are created to deal with sudden, massive requirements. Considered in comparison to the requirements of a real national emergency, the time allowed for changeover to the new system is generous. Creation of new units under the Divisional Rotation System will take about forty months to absorb the entire field army, leaving adequate time for reasonable adjustments. Being jumped through the hoop while being reformed will be therapeutic for the whole structure. As for soldiers at unit level, they have been jumping through the hoop for years with little to show for their best efforts.

THE IMPACT ON RESOURCES

The next question is, from whence will come the money and personnel for these new institutions?

All of the organizational and paperwork "systems" that the army has bought while producing the present dinosaur have been justified on the grounds that they will save money. This is reminiscent of the story of the man who put so many gas-saving features on his car that he could not drive it anywhere, because gasoline overflowed from the tank every time he turned the key. No one has ever seen such a car, or a new army system that saved money.

In a way, however, savings are inherent in these reforms, in the sense that any expenditure that produces actual military capacity is inherently a savings over current expenditures that do not. We cannot know whether the proposed reforms will save money in any bookkeeping sense, and that is not their purpose. Should the reforms prove expensive, compensatory cuts at almost any other place in the military budget will be justified. If we intend that our fundamental national security policy of deterrence be based on real military power, and not on an incredibly expensive sham, it is no exaggeration to say that virtually all of the army's current budget is wasted.

However, there is no reason why the new model army should be any more expensive to produce or maintain than the one we have now. No change is proposed in personnel or in the number of field units, their equipment, type, or basic organization. The changes are largely in the way that those personnel and units relate to each other, and in the way change itself is managed. The funding and personnel for the new institutions (largely the inspectorate) will come from others that will be absorbed or replaced. In their formative stages, the large-unit command packages will consist largely of people who are temporarily out of field units anyway, for training or schooling.

A large-scale shifting of personnel may be required initially, but many will not need to move physically. When we consider that 81 percent of army officers and men changed assignments in one year (figures from fiscal year 1980), it becomes clear that no conceivable reform would increase the costs currently generated by personnel transfers. While we will be flying most of the personnel of five-plus divisions to and from Europe every year, we will not be transporting their heavy equipment or their families, furniture, and automobiles. We will not be housing and otherwise providing for nearly the 200,000 army dependents who currently follow the troops to their overseas duty stations, there to serve as additional hostages to our allies and our adversaries. Although these dependents will still need to be housed, the money so spent will be spent domestically, and much of the expense will be absorbed by private real estate concerns. In the twelve-plus divisions that will remain in CONUS, we will not be paying for the turmoil now caused by constant movement of personnel and dependents.

By creating personnel stability we will be improving vastly the competence of unit logistical personnel, reducing the incredible waste now caused by ignorance and accident. By eliminating the current game of "Find the Excess" we will be eliminating much of the conscious waste and destruction of supplies, equipment, and spare parts. By improving enforcement of regulations against misappropriation of such material, through police forces rather than the current ineffective, paralyzing, and actively counterproductive administrative double-checks and restraints, we will better prevent costly and dangerous criminal actions. By constantly rotating equipment between old units, POMCUS stocks, and newly forming units, we will prevent losses through the obsolescing of equipment that is never used and improve the quality of higher-level maintenance performance.

These are negative savings, money that we currently waste that will no longer be thrown away. In a more positive sense, we will obtain resources from many current administrative systems that on the one hand consume money and manpower while on the other they actively interfere with units' ability to accomplish their fundamental purposes. Commanders now will determine which systems to preserve, by identifying which ones are aiding them in their quest for retention and promotion through the production of capable units. Many of these systems will atrophy rapidly. Their personnel and resources can be absorbed into the new structures. Simply throw the new jobs open to personnel now employed elsewhere in the military bureaucracy. A surprising number of these people recognize the worthlessness of their current activities and will either jump at the chance to do something worthwhile or hasten to abandon a sinking ship.

REFORM IN PERSPECTIVE

It has been in hopes of forestalling any necessity for a militarization of American life that all past American security commitments have been undertaken. American security today is based largely on nuclear forces that can be used only as a threat to take the enemy with us in a spectacular form of national suicide. To the extent that it is also based on the more rational use of conventional forces, it is founded on a sham. Capable, motivated, patriotic, and well-equipped Americans have been assembled into a hopelessly incapable military mirage. It is a mirage that seems increasingly to be believable only to American eyes, and then only to those of us who

have been paying insufficient attention to the news or too much attention
to the fictions generated by DOD.

Unless we reform our forces voluntarily now, we will inevitably suffer at
some future date some sweeping military disaster of the Dunkirk variety.
Military reform, if it comes at all, will then take place in an atmosphere of
panic. This will lead to measures executed in hasty, brutal fashion, endan-
gering the basic character of American society.

Reforms of the kind advocated here are particularly timely now, given
the lack of prospects for new infusions of money and manpower into army
forces. Because recent nuclear arms control developments require strengthened conventional forces, those who support a strong defense have no real
choice but organizational reform of some type. Advocates of further arms
control measures face the same requirement. Also, Americans of many political stripes are concerned about the actions of high military officers during
the recent Iran-Contra scandals. We should be aware that those officers'
actions and their attitudes toward rules and procedures are the inevitable
by-products of the current deranged organizational methods.

It is difficult, however, for a student of American history not to be pes-
simistic on the subject of military reform. It appears that our failure to
repair our glaringly ineffective military system is based on a fixed national
determination to keep the military element in America weak, divided, and
inefficient. On the one hand, we feel obligated in a high-threat international
environment to spend a lot of money on defense. On the other hand, we
are unwilling to risk the existence of an effective military element in our
society. We vaguely fear that such an element might pose a threat to domestic
institutions, but perhaps we fear even more that if truly capable forces were
at the disposition of the nation's leaders they might actually be used. The
political strategy that has evolved from this set of worries has been to build
an expensive, well-dressed military force that is intended to deter opponents
but can not actually fight them. Nonetheless, our useless forces continue to
be used, in pursuit of policies that, however wise or misguided, are the
legitimate expressions of our political system. The result has been a series
of well-publicized military funerals. The sharing of tragedy may build our
sense of nationhood, but it does not change the fact that these men died in
vain.

If creation of a capable military leadership will inevitably pose a threat
to American institutions, then we are indeed between a rock and a hard
place. However, this is not the case. Military organizations will always
produce characters like Lieutenant Colonel Oliver North. It is up to political
leaders to utilize them properly. We cannot eliminate the possibility of
irresponsible military action by creating military forces that are inherently
incapable of acting. The price of continued complacency in the face of our
demonstrated military incompetence will be more *Pueblos*, more Irans, more

Beiruts, more *Starks*, quite possibly on a more massive scale. If we do not intend to fix our fundamentally flawed military institutions, then we should embark on the simpler course of saving our money. Perhaps we can use it to buy protection elsewhere.

BIBLIOGRAPHICAL ESSAY

The best historical perspective on the roots of the U.S. Army's problems is provided by the writings of Russell F. Weigley, particularly *History of the United States Army* (Bloomington: Indiana University Press, 1967; use the enlarged edition of 1984), and *The American Way of War: A History of United States Military Strategy and Policy* (New York: Macmillan, 1973). Much of his argument is available in condensed form in "American Strategy from Its Beginnings through the First World War," in Peter Paret, ed., *Makers of Modern Strategy: From Machiavelli to the Nuclear Age* (Princeton: Princeton University Press, 1986). Weigley's *Eisenhower's Lieutenants: The Campaigns of France and Germany, 1944–1945* (Bloomington: Indiana University Press, 1981) is valuable in foreshadowing in an operational vein many of the organizational pathologies that were to reach fruition in Korea and Vietnam. The ambitious reader can derive much the same effect from reading the Army Historical Series works on World War II in Europe, especially if he or she includes Robert R. Palmer, Bell I. Wiley, and William R. Keast, *The Procurement and Training of Ground Combat Troops* (Washington, D.C.: Office of the Chief of Military History, 1948). Martin van Creveld's *Fighting Power: German and U.S. Army Performance, 1939–1945* (Westport, Conn.: Greenwood Press, 1982) is an investigation of the impact of American organizational or institutional methods on battlefield performance. Although some of its key arguments are challenged in Richard A. Gabriel, ed., *Military Psychiatry: A Comparative Perspective* (Westport, Conn.: Greenwood Press, 1986), in the main his analysis has held up. Michael Sherry, *Preparing for the Next War: American Plans for Postwar Defense, 1941–45* (New Haven: Yale University Press, 1977), provides a valuable look at the army's organizational thinking in those crucial years.

For Korea, probably the best single critical work is T. R. Fehrenbach's *This Kind of War* (New York: Macmillan, 1963), although the more narrowly focused combat studies of S. L. A. Marshall are just as disturbing. Roy E. Appleman's *East of Chosin* (College Station, Texas: Texas A&M University Press, 1987) examines in detail the destruction of the army's 31st Regimental Combat Team. See especially appendix A. The period between Korea and Vietnam is discussed, in a manner which relates to the current reform problem, in A. J. Bacevich, *The Pentomic Era: The U.S. Army between Korea and Vietnam* (Washington, D.C.: National Defense University Press, 1986). The volume of writing on Vietnam is reaching flood stage, virtually all of it critical in one respect or another. In general, the official historical work on Vietnam does not match the quality or objectivity of that on earlier conflicts. Andrew F. Krepinevich, *The Army and Vietnam* (Baltimore: Johns Hopkins University Press, 1986) is a good recent study. General Douglas Kinnard's *The War Managers* (Hanover, N.H.: University Press of New England, 1977) provides a penetrating look at the methods used by the American leadership to administrate that conflict. It is based on surveys of participating commanders. Philip Caputo's *A Rumor of War* (New York: Ballantine Books, 1977) provides a highly readable firsthand account of the impact of those methods on the junior leadership. For U.S. military actions from the closing period in Vietnam to Grenada, the best treatment is Richard A. Gabriel's *Military Incompetence: Why the American Military Doesn't Win* (New York: Hill and Wang, 1985). Gabriel is also the editor of a useful book on the armies that face each other in Europe. *Fighting Armies: NATO and the Warsaw Pact, A Combat Assessment* (Westport, Conn.: Greenwood Press, 1983). For another recent look at Western armies, see L. H. Gann, ed., *The Defense of Western Europe* (London: Croom Helm, 1987). A fascinating and up-to-date internal study of the workings of current units can be found in a series of five "Technical Reports" put together under the aegis of Dr. David Marlowe of the Walter Reed Department of Military Psychiatry, called the *Unit Manning System Field Evaluation* (Washington, D.C.: Walter Reed Army Institute of Research, November 1985 to September 1987). The most interesting is probably no. 5, a no-holds-barred look at training, cohesion, and leadership in the Seventh Infantry Division.

Most of the current debate on military reform dates to the Vietnam War. Paul Savage and Richard A. Gabriel, both army officers, produced a seminal work in this genre with *Crisis in Command* (New York: Hill and Wang, 1978). Their emphasis is on the ethical failings of the officer corps, and their prescriptions reflect this concern. Both have continued to write on this subject; see Gabriel's *To Serve with Honor: A Treatise on Military Ethics and the Way of the State* (Westport, Conn.: Greenwood Press, 1982). Military analyst Edward N. Luttwak writes with more concern for grand strategy, and his prescriptions tend to focus on the high command and the upper reaches of the Pentagon bureaucracy. His *The Pentagon and the Art of War: The Question of Military Reform* (New York: Simon and Schuster, 1985) is a classic description of the American military bureaucracy. Prescriptions involving a return to the draft seem, oddly, to come most often from journalists, including James Fallows, *National Defense* (New York: Random House, 1981), and Arthur Hadley, *The Straw Giant* (New York: Random House, 1986). However, most advocates of reform argue for a draft, and Fallows has also pursued the hardware route to reform. Ninety-ninth Congress, *Defense Organization: The Need for Change, Staff Report to the Committee on Armed Services, United States Senate* (Washington, D.C.: GPO, 1985), is an extremely useful overview of problems within the military and of proposals for reform. It focuses, however, on problems of interservice rivalry, command and control at the highest levels, and acquisitions. Its prescriptions are of the top-down, bureaucratic variety. This is no criticism, and the approach it takes is in some respects complementary to that of the present work. A good overview of the reform debate can be had from Asa A. Clark, Peter W.

Chiarelli, Jeffrey S. McKitrick, and James W. Reed, eds., *The Defense Reform Debate: Issues and Analysis* (Baltimore: Johns Hopkins University Press, 1984).

The best public sources for keeping up with thinking on reform within the army itself are *Military Review*, *ARMY*, and the excellent *Armed Forces Journal International*. The latter two carry extensive interviews with senior military leaders, and *ARMY* often carries articles by an interesting voice of the junior officer corps, Captain Ralph Peters. *ARMY*'s annual "Green Book" (October) issue contains articles by many of the army's top leaders and much information on programs and weaponry. The ongoing national security debate is best followed in *International Security*, a quarterly published by the Center for Science and International Affairs, Harvard University.

From the standpoint of theory, several very different works are worth examining. Barry R. Posen's *The Sources of Military Doctrine: France, Britain, and Germany between the World Wars* (Ithaca: Cornell University Press, 1984) is not a historical work, per se, but rather a refreshing example of a political scientist testing "organization theory" and "balance of power theory" against historical experience. It is a readable introduction to the formal corpus of organization theory. Posen's argument is quite relevant, even though he does not connect it to the current American situation. He concludes that genuine strategic concerns rather than parochial organizational priorities determined military policy in these nations on the eve of World War II. That priorities in American defense policy are the reverse is best shown in Luttwak, *Art of War*, and in Leslie H. Gelb and Richard K. Betts, *The Irony of Vietnam: The System Worked* (Washington, D.C.: The Brookings Institution, 1979). Martin van Creveld has written a number of works that concern military organization, but probably the most useful from our point of view, after *Fighting Power*, is *Command in War* (Cambridge: Harvard University Press, 1985), which analyzes through historical example basic approaches to handling the flow of military information and authority. For leadership theory, see Thomas J. Peters and Robert H. Waterman, Jr., *In Search of Excellence: Lessons from America's Best-Run Companies* (New York: Harper and Row, 1982), and the U.S. Army's own FM 22–100 *Military Leadership* (Washington, D.C.: HQDA, 1983). Both would be excellent guides if the army's organizational methods permitted leaders to apply any philosophy with effectiveness. As to strategic theory, see Edward N. Luttwak, *On the Meaning of Victory* (New York: Simon and Schuster, 1986), and *Strategy: The Logic of War and Peace* (Cambridge: Harvard University Press, 1987). For a coherent historical view of American national security policy, a subject that the present work does not treat but of which military effectiveness is certainly a part, see the works of John Lewis Gaddis, particularly *Strategies of Containment: A Critical Appraisal of Postwar American National Security Policy* (New York: Oxford University Press, 1982), and "The Long Peace," *International Security*, Spring 1986.

Underlying, paralleling, or at least heavily cited in most of these theoretical discussions is the work of Carl von Clausewitz. His major work, *On War*, is available in a highly readable version translated and edited by Michael Howard and Peter Paret (Princeton, N.J.: Princeton University Press, 1976); the 1984 edition with index is the most useful. The reader is advised to steer clear of other versions, many of which have been abridged in a misguided pursuit of "clarity." Although reading

Clausewitz is not quite so formidable an undertaking as it is often alleged to be, it is still best approached carefully. The best short introduction is Michael Howard, *Clausewitz* (New York: Oxford University Press, 1983). See also Peter Paret, *Clausewitz and the State* (Princeton, N.J.: Princeton University Press, 1976).

INDEX

About the Author

CHRISTOPHER BASSFORD served from 1981 to 1986 as a field artillery officer with tours in both Korea and Germany. He is currently completing his Ph.D. in history at Purdue University.